Tomorrow's Troubles

Tomorrow's Troubles

RISK, ANXIETY, AND PRUDENCE IN AN

AGE OF ALGORITHMIC GOVERNANCE

PAUL SCHERZ

Georgetown University Press / Washington, DC

The publisher is not responsible for third-party websites or their content. URL links were active at time of publication.

Library of Congress Cataloging-in-Publication Data

Names: Scherz, Paul J., author.
Title: Tomorrow's troubles : risk, anxiety, and prudence in an age of algorithmic governance / Paul Scherz.
Description: Washington, DC : Georgetown University Press, 2022. | Includes bibliographical references and index.
Identifiers: LCCN 2021049524 | ISBN 9781647122690 (hardcover) | ISBN 9781647122706 (paperback) | ISBN 9781647122713 (ebook)
Subjects: LCSH: Risk—Moral and ethical aspects. | Probabilities—Moral and ethical aspects. | Ethics. | Virtue.
Classification: LCC HM1101 .S34 2022 | DDC 303.3/72—dc23/eng/20211216
LC record available at https://lccn.loc.gov/2021049524

♾ This paper meets the requirements of ANSI/NISO Z39.48-1992 (Permanence of Paper).

23 22   9 8 7 6 5 4 3 2   First printing

Printed in the United States of America

Cover design by Nathan Putens
Cover art courtesy of Yadvinder Malhi et al., "New perspectives on the ecology of tree structure and tree communities through terrestrial laser scanning," The Royal Society Publishing, February 16, 2018.
Interior design by BookComp, Inc.

Contents

Acknowledgments

The writing of this book depended on the support, contributions, and ready ears of many people. My first thanks go to the faculty, students, and staff of the Catholic University of America. I have found a wonderful intellectual home at the university, especially among the fellow members of the Moral Theology and Ethics Area. I would also note the insights I gained from reading groups on Robert Spaemann and Alasdair MacIntyre graciously hosted by Reinhard Hütter and attended by David Cloutier, David Elliot, and Adrian Walker. The students in my 2020 course on early modern ethics helped me think through material for chapters 5 and 7 by reading the literature on probabilism, Aquinas, Machiavelli, Hobbes, and Rousseau with me. I particularly want to thank three graduate research assistants: Beth Lofgren, who developed my initial literature review; Mariele Courtois, who edited a project proposal and work on artificial intelligence; and Cristina Batt, who provided research support on many topics in the book and read through the draft manuscript. The university administration was also very helpful, including my dean, Father Mark Morozowich, and the provost, Aaron Dominguez, who supported my sabbatical application and my work on science and religion more broadly.

Support for this book was provided by the John Templeton Foundation through the Collaborative Inquiries in Christian Theological Anthropology project. I received valuable feedback on part I from other scholars connected to the project: John Bowlin, Angela Carpenter, Elizabeth Cochran, Emily Dumler-Winckler, Jennifer Herdt, Christina McRorie, Stephen Pope, Patrick Smith, and Jonathan Tran. Agustin Fuentes, Andy Yuengert, and Christiana Zenner commented on draft chapters of the work. I am grateful to the grant's principal investigators—Neil Arner, Jesse Couenhoven, and Jerry McKenny—for their suggestions and am especially grateful to Jerry for initially encouraging me to pursue risk as a second project.

I am also indebted to the Louisville Institute for a Sabbatical Grant for Researchers. During the institute's Winter Seminar, I received feedback from Eric Barreto, Miguel De La Torre, Erik Estrada, and John Fitzgerald that helped me in framing my argument.

A long-term visiting fellowship at the Institute for Advanced Studies in Culture aided the writing of the book. Conversations with other fellows— like Matt Crawford, Mark Hoipkemier, Andrew Lynn, Justin Mutter, Paul Nedelisky, and Isaac Reed—have been invaluable. Reading groups and conferences with them have inspired much of my work in chapters 7 and 8, especially the conference "Persons without Qualities: Algorithms, AI, and the Reshaping of Ourselves," which was published as a special issue in *Social Research*. Special thanks go to my frequent collaborator, Joe Davis, with whom I have discussed many of the ideas in this book over lunch during the long days of the lockdown.

This project has benefited from feedback and insights from many other friends and scholars, including Sister Juliet Namiiro, Luis Vera, and Jarrett Zigon. Through two Early Careers Scholars workshops organized by Jeff Bishop, I received comments on what became part I from Carl Elliot, Kimbell Kornu, Devan Stahl, Dan Sulmasy, and Matthew Vest. I also profited from conversations during the Working Group on Theology and the Medicalization of Risk, funded by the McDonald Agape Foundation with Farr Curlin, Stanley Hauerwas, Mary Hirschfeld, Warren Kinghorn, Brett McCarty, Peter McDonald, and Kavin Rowe. My analysis of artificial intelligence was enriched by the discussions of a working group organized by Brian Green and Monsignor Paul Tighe, which included Matthew Gaudet, David DeCosse, Mark McKenna, and Andrea Vicini.

Greg LaNave gave permission to use text from my article "Prudence, Precaution, and Uncertainty: Assessing the Health Benefits and Ecological Risks of Gene Drive Technology Using the Quasi-Integral Parts of Prudence," which appeared in *The Thomist* 81, no. 4 (2017): 507–37. Parts of it appear in chapters 6, 9, and 10. This article developed from a paper presented at a meeting of the Catholic Theological Society of America. Early versions of some of the ideas in parts I and III were developed in my articles "Risk, Health and Physical Enhancement: The Dangers of Health Care as Risk Reduction for Christian Bioethics," *Christian Bioethics* 26, no. 2 (2020): 145–62; and "Risk, Prudence, and Moral Formation in the Laboratory," *Journal of Moral Education* 47, no. 3 (2018): 304–15, although text from them does not appear in this book and the ideas have greatly developed since these early papers. Scripture quotations are from New Revised Standard Version Bible, Catholic Edition, copyright © 1989, 1993 National Council of the Churches of Christ in the United States of America. All rights reserved worldwide.

I also owe many thanks to Georgetown University Press, especially to the editor Al Bertrand, and the editors of the Moral Traditions Series, David Cloutier, Darlene Weaver, and Andrea Vicini. They, along with two anonymous readers, ensured a remarkably efficient and helpful review process that greatly improved the final presentation of my argument.

Finally, I thank my family, without whom this book would not have been possible. My mother, Elizabeth Scherz, provided countless forms of concrete support throughout the pandemic, but even more important, she has provided me with an example of how to deal with risk in later life. My children, Iggy and Lucy, have helped me to put aside this project at times so that I could enjoy the present. Finally, I thank my wife, China. Many of the ideas in this book emerged or were clarified in conversations and on walks, and she also commented on the whole manuscript. She has not only supported me personally as I tried to complete this project during the difficult days of the lockdown but is also my most important intellectual interlocutor.

Introduction

So do not worry about tomorrow, for tomorrow will bring
worries of its own. Today's trouble is enough for today.

—*Matthew 6:34 (NRSV)*

Risk management is a central task of contemporary institutions. Governments
and corporations struggle to predict in order to control the course of possible
future events, such as market downturns, wars, and pandemics. Techniques
of risk management depend, in turn, on predictions based in probabilistic
analysis. The COVID-19 pandemic illustrated the importance of probabilistic prediction as well as some of its problems. A striking feature of the news
coverage during the initial lockdown and throughout subsequent months was
the focus on possible trajectories for the disease. Different groups of disease
modelers released their predictions, usually a range of predictions, for how
the disease would progress. These predictions differed widely. Sensing a des-
peration in the public for a sense of control over the future, reporters discussed every new study and each new prediction: How many deaths could
one expect (estimates reported ranged from tens of thousands to 70 million)?
When will viral infections peak (ten days, six weeks, four months)? When
will the country hit an inflection point? Will there be a second or third wave?
Most important, when will this be over? Unfortunately, due to the nature of
modeling, especially in a crisis for which modelers lack hard data, there is
never a single answer but always a variety of possible curves, possible trajectories, possible futures. The focus on multiple possible futures itself created
problems, as uncertainty caused anxiety or different individuals committed
themselves to the reality of distinct possibilities, shaping political conflict.

This crisis dramatically illustrates our more general stance toward the
future. Action has always taken place under uncertainty. Yet there is something new today. Not only do we live in complex, rapidly changing, densely
interconnected societies, heightening the unpredictability of an action's

consequences, but techniques of probabilistic prediction have made differing possibilities a more important aspect of discerning particular action. Knowing such a range of possible scenarios can enable policymakers to respond to hidden or emergent dangers. Yet this mode of temporality, this stance toward the possible future, is not confined to policy elites. Almost everyone is called to participate in it. The news media was desperate for details about the multiple COVID trajectories precisely because their consumers desired, or at least were encouraged to desire, knowledge of them. To take another example, news coverage in the days preceding the 2020 election largely occurred in the future tense: predictive models of voting, how different states breaking different ways could affect the models, whether violence would result from the election. This kind of news reflects the scenario planning that people are called to do in everyday life: business strategies, retirement planning, medical decisions.

Not everyone, however, receives the same vision of the future. Social media news feeds directed some users to the direst predictions of COVID. In contrast, other news feeds were filled with optimistic projections or criticisms of catastrophic scenarios. These alternative news feeds were also shaped by probabilistic prediction. Based on past viewing habits, a person's contacts' habits, and other elements of his profile, the algorithms governing his social media feeds would fill them with the content that he was most likely to click on and view for the longest time. Generally, this content would match his and his contacts' preexisting views. In this way, probabilistic prediction created communities exposed to different narratives of the present, accelerating trends already emerging in older forms of media. The different visions of the future accentuated moral and political disagreement, undermining the collective political action necessary to combat the pandemic. At its worst, such algorithms can encourage conspiracy theories, such as denials that COVID even exists. Such conspiracy theories generate lengthy engagement with a website, increasing sites' revenues and fulfilling the algorithms' imperatives. Probabilistic prediction shapes attention, discourse, knowledge of the world, and thus action.

A final example shows that problems can arise even when prediction occurs at a more individual level. Early during the pandemic, there were debates as to how to distribute ventilators in overcrowded intensive care units. The most widely discussed debate was over whether to use age and predicted quality of life in making these decisions, criteria that would discriminate against older adults and people with disabilities.[1] Most religious ethicists argued for a more objective test for rationing, something like a sequential organ failure assessment (SOFA) score. SOFA scores predict the risk of death based on clinical indicators such as heart, liver, and kidney function. Although seemingly objective, scholars noted that a racial bias is baked into such rationing.[2] Minority patients are more likely to have worse SOFA scores because they have a greater chance of suffering from comorbidities due to conditions like diabetes and high blood pressure. This disproportionate burden of poor health is due in turn to poverty or lack of health care caused by a long legacy of historical injustice.[3] In this way, probabilistic prediction could perpetuate past wrongs as their consequences become integrated into metrics based on probabilistic risk assessment.

In each of these examples, we see the probabilistic prediction of risk in action. It is embedded in basic bureaucratic procedures as well as in everyday technologies like social media. Many of these technologies depend on machine learning, a form of artificial intelligence, to deliver predictions. Epidemiological predictions also rely on massive computing power. For this reason, today, probabilistic risk assessment is deeply intertwined with emerging forms of artificial intelligence, making it an important locus of analysis.

This book investigates this framework of probabilistic prediction of risk, founded upon the mobilizing of multiple futures at both the individual and social levels. It examines how this framework shapes contemporary consciousness, systems of power, and technology. The subsequent chapters explore its historical and theoretical foundations, its effects both on the acting subject and society, and its problems. Part III of the book asks what alternatives there are. Can and should Christians think otherwise about action?

RISK AND PROBABILITY IN CHRISTIAN ETHICS

Although the COVID-19 pandemic has strikingly highlighted the role of probabilistic prediction and risk, more and more areas of daily life—including work, shopping, online interactions, and investments—are shaped around probabilistic risk assessment. The rise of probability theory since the seventeenth century has formed our entire mental apparatus: in public health, but also in physics, biology, medicine, finance, and law. It would be difficult to find a field of thought not affected by the probabilistic revolution. In this book, I address its use primarily with regard to practical reasoning at personal and social levels.

This investigation involves a focus on two forms of thought. First, there is decision theory, a way of using predictions of the probability of future states of affairs to choose a course of action. Although its roots stretch back to the origins of probability theory, a risk-based decision theory was not fully formalized until after World War II, when there was an explosion of work on topics like game theory, rational actor theory, and risk/benefit analysis. Since that time, it has moved from being a tool of military strategy, business, or policymaking to being considered the idealized form of rationality for all practical reasoning. For many policymakers, every citizen should be a rational actor conscious of future risks. When they are not, these deviations are deemed biases, thus showing that this model of thought has become normative.

A second domain involves a public policy rationality that considers people in terms of populations. Populations have specific characteristics, such as disease risks, risk of death due to accidents, distribution of traits, and consumer habits. In this view, risk is "a statistical and probabilistic technique, whereby large numbers of events are sorted into a distribution."[4] In this form of rationality, the decision-maker first analyzes the statistical characteristics of a population and then manipulates them to achieve her ends. These ends could be increasing the sales of a product by manipulating the propensities of a consumer population. Or it could be an attempt to improve the health of the population by changing social conditions or individual behaviors to reduce certain risks. In the contemporary world, governments and corporations implement these modes of behavioral intervention through forms of artificial intelligence. Both modalities, decision theory and population-based governance, require the quantitative prediction of risk.

Despite the centrality of these modes of thought for society, relatively little work has been done on them and their implications in religious ethics.[5] One might think that the long-running debates surrounding consequentialism, the mode of ethics that determines the morality of an action based on its ratio of costs and benefits, would address these modes of thought. Yet these debates tend to focus primarily on the important question of whether any kinds of actions are inherently immoral, regardless of the consequences, or on whether certain kinds of rights may be violated. In the Catholic tradition, the most important instance of this debate occurred in the proportionalist controversy from the 1960s to the 1990s.[6] Proportionalist theologians, as they are commonly called, argued that the morality of an action depended primarily on whether the amount of harm, like death or economic loss, caused by the action was proportionate to the goods achieved by the action. Was the value aimed at best achieved by the action or undermined by its unintended consequences? To determine the ratio of goods to evils, some proportionalists tried to integrate probabilistic styles of policy decision-making into Catholic ethics. For example, they made the determination of the speed limit, with its balancing of the economic costs (and thus decreased resources to spend on health care and fewer jobs) of a low speed limit with the increased traffic deaths of a high speed limit, a key paradigm for practical reason.[7]

In the end, however, the debate turned away from the difficulties of using this mode of reasoning, circling instead around the proportionalists' rejection of the idea that any physical action type is intrinsically evil. Although important, especially as it affects the evaluation of technologies like contraception, the question of whether seemingly immoral actions can become moral due to their consequences affects only a narrow band of human action. Most of the time, people are not deciding the dramatic questions that inspire the paradigmatic thought experiments of the proportionalists: whether to push an obese man in front of a trolley, perform a craniotomy, or lynch an innocent person to appease an angry mob.

Debates over proportionalism and other forms of consequentialism thus tended to neglect the difficult negotiations of consequences in everyday life, the common prudential decisions that can have large effects, such as whether to allow a certain chemical into widespread use, whether to have a genetic test for breast cancer, or how much to invest for retirement. This book addresses these more mundane actions rather than more dramatic cases like direct killing or contraception. Everyone accepts that the ratio of good to bad consequences from an action should be proportionate, but no one can really say what that means, even consequentialists. Moreover, consequentialism takes our emerging form of probabilistic prediction as a given, failing to address how it is changing our perception of the world and our actions in it. As debates surrounding decision theory and the precautionary principle that I discuss in this book suggest, policymakers recognize that human finitude limits the number of future consequences that one can consider, but it is how to draw these limits that should be the actual focus of debate. To take the example of proportionalism again, its proponents' theoretical system was foundering on the meaning of proportionate reason even before its papal condemnation.[8]

Virtue ethics could engage these last questions concerning practical reason, although risk and decision theory have not been central to its agenda. Some important work in the field has addressed contingency, but largely in relation to the classical category of fortune or moral luck rather than to the contemporary probabilistic prediction of risk.[9] More recently, philosopher- and theologian-economists like Andrew Yuengert and Mary Hirschfeld have criticized the weaknesses of rational actor theory as a model of practical reason, suggesting that it fails to truly describe the human good and human desire.[10] They have criticized the background assumptions and methodological developments of this mode of thought, a critique upon which my analysis builds. Like me, they have turned to virtue theory as an antidote. However, their discussion has understandably focused primarily on the economic domain, whereas this book looks at the effect of risk-based practical reason in other areas, like health, technology, and daily life.

Some virtue ethicists address new technologies such as artificial intelligence and social media.[11] Much of this literature considers general virtues for a technological society or for engagement with a specific technology. Although these efforts are valuable, considerable insights may be gained by evaluating human interactions with these technologies against the broader background of the probabilistic prediction discussed here. One starts to see consistent patterns of engaging the world, those that operate beyond the use of technology. Such an analysis also provides deeper insights into the philosophical anthropology and model of practical reason that supports these technologies.

Perhaps the best discussion of the broader implications of probabilistic prediction for human character occurred at the very origins of the contemporary recovery of virtue. In *After Virtue*, Alasdair MacIntyre condemned the predictive game theory operative in the social sciences, a condemnation of bureaucratic manipulation that inspires much of my own analysis.[12] However, as I and others have argued, MacIntyre's thought tends to idealize communities isolated from the contemporary world.[13] Although his most recent work has tried to provide a few examples of contemporary communities of virtue, like school boards, he is still most enthusiastic about articulating the virtues of the fishing village.[14] Yet it is much more difficult to see what social forms might arise in the present that would not engage bureaucratic rationalities. In this book, I suggest how probabilistic prediction of risk can be appropriately used in many instances but not universally, and I also identify social forms that could constrain them.

This book attempts to address these lacunae in current virtue theory and religious ethics more generally by examining other effects of probabilistic risk assessment on subjectivity, relationships, and social systems. It morally forms people, in the sense of shaping dispositions, worldviews, and affects. Moreover, it is transforming society. As many have noted, we now live in a risk society, oriented toward fears of the future: risks of cancer, environmental degradation, precarious jobs, economic debt, terrorism, crime, and on and on.[15] Probabilistic prediction grants us amazing control, but paradoxically increases our fears exponentially at the same time.

My argument is that dangers arise when probabilistic prediction expands beyond its appropriate domain and becomes a worldview. But the problems of probabilistic risk analysis that I chronicle here are not inevitable. There are applications today and historically in which they have not engendered such dangers. As the coming chapters note, the Enlightenment figures who developed probabilistic techniques did not see their mathematical analysis as the fundamental interpretation of practical reason but instead adjusted their mathematics to fit the prudence of the wise person. Many economists have recognized decision theory as the formal abstraction that it is. Risk analysts themselves accept the limitations of cost/benefit calculations. When such limitations are acknowledged, these technologies can be incredible tools for serving human flourishing, as I discuss in chapter 10. Insofar as we are embodied creatures facing the dangers of an uncertain, fallen world, risk analysis is a useful tool for caring for ourselves and others.

Today, however, this rationality is capturing more and more domains of life, spreading beyond particular policy and business decisions into the sphere of private action. It threatens to become the paradigmatic form of rationality against which all decisions are judged. In its use in governance, probabilistic prediction of risk also supports a particular vision of the human. Chapter 7 describes this behaviorist understanding of the individual as a stimulus/response machine operating through a probabilistic calculus. It is this vison of the human that supports manipulative forms of power. Parts I and II of the book are dedicated to exploring the dangers that arise when this form of rationality expands to shape all spheres of life and becomes a worldview. However, throughout the book, and especially in part III, I point out ways to positively appropriate probabilistic forms of rationality so that they serve rather than undermine human goods.

AN ETHICAL FRAMEWORK

Two interrelated questions or themes appear especially important for the ethical assessment of probability theory. The first regards a new relationship to the future. Probabilistic risk assessment promises a knowledge of this future. More specifically, it promises a knowledge of how likely it is for a particular future to come to fruition. Through the techniques of risk assessment, the agent seems able to see all possible futures and their chances of realization. This knowledge gives him the power to prepare for and perhaps even select the future he desires. Scholars often criticize the Promethean pretentions of technology. It is appropriate that "Prometheus" literally means "foresight"; these technologies gain much of their power through their claimed prediction of the future. What does this mode of engaging the future in terms of prediction and control over multiple possibilities portend for character and practical reason? Second, given this possible control over the future, what is the agent's responsibility for it? It might seem that she can take steps to mitigate every possible harm, so, at a policy level, it invites regulatory and technological control. Yet, as we shall see, every step of mitigation creates new risks. What responsibility does she, as an individual or policymaker, bear for the realized risks? Moreover, because people are embedded in bureaucratic systems attempting to control them, does the individual bear any responsibility or does responsibility lie at the level of systems?

This second question of responsibility for the future becomes especially pressing for Christians as it relates to our trust in God's providence. Christian ethics faces the question of how to live in a society hyperfocused on predictive control of the future when Christ tells us to not be overly solicitous about tomorrow, even with regard to basic needs like food and clothing.[16] The Sermon on the Mount, which will be central to my analysis, and countless parables condemn these concerns, and the Church Fathers tie such anxious solicitude to greed and vicious forms of power. These concerns over whether human attempts at control show lack of faith in God's action stretch back into the Old Testament and Israel's faith in God's saving work. Central to this work is discerning how one should use these tools in the face of these warnings.

In framing these questions, I draw on Stoic virtue ethics. Stoicism was deeply concerned about what the individual can be responsible for in the face of life's uncertainties. These questions were pressing, given the negative constraints of their social position in a highly stratified society. In the Hellenistic period and the early Roman Empire, nearly every free person was an intermediary, dependent on more powerful patrons but also serving as a patron to subordinates. Stoicism was an ethics designed for intermediary actors, who attempted to do the good they could within the constraints of power.[17] On the positive side, Stoics trusted that the decrees of divine providence will always be realized in history, no matter how the individual acted. They merely needed to conform their judgments with the providential rationality of the natural law governing the cosmos, whatever the predicted consequences. Uncertainty, social position, and providence severely constrained Stoics' responsibility, in the sense of liability for consequences. Yet this did not mean that they eschewed responsibility in terms of care for others and for society. Indeed, much of their ethics was designed to allow them to meet their duties of care.[18] Stoics thus encouraged agents to pursue ends in action that corresponded to human nature, what they call natural functions, or *katechonta*; but they also recognized that ensuring success in achieving such ends was beyond human capability. Recognizing these intellectual advantages, Christian ethicists drew on Stoicism in the responsibility ethics that developed in the last century. For these reasons, Stoicism is a useful framework in which to consider both duties to others while also recognizing constraints on action. Moreover, considerations of temporality were central to Stoics' ethical system, and developing a focus on the present served as a major goal of their spiritual exercises.[19] My analysis does not focus on the particular virtues, because Stoicism is much more concerned about how habits and practices shape perception of the world as well as how these interpretations are translated into action.

Though my analysis is inspired by Stoic ethics, it still has ramifications for Aristotelian, Thomistic, and other forms of virtue ethics. In many ways, these different systems have already influenced each other over the course of history. For example, my attempt in chapter 10 to meld probabilistic risk assessment with the virtue of prudence uses the Thomistic model of practical reason, which itself is a blend of the Stoic and Aristotelian understandings of prudence. Further, the conclusion discusses how to translate the arguments in this book into the framework of the seven Thomistic virtues. Though Stoic in inspiration, this study has implications for any virtue ethic.

A THEOLOGICAL FRAMEWORK

The early Christian adoption of Stoicism fundamentally modified the Stoics' understanding of the person and action, due to doctrines like a personal God, the Paschal sacrifice, the Resurrection, and grace. Although there are many continuities between Stoicism and Christianity, moral theologians must take note of important differences in their anthropologies and even more so their mutual differences with contemporary conceptions of the person. Every critique is based on a positive vision, and my critique of the contemporary understanding of the person that is tied to probabilistic prediction of risk arises out of my commitment to a Christian anthropology that envisions the human person in relation to God. In this work, I embrace a broadly Thomistic theological anthropology—"broadly" because it will become clear that the analysis presented here differs from that of Aquinas in many ways, primarily in terms of different emphases, such as a more Stoic approach to some questions, and a rejection of some aspects of Aquinas's thought, such as his faculty psychology. Nor does this book provide an exegesis of Aquinas's works, though exegesis is important in some chapters. The book also draws on many resources unavailable to Aquinas, such as social theory and phenomenology. I deploy Thomistic thought as a general framework, while differing in some details, in the way that much of contemporary Catholic moral theology draws on Thomistic themes.

Aquinas's anthropological vision is founded in the understanding that men and women are created in the image of God.[20] Although this concept is complex, Aquinas defines it using John Damascene's understanding of the image as implying "an intelligent being endowed with free will and self-movement."[21] In their intellectual capacities, humans reflect God, who freely and contingently creates the world out of nothing, ordering it through His rational Logos. Aquinas also draws on Augustine's picture of what God is in Himself apart from Creation, what is known as the immanent Trinity: God the Father knows Himself through His Word, who is the Son, and from this knowledge springs forth love, the Holy Spirit.[22] People are thus rational agents with reason and free will, and any attempts to undermine that rational agency, as appears in the forms of governance of populations through risk and algorithms discussed in chapter 8, offend against the image of God in the person.

Because of the multiple contemporary meanings of reason and free will, this theological anthropology can be easily misunderstood. Though practical reason is an important aspect of human intellectual ability, the highest form of intellectual activity for the Thomistic tradition is contemplation, gaining insight into the essence of things and the causal structures of the world.[23] Therefore, reason is broader than the calculative rationality of decision theory. As many scholars have noted in debates surrounding artificial intelligence, human intellect cannot be reduced to probabilistic prediction and choice but must include other essential capacities, such as the ability to grasp meaning.[24] Ultimately, human intellectual faculties are aimed at the contemplation of God. It is in knowing and loving God that persons most closely image God, who knows and loves Himself. It is in this Beatific Vision and sharing in the eternal life of God that humans reach their ultimate end.[25] Thus, we must reject any attempt to make probabilistic theory aimed at achieving temporal goods the sole or even paradigmatic form of human intellectual activity, as scholars of decision theory discussed in chapters 2 and 7 attempt to do.

Second, a truly free will is not arbitrary, aimed at whatever momentary desires a person might have. Instead, the will is ordered toward attaining human flourishing through fulfilling the goods of human nature. In Servais Pinckaers's words, it is a freedom for excellence rather than a freedom of indifference.[26] The modern revival of virtue ethics is closely tied to this appreciation for teleology, meaning both that every action is for an end and that moral ends must conform to our natural teleology, the goods appropriate to the kind of creatures humans are, such as health, social relations, family, and intellectual pursuits.[27]

For Aquinas, the highest good, the most complete realization of human capacities, is to know and love God. Loving God means uniting one's will with His. As chapter 9 discusses, Christian practical rationality, reflecting the Lord's Prayer, entails seeking that His will be done. For the Christian, the fiat of Mary at the Annunciation and Jesus in the Garden of Gethsemane serve as the model of all action. In the ancient philosophical tradition and in Patristic theology, the turn away from God's will toward one's own is ultimately a form of enslavement to the passions or to others rather than true freedom. Thus, the turn toward temporal goods described in chapters 3, 4, 7, and 8 that are coincident with modern forms of probabilistic rationality lead to problems like anxiety, addiction, loss of agency, and unhappiness.

But it would be a mistake to believe that the accomplishment of God's will is in doubt. God not only creates but also governs the universe through His providence. As in the Stoic conception, all events occur either by His express will or at least by His permission (in the case of evils). God's providence has become theologically and philosophically controversial, so I devote much of chapter 4 to defending it. Yet, in essence, the concept of providence assures us that we have no need to fear nor take excess responsibility for the future because God will make all things work for the good. This idea of providence does not lead to a deterministic universe, as some have feared, because God works through both necessary and contingent causes.[28] God allows creatures to have their own causality, with God's governance even working through human wills. Though God is never the cause of sin, His grace is necessary for a person to do good. At the same time, this involvement of God in human action does not negate human freedom, because God, as Creator, is not merely another cause acting in the world in competition with human causality. God's action transcends the network of natural causality. How exactly to reconcile the role of God's providence and human free will is a highly debated point, which this book cannot solve.[29] It merely accepts that the divine and human contributions to action occur in a noncontrastive way.

Finally, this vision of humanity is fundamentally relational. Humans are made for communion with God through knowledge and love. Through God and the Body of Christ, we are made to relate to other people as well. Even at a natural level, humans are political and social creatures depending on others for meeting their basic needs as well as the need for full human flourishing. Humans seek a common good in the shared life of society. Any individualistic picture of the self, as one finds in the decision theory sketched in part I, is incorrect. As chapter 11 discusses, people must support each other in their weakness through appropriate social structures that manage risk. At the same time, others must always be recognized as persons who themselves have agency. They cannot be cared for merely as statistical lives or objects of policy, as the governance mechanisms described in part II attempt to do.

Care must always be intersubjective in nature, helping others to fully participate in society.[30]

The foregoing description is the broadly Thomistic anthropology that will inform my analysis, one shared by much of contemporary Catholic moral theology. This anthropology is itself shaped by a very classical doctrine of God, who is understood as eternal, omnipotent, omniscient, and the like—all of which attributes are entailed by God's simplicity and status as Creator. There are many other possible theological anthropologies, and many theologians who would reject aspects of this framework: many theologians of technology desire a greater emphasis on human freedom and cocreation; other theologians are concerned about the focus on rationality found in it; feminist theologians are dismayed by the seeming individualism of this image of God; some Protestant theologians dislike tying the image of God to human nature; and others would see the image of God in Christ alone.[31] These are all important considerations, and ones that this Thomistic framework can address, but it would take another whole book to adequately confront them.

Here, there is only space to give merely the positive reason as to why this theological framework is so helpful for this project: its richly synthetic nature. MacIntyre has shown that Aquinas's work is structured in the form of an ongoing debate.[32] It addresses the best arguments presented on an issue so far and subsumes them into a broader synthesis. Aquinas himself provides perhaps the most complete synthesis of Patristic thought. He also combines the largely Augustinian theology of his time with the new Aristotelian philosophy. In so doing, he provides a synthesis of Stoic and Aristotelian concepts of action, as I have noted. This structure also allows him to develop Augustinian ideas of temporality while engaging the most advanced forms of natural philosophy available to him.[33] This multifaceted structure gives this tradition the ability to confront new social situations, much as it did in the medieval period.[34] In the last century, thinkers have used broadly Thomistic premises to address and absorb social theory, labor issues, phenomenology, personalism, and human rights discourse, among other developments.[35] I am convinced that this is the theological framework with the greatest ability to engage new ideas and developments while retaining the best aspects of the tradition.

STRUCTURE OF THE ARGUMENT

To make its argument, the book is divided into three parts. These parts mirror distinctions in probability theory itself, which has two main theoretical schools for interpreting the meaning of the mathematics of probability. The first, the subjectivist school, understands probability as individual, subjective estimates of the likelihood of events. Part I therefore examines the use of probability by the individual actor. The second, objectivist interpretation holds that certain probabilities are objective features of things, situations, or collectivities in the world, like a container of gas molecules or the population of a city. Therefore, part II examines the way people are now made the object of probabilistic calculations to govern their behavior. The early chapters in parts I and II do not engage in much theological analysis and critique but instead aim at explaining these phenomena on their own terms. This form of rationality is so common today that it appears natural to us. Because of this seeming naturalness, I spend many pages developing historical, social scientific, and phenomenological analyses so that the reach of this way of thinking becomes recognizable. I try to describe these concepts and social programs in a way that is fair and that the authors of these systems would largely accept, while at the same time allowing them to stand out in their distinctness. One of the best ways to make this new way of thinking stand out is to compare it with previous models of practical reason or moral judgment. My aim in the early chapters of parts I and II is not so much to proclaim these earlier ways of thinking as better but to show that risk analysis is relatively new and contingent. Only once the phenomenon appears can I fully subject it to theological and ethical analysis, as I do in the later chapters of parts I and II. Part III then develops a Christian way to engage the questions raised in the first two parts.

The book begins with an overview of probability theory, especially how it differs from older Aristotelian models of contingency. Probability theory introduced not only a new form of mathematics but also a new way of understanding contingency and uncertainty. Chapter 2 discusses how this new understanding has shaped practical reason through decision theory. Here again, one sees a shift from classical and medieval thought. As other authors have discussed, the agent in decision theory no longer focuses primarily on an end to be achieved through action. Instead, she envisions possible futures arising from decision situations, surveys the benefits and dangers emerging from each scenario as modified by their likelihood, and then chooses between these possible futures. This framework creates a radical instability in the agent's relationship to ends.

This form of decision theory also transforms the person's relationship to the future, as is described in chapter 3. Instead of focusing on an end, the actor must conjure all the likely possible futures and meditate on them. This way of engaging the future leaves the person unprepared for true novelty because it suggests that the possible futures can be known in advance. Not only is this a philosophically deficient way of envisioning temporality but it also creates problems for the actor through its psychological effects. As alternative futures are made concrete in the actor's mind, she realizes what she must forgo in making any choice and anticipates how she will feel in the future knowing what was lost. Research in psychology and economics suggests that the resulting anticipatory regret in relation to forgone goods has become a major problem for contemporary actors. This should be no surprise, as existentialist philosophers such as Kierkegaard and Heidegger discussed how closely related a focus on possibility is to feelings of anxiety.

Because of this anxiety, probability theory tends to encourage desires for security, as chapter 4 examines. Indeed, decision theory was designed to stabilize the nuclear balance of terror. It seems to promise a system of control. Yet theologians see this desire for security provided through one's own efforts as dangerous. Because a person can never have enough money or resources to ensure future security, he falls prey to greed. He seeks to earn ever more money without risk, which was the great problem scholastics saw in usury. More fundamentally, seeking to ensure security through one's own efforts undermines trust in God's providence, a stance that is at the heart of the Sermon on the Mount.

Part II addresses how this desire for security is instantiated in politics through the use of probabilistic risk analysis. Before getting into the heart of these issues, chapter 5 examines the shifting meanings of the word "probability," giving a historical overview of how these different meanings have had an impact on understandings of interpersonal relationships. In ancient and medieval thought, the probability of something referred to its trustworthiness. This probability could refer to things like arguments and evidence, suggesting their strength. More essentially, however, probability judgments relied on relationships of intersubjective trust. This trust could be as to whether a witness was credible or, in the theological system of probabilism, whether a probable opinion was one held by a trustworthy authority, a moral theologian approved by the Church. This changed with Pascal's simultaneous assault on casuistry in his *Provincial Letters* and his development of the mathematics of probability. Probability became tied to either one's subjective judgment or to objective features of the world. The intersubjective aspect of trust in a tradition's authoritative figures was lost.

Chapter 6 explores how the objective notion of probability shaped politics through differing notions of responsibility for risk. On one hand, politicians seemed to become more responsible for the consequences of their actions, consequences that could now be calculated with greater accuracy. Indeed, the development of statistics showed that citizens could be understood in terms of populations that had different distributions of characteristics. Politics became responsible for the risks run by the population, driven to manipulate statistical variables through mechanisms like insurance and regulation. All possible futures were analyzed through risk/benefit calculations. Yet it became apparent that technological attempts to provide security through new medical treatments, pesticides, power sources, and so forth were creating new risks. The limits of prediction became apparent as cost/benefit analyses proved false due to unintended effects of policies. These problems gave rise to another form of managerial responsibility, a precautionary approach intending to prevent future disasters. Given the risks unleashed by any action, however, this approach could stymie all policies. In response to these problems and the increasing regulation of risk, a completely different mode of responsibility became popular, one similar to older liberalism. This mode called for everyone to be responsible for himself and to embrace uncertainty. If the prior managerial mode depended on the providence of politicians, this neoliberal form depends on the providence of the market.

One of the chief sources of uncertainty to be controlled in all these forms of governance is human action. Humans are unpredictable and possibly dangerous, not only through malicious intent but even through innocent behaviors that increase risk, such as smoking. Much technology development has dedicated itself to making people more predictable and thus directing this behavior. Chapter 7 explores three examples of these new technologies (nudging, labor management, and surveillance capitalism) and the model of human nature that underlies them. This model, ultimately stemming from behaviorism, sees people as faulty rational actors, responding to environmental stimuli in predictable ways based in probabilistically distributed rewards or biases in calculating those rewards. As such, experts can design technologies to influence individual behavior by manipulating the environment to direct them to certain ends, generally based around temporal goods. To make such predictions, artificial intelligence systems require expert probabilistic predictive analysis of behavior, relying on massive amounts of data gained through intensive technological surveillance.

Chapter 8 analyzes the dangers of this approach. On one level, it centralizes power in ways that threaten abuse, allowing the manipulation of the objects of this power by those who possess the surveillance databases and control the implementation of algorithms managing social institutions. It also systematizes and expands bias against marginalized groups. At a deeper level, it does not address people's reason and free will, failing to recognize them as made in the image of God. Instead, it treats them as predictable stimulus/response machines. At its worst, as described in Natasha Dow

Schull's ethnography of addictive programming, these systems can entice people to acquiesce in voiding rational agency altogether by embracing a compulsive pushing of buttons for psychic rewards. Drawing on Romano Guardini's discussion of the demonic, the chapter describes how these strategies embody an intensification of one tendency of modern systems of power, a tendency to eliminate responsible agency.

Given the dangers of either the abdication of or overweening forms of responsibility, chapter 9 begins part III by examining theological frameworks of responsibility developed in the twentieth century. These frameworks focus on the Christian's response to God's will in a specific situation. Practical reason is envisioned as the attempt to discern, based on past experience, both one's own and that contained in the Christian tradition, what God calls the person to do in the particular moment. The focus is not on future scenarios and consequences but on the present and thus avoids the problematic temporality of much risk-based decision theory.

This framework does not deny that consequences play some role in right practical reason, as God gives each person responsibility for particular others. It is a limited responsibility, however, because of trust in God's providence and a recognition of others' agency. This recognition of consequences means that there is a defined role for probabilistic risk/benefit analysis, primarily at the policy level, as discussed in chapter 10. Such analysis is especially needed when confronting new technologies or situations for which the past provides little guidance. This mode of analysis is not determinative, however; it's merely a step in the process of counsel, one of the components of a fuller vision of prudence.

These forms of responsible, prudent agency can fully operate only in supportive social structures. Chapter 11 examines Scripture for principles for properly addressing common risks. Although the Wisdom Literature outlines modes of personal providence, the Law suggests forms of social structure that limit the effects of realized risks, such as the Jubilee Year. These sources also suggest the role of organizations based on intersubjective engagement for supporting the suffering and those who are at risk. This chapter sketches elements of a better social approach toward risk, one that limits types of harm through social structures and safety net programs while providing interpersonal systems of support based in subsidiarity. Through these measures, society can escape the manipulation, objectification, and unintended consequences that bedevil more managerial forms of risk control.

This book provides only a sketch of a Christian response to the growth of probability-based mechanisms of governance and action in our society. To address it thoroughly, however, we must at least begin to recognize this problem and bring forth some of the theological resources for addressing it. That has been my goal here, to make a beginning. For that, one must understand, in some depth, the distinctiveness of modern understandings of uncertainty. Chapter 1 begins the body of the book with this very task.

NOTES

1. For two important contributions to this debate, see Emanuel et al., "Fair Allocation"; and Joint Statement, "Moral Guidance."
2. Menconi, "COVID-19 Ventilator Allocation Protocols"; Tartak and Khidir, "US Must Avoid Building Racial Bias into COVID-19 Emergency Guidance"; Schmidt, Roberts, and Enanya, "Rationing, Racism and Justice."
3. Farmer, *Pathologies of Power*; Marmot, "Social Determinants of Health Inequalities."
4. O'Malley, "Governmentality and Risk," 56. This analysis of risk as governmental technique has its origins in the work of Foucault et al., *Foucault Effect*; and Foucault, *Security, Territory, Population*. But other schools of sociology examine the reflective focus on risk under the moniker of the risk society. See Giddens, *Consequences of Modernity*; Beck, *Risk Society*; and Luhmann, *Risk*.
5. An important exception is Welch, *Feminist Ethic*. Welch provides an insightful critique of game theory from a womanist perspective. Most theological analysis of risk has tended to focus on God's risk in Creation, such as Gregersen, "Risk and Religion." These latter works depend on a very different doctrine of Creation and God than that found in this book.
6. There is no neutral label for these prominent Catholic moral theologians—including Richard McCormick, Bruno Schuller, Charles Curran, Josef Fuchs, and Peter Knauer—who attempted to rethink practical reasoning in the wake of Vatican II and the debate over contraception, because each term (proportionalist, revisionist, etc.) reflects a certain perspective on the controversy. I use "proportionalism" merely because it is a commonly recognized label. For historical overviews, see Odozor, *Moral Theology*; Keenan, *History of Catholic Moral Theology*.
7. Knauer, "Hermeneutic Function," 11–13; Janssens, "Ontic Evil and Moral Evil," 63–64, 79.
8. For a discussion of these difficulties, see McCormick, *Ambiguity*; McCormick, "Commentary on the Commentaries." For papal condemnation, see John Paul II, *Veritatis splendor*.
9. Williams, *Moral Luck*; Bowlin, *Contingency and Fortune*; Nussbaum, *Fragility of Goodness*.
10. Yuengert, *Approximating Prudence*; Hirschfeld, *Aquinas and the Market*.
11. E.g., Vallor, *Technology*; Bennett, *Aquinas on the Web?*; Vera, "Augmented Reality."
12. MacIntyre, *After Virtue*, 88–108.
13. Scherz, *Science and Christian Ethics*, chap. 5.
14. MacIntyre, *Ethics in the Conflicts of Modernity*, 167–80.
15. Beck, *Risk Society*.
16. Mt. 6:25–34.
17. Foucault, *Care of the Self*, 88. For a discussion of my interpretation of Foucault on these points, see Scherz, *Science and Christian Ethics*.
18. For care in Stoicism, see Reydams-Schils, *Roman Stoics*; Scherz, "Grief, Death, and Longing."
19. Hadot, *Philosophy*; Scherz, "Living Indefinitely."

20. Gn. 1:27; Thomas Aquinas, *Summa theologica*, I.93; Merriell, *To the Image of the Trinity*.
21. Aquinas, *Summa theologica*, I-II.Pref.
22. Aquinas, I.93a6.
23. Maritain, *Degrees of Knowledge*.
24. Dreyfus, *What Computers Can't Do*; Searle, "Minds, Brains, and Programs"; Larson, *Myth of Artificial Intelligence*.
25. Aquinas, *Summa theologica*, I.93a8, I-II.3a8; Peter, *Participated Eternity*.
26. Pinckaers, *Sources of Christian Ethics*, 327–99.
27. MacIntyre, *After Virtue*; MacIntyre, *Dependent Rational Animals*; Porter, *Nature as Reason*; International Theological Commission, "In Search of a Universal Ethic."
28. Aquinas, *Summa theologica*, I.105.
29. The literature is vast, but for discussion of these topics, see Tanner, *God and Creation*; Burrell, *Freedom and Creation*; Freddoso, "Introduction"; Byers, *Perception*; Rist, *Augustine Deformed*; Wawrykow, *God's Grace and Human Action*; and White, *Fate and Free Will*.
30. For a discussion of participation and the common good, see Hollenbach, *Common Good*.
31. A few representative examples of these concerns include Hefner, *Technology and Human Becoming*; LaCugna, *God for Us*; Wolterstorff, *Justice*; and Tanner, "Grace Without Nature."
32. MacIntyre, *Whose Justice?*; MacIntyre, *Three Rival Versions*.
33. Peter, *Participated Eternity*.
34. Porter, *Natural and Divine Law*.
35. E.g., Leo XIII, *Rerum novarum*; Stein, *Potency and Act*; Petri, *Aquinas and the Theology of the Body*; Tomczyk, "Presence of Virtue Ethics"; and Maritain, *Person and the Common Good*.

PART I

The Subjective Experience of Risk

1

From Contingency to Probability

So too that chance which seems slack-reined to roam,
endures its own bridle, and itself moves by law.

—*Boethius*

Before addressing the ethical ramifications of these phenomena, let us begin with a more basic question: What is risk? What is the associated concept of probability? Perhaps the easiest way to understand risk is to first distinguish it from what came before, from prior concepts by which philosophers and theologians considered future uncertainty. This is not an easy task. Although the ideas of probability and risk, especially as they are mathematically expressed, are not intuitive, they now possess a certain everydayness. Given the ways in which we are inculcated with and shaped by probabilistic thought, many people may think of these concepts as basic to the human conceptual apparatus. Yet they arose late, in the mid–seventeenth century. Today, even experts have difficulty using them in day-to-day life, showing their nonintuitive nature. Although there were ideas about uncertainty and the contingent future before this period, they were not expressed in terms of quantitative probabilities. So how are probabilistic notions different from prior modes of thinking about uncertainty? This chapter describes these different modes of approaching uncertain action, the difference between contemporary understandings of probabilistic risk and the Aristotelian model of contingency that guides virtue ethics. With these distinctions in place, their relevance for action will become apparent in later chapters.

ARISTOTELIAN CONTINGENCY

The first major problem with relating virtue ethics to contemporary risk society is that ancient virtue theorists had no concept of probabilistic risk.

The idea of risk did not develop until the late medieval period, and mathematical probability theory did not emerge until about 1654. For this reason and because of other theoretical concerns, ancient virtue theorists were committed to a certain kind of causal determinism, which could be quite rigid, depending on the school.[1] For example, a deterministic causal nexus was central to ancient Stoic ontology, serving as the vehicle of the divine providence of their immanent god.[2] This determinism was one of the many areas of contention with their chief philosophical rivals in Antiquity, the Epicureans, who believed in a nondeterminist universe shaped by the arbitrary swerve of atoms that were the fundamental particles of reality.[3] This randomness served to undermine ideas of providence in the Epicurean system and thus justified freedom and unconcern with the gods. As later chapters explore, questions of determinism are closely tied to concerns about freedom and divine action.

Though Aristotle was much more attentive to the effects of the unforeseen on human action than the Stoics, he too conceived of a largely causally determinist universe. It is true that he accepted chance as an efficient cause,[4] but his understanding of chance was not the same as the contemporary understanding of probability.[5] As Bernard Lonergan says, Aristotle explicitly "repudiated the possibility of a theory of probability. . . . Hence, while Aristotle recognized statistical residues and concrete patterns of diverging series of conditions, he had no theory of probability to bring them to heel within the field of scientific knowledge."[6] There is no deliberation about chance events, nor is there a science of chance in Aristotle.[7]

The closest concept in Aristotle to our ideas of probability was contingency, as contrasted with necessity. For some causal agents, effects follow necessarily from the action of the cause. For other causal agents, including most things in the sublunary realm, effects follow contingently upon the action of the cause—meaning that ordinarily and for the most part, a certain effect proceeds from the cause but that these effects can be interrupted by some other influence or by a failure on the part of the causal agent. Note that this is not a probabilistic understanding—it does not mean that, following an action, event x happens a certain percentage of times and event y happens a different percentage of times. It means that x generally happens unless z intervenes, which would give y. It is not a position based on probabilities.

Instead, Aristotle viewed the world as containing sets of determinate causal chains. In some interpretations of Aristotle, many of these deterministic causal chains can always be traced back to some sort of indeterminate event—such as an accident, a failure in the power of the agent, or a free choice of a rational agent—so it is not a completely determinist universe.[8] Moreover, these causal chains were not predictable, because sometimes these chains intersect in disruptive or productive ways, giving rise to unexpected outcomes.[9] Two of his examples of contingency show how this works. First, a farmer digging a hole in a field discovers buried treasure.[10] Two causal chains, someone who buried treasure and a person performing manual labor, come together to bring about a contingent event. In the second example, a person goes to the market for some reason.[11] He runs into a second person, who owes him money, so he is able to collect his debt. The first person does not go to the market for the purpose of collecting his debt, nor does the second person go to the market to pay his debt. Two unrelated sets of intentions and independent causal chains are at work. These causal chains intersect, giving rise to an unforeseen event that resolves a third chain, the loan and repayment of a debt. There is nothing in this explanation of events that hints at probability, just coincidences caused by intersecting determinist causal chains. This Aristotelian understanding of chance causality was tremendously influential. Later commentators again and again use the example of the farmer digging in a field finding gold, and this became the standard explanation of chance in the medieval tradition of Aristotelian commentary. For Christian authors like Boethius, however, chance is enfolded in providence: "We may therefore define chance as the unexpected event of concurring causes among things done for some purpose. Now causes are made to concur and flow together by that order which, proceeding with inevitable connexion, and coming down from its source in providence, disposes all things in their proper places and times."[12] The ethical importance of the theological tie between chance and providence will become apparent in chapters 4 and 9, where this tie becomes a balm for anxiety and an overinflated sense of responsibility.

PROBABILITY

Although recent Aristotelian and Thomistic commentators are clear that Aristotle had nothing like our contemporary concept of probability, they do not always make their justifications for this claim as explicit or detailed as one might desire. Few of these works make a clear distinction between how contingency operates and how probability does. To remedy this absence, we must look at what probability itself is to fully understand the difference it makes for ethics.

However, once one turns to the question of the definition of probability, there is an immediate problem: philosophers and practitioners disagree over their interpretations of probability. These disagreements do not affect day-to-day work in statistics, the practical techniques of which are highly developed and agreed upon by all statisticians, but they do make an impact on a theoretical grasp of probability. Though there are a wide variety of interpretations, these can be simplified into two broad groups: an objective and a subjective understanding of probability.[13] Historians of probability have shown that these two interpretations were interlinked for the first two centuries of probability theory, only becoming distinguished in philosophical debates in the nineteenth century.[14]

The Objectivist or Frequentist Interpretation

In the objectivist or frequentist interpretation, a probability is a feature of a distinct area of the world—what the philosopher Ian Hacking calls a chance setup.[15] The simplest, most obvious case regards those games of chance that lie at the origins of probabilistic thought. A coin has a 50 percent chance of landing heads or tails; each face of a die has a one-sixth chance of appearing after a roll. It is just a condition of the situation that there are a certain number of possible results. Note that each of these results or events is equiprobable. This is what the influential economist and philosopher of probability John Maynard Keynes called the principle of indifference: given a certain set of outcomes, one can determine the probability of a result by adding together the number of outcomes that give a certain result and dividing over the total possible outcomes.[16] The probability of getting an even face of the die is the sum of the three even sides divided by the total of six sides (three-sixths, or one-half). Probability is a combinatorial type of logic; one examines all possible combinations of results.

Of course, most events in the world about which one is interested are not equiprobable because not everything is like a roll of an equally weighted die. People are more likely to die of a heart attack than in a plane crash. A winter day is more likely to be cold than to be warm. Human action also alters probabilities. A smoker is more likely to die of lung cancer than a nonsmoker. A driver is more likely to crash if texting while driving than if not. Thus, a more general conception focuses on the distinct, long-run frequencies of different classes of events. Drawing on the law of large numbers, the idea is that as one gathers more and more instances of a certain chance setup—or collective, as Richard von Mises termed it—the relative frequency of certain events will settle down at a particular value.[17] If we gather more and more data on the mortality of smokers, we should find that a certain percentage, x, will die of lung cancer; a certain percentage, y, will die of heart disease; and that these percentages will be stable over time. In this interpretation, the collective at which one looks is essential; different collectives will have different relative frequencies of events. If we turn to the general population instead of just smokers, we find that a different percentage, *a*, die of lung cancer and another percentage, *b*, die of heart disease. This is why proper sampling is so important in scientific studies and surveys. For this reason, von Mises entitles a subsection of his first chapter "First the Collective—Then the Probability."[18] It is tremendously important to carefully specify the space of events that you are examining when considering objective probabilities. This determination of a collective, a population, becomes important in the discussion of probabilistic governance in part II, as it raises concerns over treating human collectives in the same way as groups of gas molecules and other material objects.

In this objectivist interpretation, probability becomes a property of a certain situation in the world. As Hacking puts it, "I have called long-run frequency a property, as one might call density and length properties. . . . A particular long-run frequency of something may be a property of some part of the world."[19] In this, it is dissimilar from the intersecting lines of causation in the Aristotelian vision of contingency. A probability of some occurrence is a real property of something in the world. Here is where Aristotelian commentators have concerns. Some Thomistic commentators, such as Bernard Lonergan, argue that probabilities are not in themselves real properties, just indicators of complexity; we just cannot predict all the different factors at play. A probability merely indicates our lack of knowledge. In this view, the probabilistic nature of events is similar to Aristotle's schema of intersecting deterministic causes, in that, for example, the toss of a coin is inflected by sets of causes like starting position, angular momentum, and the like.[20] The outcome of a journey by ship is shaped by deterministic but unpredictable weather systems. The problem is that the influences and intersecting causal chains are of such a vast number that it is nearly impossible to disentangle them. Most actions take place in systems that are so incredibly complex that they cannot be resolved into their determinate causal structures. Such an interpretation may work for some things, like coin tosses, but not for other physical processes, like those found in quantum mechanics or mutation rates in genetics. These probabilities seem much more inherent to the situation. In any case, this understanding of probability creates a very different picture of contingency than Aristotle paints. As Hacking describes it, "The most decisive conceptual event of twentieth-century physics has been the discovery that the world is not deterministic. Causality, long the bastion of metaphysics, was toppled, or at least tilted: the past does not determine exactly what happens next."[21] Indeterminism becomes a fundamental feature of certain aspects of the world. It is likely that this new indeterminism has exacerbated increasing doubts about the idea of providence, raising questions of how God acts outside a deterministic causal order.

There is a way to incorporate aspects of this framework into an Aristotelian ontology, if not into Aristotelian understandings of contingency. This becomes clear in Thomistic engagements with the probabilistic nature of contemporary scientific fields like quantum mechanics. The mid-twentieth-century Thomistic philosopher and theologian Charles De Koninck explained the probabilistic nature of such fields by pointing to the indeterminacy of Aristotelian prime matter.[22] As one gets closer to examining the fundamental stuff of the world, such prime matter will lack form, which is what determines the action and properties of substances. It is therefore not surprising that lower levels of nature would be indeterminate. This is an intriguing response worthy of further explication, but it does not quite address the regularity of the outcomes, the fact that though the physicist cannot predict exactly what would happen in each occurrence, she can predict with mathematical precision the different frequencies of different outcomes in a large number of cases. Nor does it explain the wide variety of macrophenomena that are also probabilistic, such as the social regularities discussed in chapter 6. It is these broader aspects of the world that affect human action.

Many scholars have found the objective interpretation of probability unsatisfying for a different set of reasons. First, it requires that one define the parameters of a collective before one starts experimenting. Such a definition is not possible in many of the uses that scientists want to make of statistics, which involve starting out with statistics and then using these data to distinguish different groupings. Second, there are technical issues with this model, which are generally not material to my argument.[23] Most important for practical reason, the relative objective, long-run frequency interpretation, tells us nothing about single events.[24] It only speaks of a large group of events, what frequency a certain event is likely to have in a collective. It does not predict what will occur in a particular instance of a collective. Thus, it is not helpful for action guidance in most situations where one does not have a large sample to which to refer. Nor will it help in directing a person in a single decision, even if she does have a large sample. An actor cannot tell if her situation fully fits the parameters of the appropriate collective. Practically, one cannot simply follow the odds in life. If everyone followed the odds, then no one would start a new business (most fail) or become a premed student (most will not end up getting into medical school).

The Subjectivist and Bayesian Interpretation

Because of these and other problems, an alternative understanding of statistics has become prominent. In this subjectivist interpretation, probability reflects the subjective certainty with which a person believes a proposition is true. It is a statement of one's strength of belief. The subjective model received its most detailed theoretical analysis in connection with games, especially games of chance. Some interpretations rephrase the question of probabilities into the forms of bets: What odds would an agent accept in order to bet on an event coming to pass?[25] What he considers even odds tells us the probability he assigns to an outcome. For example, with a coin toss, a person would require at least equal odds to bet on heads. However, this also allows one to apply probability to single events. The odds a person assigns to the outcome of the Super Bowl tells what he considers the probability of a certain team winning. There is no long-run objective probability in such a case. A person's subjective probability will be based on his own past experiences and the information available to him. This framework can be expanded into any number of different fields. It is in the subjectivist interpretation that Blaise Pascal's necessity of gambling discussed in chapter 2 is realized.

One of the benefits of this approach is that it allows a method for adjusting one's probability judgments in light of new evidence according to how much such evidence supports a particular hypothesis. For example, if a person were trying to determine if a die was fair or weighted, she might begin by assuming that it was fair. But as she rolled and saw that six was coming up half the times after twenty rolls, then she would start to assume that it might be weighted. After eighty rolls in which six came up thirty-eight times, she would be fairly certain that someone was cheating her. This insight into how to gradually adjust probability judgments in light of evidence is the foundation of Bayesian statistics, the most important form of subjective probability theory.

A problem with this whole framework is how to determine the initial bet on a single event, what is called a prior probability. Although using Bayesian methods to analyze a long run of data might lead different people to converge on a similar probability of an event, how this occurs will depend on the different initial bets they make of the likelihood of any event. If a person started out 99.99 percent sure that the die was fair, it will take much more evidence to convince him that it was weighted than it would take to convince a person who was only 60 percent sure that it was fair. This becomes especially problematic when probability theory is applied to a single event with no prior data. In that case, there is no objective way to determine what the probability should be. Probability estimates can thus seem arbitrary. Take the example of COVID-19. At the beginning of the outbreak, disease modelers came up with widely different pictures of how the pandemic would progress, in part because they used different prior probabilities and different models and assumptions about the disease. There was very little information on the infection fatality rate, how transmissible it was, and who was spreading it. Thus, the models were based on bets. This method can become problematic when used in public policy. Different interest groups may set vastly different probabilities on an event, like an environmental disaster, with industry groups thinking it unlikely and environmentalists thinking it very likely. Further, critics are concerned with using such a subjective method to engage with what should be an objective science, like epidemiology. As this discussion suggests, there are strong arguments for and against both the subjective and the objective models.

CONCLUSION

Both these modes of thinking about probability have shaped contemporary ethics. This is especially clear with subjectivist models. Economic theory has used it to rethink the market as a number of bets people make on future prices based on the information available to them. It was also developed into a whole decision theory, whose development was deeply shaped by the Cold War.[26] Objectivist models also play their role, however, especially in public policy, which determines the statistical frequency of certain characteristics in the population and intervenes to manage them. Thus, both forms of probabilistic thought affect contemporary action.

The next two parts of the book address the ethical issues arising out of each of these models of applying probability theory to life. Part I addresses how decision theory based on subjective probability shapes individual practical reason. It analyzes the problems that arise out of the consideration of multiple futures, anxiety over choice, the determination of ends, and a focus on security. It describes how the eclipse of ideas of providence that were tied to earlier models of chance as a deterministic causal nexus is implicated in these problems, because losing providence undermines certain aspects of human agency. Part II analyzes the abuses that can occur when individuals and society are thought of in terms of a population with objective statistical properties. The abstraction from the concept of the individual as a person—with rationality, relationality, and freedom—opens policymakers to dangerous dreams of complete control over others. Part III turns to a Christian response to these issues, exploring how to use the insights of probability theory and risk analysis well in practical action.

NOTES

Boethius, "Consolation of Philosophy," 5.1.10.

1. The change from a deterministic worldview to a less deterministic one occurred slowly. Many scholars used probability theory while still embracing a strict determinism, perhaps most famously Laplace. It was not until the late nineteenth century that scholars truly envisioned a probabilistic world. Hacking, *Emergence of Probability*.

2. Long and Sedley, *Hellenistic Philosophers*, 333–43; Bobzien, *Determinism*.

3. Long and Sedley, *Hellenistic Philosophers*, 102–12.

4. Aristotle, *Physics*, 2.5; Junkersfeld, "Aristotelian-Thomistic Concept of Chance," 12.

5. Junkersfeld, "Aristotelian-Thomistic Concept of Chance," 78–79.

6. Lonergan, *Insight*, 129; Hacking, *Taming of Chance*, 12.

7. Aristotle, *Nicomachean Ethics*, 3.3; Junkersfeld, "Aristotelian-Thomistic Concept of Chance," 14; Dudley, *Aristotle's Concept of Chance*, 7.

8. Dudley, *Aristotle's Concept of Chance*, 306–7.

9. Junkersfeld, "Aristotelian-Thomistic Concept of Chance," 74.

10. Aristotle, *Metaphysics*, Delta, 30.

11. Aristotle, *Physics*, 2.5.

12. E.g., Boethius, "Consolation of Philosophy," 5.1.53–58.

13. This division follows standard treatments of probability, such as that of Hacking, *Introduction to Probability*; and Childers, *Philosophy and Probability*. There are many disagreements within each of these camps, which are highly technical and irrelevant for my broader argument. Readers should remain aware that this is a simplified ideal type of these positions.

14. Hacking, *Emergence of Probability*; Gigerenzer et al., *Empire of Chance*; Daston, *Classical Probability*. As chapter 5 discusses in more depth, some historians have pointed to the application of early probability theory in legal theories of evidence as in part causing this overlap. Others look to the importance of expectations in early discussions of aleatory contracts and division of winnings in unfinished games of chance. Hacking, in a disputed explanation that draws on Michel Foucault, points to the fact that objective evidence in nature was seen as signs implanted into it by God, making such evidence subjectively understood markings of objective order. See Hacking, *Emergence of Probability*, 39–48; and Foucault, *Order of Things*.

15. Hacking, *Logic of Statistical Inference*.

16. Keynes, *Treatise on Probability*, 41–64. Variants of this principle were stated very early in the development of probability theory, as noted by Hacking, *Emergence of Probability*, 122–33.

17. John Venn discussed this framework, but it was most famously stated by von Mises, *Probability, Statistics, and Truth*. See also Hacking, *Logic of Statistical Inference*; and Popper, *Logic of Scientific Discovery*, 133–208. Karl Popper developed a slightly different, propensity interpretation; the relative frequency describes the propensity for certain events to occur in a particular setting. See Popper, "Propensity Interpretation of Probability."

18. von Mises, *Probability, Statistics, and Truth*, 24.

19. Hacking, *Logic of Statistical Inference*, 2.

20. Lonergan, *Insight*, 60–61.

21. Hacking, *Taming of Chance*, 1.

22. De Koninck, "Problem of Indeterminism"; De Koninck, "Reflections on the Problem of Indeterminism."

23. These technical issues arise from the fact that the objective interpretation is hard to align with some aspects of the accepted mathematical formalization of probability by A. N. Kolmogorov into a series of axioms from which he derived mathematical statistics. This formalization is a highly abstract model of set theory that corresponds poorly to any philosophical understanding of probability, but especially with the objective interpretation. One technical issue involves how to define randomness. The objectivist interpretation requires that the investigator be able to randomly sample from a collective. For the equations to work, it cannot be the case that one could predict patterns in the occurrence of single events (e.g., when heads will come up on a particular toss), merely the overall frequency. It is incredibly difficult to specify a formal definition of randomness that works with the mathematical formalization of probability theory.

24. Keynes, *Treatise on Probability*, 95–97.

25. Childers, *Philosophy and Probability*; Keynes, *Treatise on Probability*; Savage, *Foundations of Statistics*.

26. Edwards, *Closed World*.

2

Practical Reason and Probability Theory

You must wager. It is not optional.

—*Blaise Pascal*

With this meditation and the similar discussion in the *Port-Royal Logic*, Pascal initiated a new rationality for human action. A brilliant polymath—making fundamental contributions to science, mathematics, and philosophy—Pascal developed mathematical probability theory after a gambler asked him how to divide the pot if a game was interrupted. He soon applied his new theory to human action. Because of his involvement in seventeenth-century theological debates over Jansenism (discussed in chapter 5), it was almost inevitable that his specific application would regard the belief in God. As he described the situation, if a person believes in God, then she gains the infinite good of eternal life. If she does not, then she gains the pleasures of life followed either by nothingness or everlasting suffering. The only good coming from the lack of belief is thus the pleasures of earthly life, which are as nothing in comparison with eternal life, no matter what the probability of the existence of God. She is therefore well advised to take up the habits of the believer so that she might be formed in faith.

In Pascal's practical rationality, the individual must survey the combinations of possible courses of action open to her (to have faith in God or not), assess the gain to be made from each possibility (infinite or nothing), adjusted by their probability (here immaterial), and choose the largest expected gain. The fact that this framework of argumentation is first tied to belief or rather to the adoption of the habits of a believer (going to church, daily prayer, devotional reading) is merely a detail. It is applicable to all areas of life. Although Pascal only considered the necessity of wagering on our eternal fate, in truth, this rationality forces us to gamble in all areas of our lives. In this, Pascal initiates a new form of practical reasoning, one greatly developed in the twentieth century in the form of decision theory.

In the virtue ethics that was dominant before the modern period, prudence was thought to help people make singular decisions under conditions of uncertainty, which is the basic problem of risk. Yet prudence, for all its seeming utility in addressing these questions, is very different from the probabilistic decision theory described by Pascal that is the focus of this book. Virtue ethics, originating in ancient and medieval thought, was not formulated with probability and risk in mind, for the simple reason that these concepts did not yet exist. Without a concept of probability and the corresponding style of decision-making, classical analyses of virtue envisioned a very different procedure for deliberating about a decision. This lack of correspondence between contemporary and older styles of deliberation needs to be addressed if one hopes to develop an adequate ethic of risk in continuity with older forms of ethics.[1]

It is not that the lack of a concept of probability in itself is such a problem for virtue-based action theory. Instead, the development of probability theory led to a very different relationship to the future and future action. Older action theories described action in terms of the agent selecting an end and then seeking the means to that end or in terms of responsiveness to present situations. Newer models of action instead portray the agent laying out an array or rather a set of branching arrays representing possible courses of action along with the totality of each course of action's costs and benefits, modified by their likelihood of occurring. Comparing these possibilities, the agent chooses the optimal combination of expected costs and benefits. These distinct relationships to contingency and the future entail a very different model of action. These differences, in turn, are at the heart of the moral problems latent in this model of action. Although, in the epigraph to this chapter, Pascal was addressing the necessity of existential gambles, this model of action has invaded much of personal and professional life. Contemporary technology is designed with this model in mind, and individuals are trained into it. It is not that these ideas alone have caused the shifts I discuss here, but these ideals have shaped our institutions, daily practices, and education. The whole of political policymaking and even personal decision-making are now being forced into the form of a gamble on probabilities. To be rational now means to gamble.

PRUDENCE AND DECISION THEORY

One sees aspects of a changed mode of thinking about practical action already emerging in the Renaissance when comparing the differences between how Thomas Aquinas, dwelling in the medieval Aristotelian tradition, and Niccolò Machiavelli, who lies at the Renaissance origins of contemporary political thought, characterize the decision to found a city. Aquinas first states the primary goal of the prince: to lead his people to beatitude.[2] At its heart, there is a focus on an eternal goal and its realization. He then lays out the conditions necessary to achieve such a goal through the construction of a well-run kingdom and then proceeds to outline the requirements that such a city and its surrounding countryside must have to meet such conditions.

In contrast, Machiavelli first describes two possible ways of organizing cities and the effects of each of these systems of organization.[3] The first, like Venice or Sparta, had a stable set of elites who governed for a long period of time. Because these elites possessed legitimacy, there were few tumults or other civil disturbances. However, because these states would not use the common people to fight their wars, their possibilities for expansion were limited. The second kind of city is like Rome, which had many tumults and much instability; but these were tied to the fact that its form of organization allowed for conquest. Because Rome used its common people in its armies, they desired and fought for a greater share of power and spoils.

Machiavelli then leaves it to the reader to decide which course of action to choose: a republic that will stably last a long time or one that can aim at possible greatness: "And so, in every decision of ours, we should consider where are the fewer inconveniences and take that for the best policy, because nothing entirely clean and entirely without suspicion is ever found."[4] For Machiavelli, there is no safe course because all courses of action are risky: "For in the order of things it is found that one never seeks to avoid one inconvenience without running into another; but prudence consists in knowing how to recognize the qualities of inconveniences, and picking the less bad as good."[5] Machiavelli's ruler must become adept at judging the relative risks of various courses of action to achieve the best outcome, all things considered, whereas Aquinas's ruler is focused on finding the most secure route to achieve a certain end. Yet Machiavelli is not quite yet in the modern mode. First, he does not quantify the likelihood of the different possibilities. More important, he still uses a heroic standard to choose between a basic binary of long life or glory. In this, he harks back to the framework of the prephilosophical, heroic Greek past. In the *Iliad*, Achilles makes a similar choice between staying home and joining the Trojan War. Machiavelli follows Achilles to choose glory with the Roman form of state.

As this example suggests, there are two major differences between these modes of practical reason: first, a shift from a focus on ends, on goods sought, which is a teleological conception of action, to a weighing of outcomes, and, second, a changed relation to possible futures. In the Aristotelian and Thomistic system, a prudential judgment begins by envisioning a particular goal that is to be sought.[6] Intention is central to Aristotelian action theory, and intention is of a certain end.[7] How this end enters the actor's intellectual perception is less clear, but the rational intention of an end is the origin of all human action.[8] Once the end is in sight, the actor deliberates about what kind of action is necessary to achieve that goal, what means should be used. Only in this period of deliberation does the actor consider multiple possible futures, but even this occurs in a way different from surveying a multitude of combinatorial possibilities. She reasons backward from the end, trying to discern steps of causal relations that get her from her current position to the attainment of the end. There may be multiple such causal pathways. After determining a means, she prepares for a set of common negative contingencies that may affect the causal chain she sets in motion.[9] Aristotle recognizes that certain arts are stochastic, in that they do not always have determinate outcomes and must make do with the contingencies of the natural world. For example, the captain or pilot of a ship may set a course but is prepared to confront a storm that might arise. The prudent captain will not sail at times of the year when the contingency of a storm becomes more likely, such as winter. The future with regard to action is thus seen in terms of an end to be achieved, the means to achieve that end, and things that might disrupt that process.

The Aristotelian framework is not the only approach to future action found in classical ethics. In Stoicism, one finds a very different relationship to the future, a sort of nonrelationship, that is even further from contemporary decision theory. The future is nonexistent for Stoics; one can find happiness only by focusing on the present.[10] As chapter 3 discusses, they are concerned that anxiety over future achievement and consequences drive one from the present and thus from happiness. This framework makes dealing with fears over contingency a central part of Stoic practical ethics; one has little control over outcomes, so one should not be greatly concerned about them. This lack of concern is exemplified in Stoics' metaphor of the archer: the archer's goal should be to do all he can to hit a target rather than to actually hit the target.[11] The effort to shoot well is the ultimate aim, because hitting the target can be impeded by any number of contingencies, such as a strong wind. Instead, perfection as an archer comes in shooting the shot well at the moment the arrow is released. Although one does aim at some form of future goal, virtue is found in the moment of action. Indeed, Stoics' favorite metaphors for practical reason lay in the kinds of actions that have no future goal, like boxing or dancing, in which what is aimed at is responsiveness and flow in the moment. The uncertainty of achieving ends does not lead to anxiety because of Stoic, and later Christian, trust in divine providence. If we do all that is up to us but do not achieve our aim, it only means that we were not meant to succeed. God will bring something better out of this result.

This unconcern about future consequences reappears in Stoic-influenced modern ethics, such as deontology. Immanuel Kant argues that the only good thing is a good will, thus relativizing the achievement of temporal goals.[12] In the same vein, the legal philosopher John Finnis, while recognizing that right actions should aim at efficiently achieving some good, denies that future consequences should play a major role in the considerations of moral action.[13] One even sees a variant of this in Aristotle. Though the prudent person generally will succeed in achieving her end, the thing that differentiates action from craft is the effect that occurs in the person herself. As Aristotle argues, "For production has its end in something other than itself, but action does not, since its end is acting well itself."[14] That end occurs in the moment of action. Thus, most forms of traditional action theory either downplay the future or take it into consideration under the formality of a good to be achieved. Both strategies begin with an end.

Modern practical policy decision-making proceeds differently in that it begins by laying out all the possible courses of action facing the actor in a situation before judging between them. In this, it reflects the methods of utilitarianism (or, rather, the methods of utilitarianism reflect these shifts in political decision-making). For the early-twentieth-century consequentialist philosopher G. E. Moore, defining a duty requires knowing the effect of actions on the happiness of the universe: "We must also possess all this knowledge with regard to the effects of every possible alternative; and must then be able to see by comparison that the total value due to the existence of the action in question will be greater than that which would be produced by any of these alternatives."[15] Of course, such total knowledge is impossible, so ethics should aim at "shewing which among the alternatives, *likely to occur to any one*, will produce the greatest sum of good." The important thing here is that the focus is on the comparison of the results of different series of actions. But not only utilitarians engage in this model. Even John Rawls frames his influential contractarian approach in terms of principles for deciding between different institutional structures based on the sum of their effects.[16] For Rawls, the aim is to reach a Pareto optimality in which no one's situation can be improved without worsening the situation of someone else. To do so, one must have a sense of all the courses of action, their probabilities, and the events laying before one.

In this, modern decision theory reflects the methods of probabilistic analysis, in which one seeks to know all combinatorial possibilities. Once the actor places possible courses of action before himself, then he can determine the action with the most preferable outcome. Yet this procedure is difficult because of the challenges of determining all future effects and the uncertainty involved in this process. Because no outcome is assured, the actor must use probability theory. He must weigh the risks of future action, weighing the probability of each potential possible outcome. He calculates the amount of benefits weighted by likelihood of outcome versus the dangers weighted by likelihood of outcome. These benefits and costs will be connected to diverse kinds of ends, not to a single end, so issues of commensuration arise. There is no final, eternal end at which all action aims, as in Aquinas. As discussed in chapter 1, it is important to note that in this probabilistic framework, indeterminateness lies not in possible intersections of causal series, as in Aristotelian models of chance, but in the action itself.

This relationship with the future as a spread of possibilities appears even in the mathematical framework of probability theory. This theory proceeds by envisioning all possible events as lying on a plane. One then makes groups of certain kinds of events. Think of a Venn diagram, a figure originally described by one of the major nineteenth-century probability theorists. Circles surround groups of events, with the relative area of the circle determining the likelihood of the event, the number of times the event will possibly occur. Different kinds of events may overlap in some way. In another widely used visualization framework, experts in risk communication suggest using diagrams outlining all possible outcomes to communicate risks. Say a certain medical procedure for a condition—surgery, for example—will result in 23 percent of patients dying of the condition, whereas if patients with the condition do not have the surgery, 45 percent will die of the condition. There is also a 2 percent risk of a patient dying from complications from the surgery. The doctor translates these numbers into pictures of the number of people out of 100 who will die in each situation: 25 people die in the case of the surgery, whereas 45 die without it. The patient can look at all possible outcomes together. What this mode of thinking presumes is that all possible future events are available to the actor's awareness, lying before her so that she might judge between them. She compares these possible futures and determines which bundle of outcomes she most prefers, choosing that one.

THREE EXAMPLES

Let me give three examples to illustrate how decision theory constructs the world with regard to multiple incommensurable ends and sets of branching arrays of the effects of future action. First, one sees this mode of decision in utilitarian discussions of procreative beneficence. This is an argument put forward by the ethicist Julian Savulescu: one has a (weak) moral duty to produce the best offspring possible, the one most optimized for success.[17] If this were limited to a duty not to injure future offspring or intentionally choose a disability, it would be fairly defensible from an Aristotelian perspective. But what is distinctive about Savulescu's argument is how it is framed, the images that accompany it. He frames it in terms of preimplantation genetic diagnosis, when, after in vitro fertilization, potential parents obtain genetic information on all the embryos to determine which to implant. He argues that the parents should implant the best one—the child with the least chance of disease, the highest likelihood of intelligence, and the like. What is interesting is the image that his approach conjures of all the embryos lying before one—actually, the genetic propensities of the embryos—allowing one to predict the likelihood of a whole array of future consequences before deciding which one to use to continue the process of artificial reproduction and which to consign to the trash or freezer. Savulescu argues that we should develop artificial gametes so that we can even more closely approximate the utilitarian ideal. With artificial eggs and the father's sperm, doctors could generate hundreds of embryos for genetic testing. Think back to the diagrams of surgical risk, converted into personal characteristics: of the one thousand, twenty are likely to have a high educational attainment, fifteen to have exceptional athletic ability, and so on. There are different kinds of goods difficult to compare: beauty, intelligence, temperament. Moreover, each would set the child up for a different kind of life and different decisions that will arise as that life proceeds. The parent has hundreds of act functions from which to choose, shaping the entire future of a life. It is this synoptic gaze over future possibilities that makes this an ideal paradigm for contemporary decision-making.

This need not apply only to science fiction scenarios but also inheres in everyday decision-making. Consider picking an investment. If acting with due diligence, the investor should look at a certain investment, Amazon stock for example, and consider the expected growth and returns on that stock. She must also consider the various events that might occur that would affect that stock: an economic downturn, government regulation, the emergence of competitors, a consumer turn back to brick-and-mortar stores, intensified global warming, computer hackers, crises in Jeff Bezos's personal life, a war, and so on. How would the company respond to these situations? An investor ought to take all these scenarios or at least general subsets of them, calculate their possible effects on the stock, and weight them by their expected probability to determine a fully accurate prediction of the stock's future. She should also determine whether these risks can be insured against. But a rational economic actor will not stop there, because she must take into account the opportunity cost of forgoing other alternatives. Indeed, the investigation of Amazon stock is already a limited subset of a much larger space of possibilities, including other potential stocks, bonds, savings accounts, direct investment into a business partnership, or what have you; their potential earnings; and their potential risks. It is only with a comparison between these vast panoplies of future scenarios that she can truly decide whether a certain investment is a good idea. In this example, the end may seem clear, tied to the ultimate commensurable good, money, but even here she must balance the end of maximization versus ends of security in the face of risk.

An even more mundane example that clearly illustrates a multiplicity of ends and futures available in a decision is choosing what to do on Friday night. After a busy week, a person may be torn between many options. He has been invited to a party, which may be energizing and fun but also exhausting. It is important to consider the likelihood of who else might be there and how that would change the night's outcome. How might he respond to different people who might attend the party? He is so tired that he might just stay in and read a book. Or there is a movie that he had been wanting to see. How would he feel depending on whether he liked it or not? He could go to dinner with a friend, which would be relaxing but also engaging. Then there is the choice of which friend to ask and which restaurant; each would have its own advantages and disadvantages. All these possibilities lay before him, with no clear goal, aside from the general one of having a good evening, but with a number of different goals at play that could be realized in varying degrees in the different actions, depending on how events unfold. Decisions here must be made without the commensuration of monetary results.

There are some important commonalities between all three examples. First, there is no one fixed end but rather an incommensurable jumble of possible goods to be more or less realized in various scenarios: fun, relaxation, and social support in the night out; different qualities in a child. Even the investment decision, which seems to seek a commensurable good, money, actually balances various ends: the ends of more money, security, anxiety over the future, and, depending on how socially conscious she is, the effects of the investment on the world. Implicit in this first aspect of these decisions is a second: the actor must weigh the problems and benefits of the various results. The person is given a menu of possible futures realizing various goods from which to pick a preferred outcome. Finally, decisions result in more decisions; the tree of scenarios is ever ramifying. Choosing dinner with a friend leads to the choice of restaurant, which leads to selecting from a menu, and so on. As Jorge Luis Borges put it, time is a garden of forking paths.[18]

Practical reason cannot ignore these infinitely ramifying possibilities of action. Leonard Savage, the father of decision theory, says that "what in the ordinary way of thinking might be regarded as a chain of decisions, one leading to the other in time, is in the formal description proposed here regarded as a single decision."[19] In deliberation, the actor must include not only the concrete possible consequence of a decision but also the further decisions that are consequent upon that decision as well as the consequences of those decisions. All these possible outcomes will affect the desirability of each option in the first choice. The actor must consider as much information as possible in that first choice. As Savage puts it, the ideal would be that the rational actor would only make one decision in her life, a decision that would include all possible future decisions.[20] This remark highlights the idealistic picture of human rationality found in this model, which is comparable to the intellectual ability of angels and demons who likewise make a single determining decision for their entire existence.[21] Although an impossible ideal to realize, it does set the framework for thinking about individual decisions. It also emphasizes the timeless ideal of rationality under consideration: "Acts and decisions, like events, are timeless. The person decides 'now' once for all; there is nothing for him to wait for, because his one decision provides for all contingencies."[22] This mode of action reaches beyond the possibilities for time-bound human action. It tries to capture God's omniscience by taking a synoptic view of the entirety of possible futures, transcending time, not through God's eternity but through mathematical formalism. For both Savage and Pascal, the stake of these decisions is our entire life.

CONCLUSION

My argument of course is not that this is an accurate, universal reflection of human practical reason or even that this is how every person deliberates at all times. Many critiques have been written regarding rational actor theory cross-culturally, showing that most people even in Western societies fail to embody it. However, this mode of thought has become normative. Early in the theory's development, economists like Maurice Allais had noted that the deliveries of theory departed from commonsense intuitions. Yet Leonard Savage responded to these critiques by saying that commonsense intuitions must therefore be reformed: "A person who has tentatively accepted a normative theory must conscientiously study situations in which the theory seems to lead him astray; he must decide for each by reflection . . . whether to retain his initial impression of the situation or to accept the implications of the theory for it."[23] Risk-based decision theory is not merely attempting to describe ordinary prudential reasoning, as was early probability theory. Instead, it is prescriptive and normative. Deviations from it are now termed biases that must be controlled through nudging, as we shall explore in later chapters.[24]

As a form of thought becomes culturally normative, people will be formed in this modern decision theory. This is what we see today; this rationality emerges from restricted settings like the corporate and government office to seep into private life. For example, Xinyan Peng provides an ethnographic description of the parenting strategies of young professional Chinese women.[25] These women use the tools they have learned at work to rationalize their parenting, treating their children as projects. To balance workloads with their husbands, they use spreadsheets to quantify and visualize home labor, developing a points system; by performing home and childcare tasks, each spouse can earn points. These points can be redeemed for rewards like a night out with friends. By transforming home life into this kind of game, each spouse can develop strategies to maximize their rewards, which has led to the need to further hone the points systems because one spouse might try to work overtime (earning points due to increased salaries) to dodge home tasks. These strategies are based in probabilistic decision theory. Relationship apps in the Western world similarly gamify private life, allowing spouses to compete against each other and other couples to earn points from things like chores.[26] Quantification and gamification are allowing the increased application of decision theory to daily life.

Other influences encourage decision theory's spread. Finance classes shape people in it. Policy elites are trained in it. Children are educated in it. As chapters 7 and 8 discuss, apps and other technologies encourage it. Even those who criticize it as an inadequate theory of rationality, who recognize its historical contingency in the human sciences, suggest that training in it is essential to citizenship.[27] It has thus become the most publicly important action theory.

The argument of this part of the book is not that the Aristotelian and risk-based decision-theoretical views of the uncertainty of action are completely unrelated or that they are irreconcilable. Candace Vogler is correct that one could think of this kind of deliberation as related to intention: a person regards the future probabilistically when he has no clear end in view. In such situations, he undertakes a calculative process in choosing a certain end.[28] But I am not sure that this is what contemporary actors are doing when they undertake this form of decision making. These are very different emphases to consider when embarking on action, depending on one's mode of reasoning. Neither am I arguing that we must reject decision theory. However, those championing earlier modes of understanding prudential judgment must at the very least take into account these changed considerations in modern decision-making. On one hand, this changed form may suggest that virtue theory ought to take into account some insights from consequentialist risk/benefit analysis because of its power in predicting and possibly mitigating future dangers, as chapter 10 discusses. Yet it also means that virtue theorists should be ready to analyze and critique problems in such forms of decision-making, as much of parts I and II outline. If ethicists fail to make these distinctions, too quickly attempting to combine these two forms of deliberation, problems will arise. The rest of this part explores the possible problems with this mode of decision-making from the subjective perspective of the acting person. Chapter 3 begins this exploration by more deeply interrogating the problems of the temporality of multiple futures inherent in decision theory. After this examination, the subsequent chapters delve into the second difference between Aristotelian and probabilistic action, involving responsibility for the multiplicity of ends.

NOTES

Pascal, *Pensées and the Provincial Letters*, 81.

1. My analysis draws on Yuengert, *Approximating Prudence*; and Hirschfeld, *Aquinas and the Market*.
2. Aquinas, *On Kingship*, 2.1–4. Such practical manuals are invaluable for understanding how reasoning was to take place in practice. Although Aquinas is traditionally listed as the author of this work, it is unclear how much of it he actually wrote and how much was completed by his student.
3. Machiavelli, *Discourses on Livy*, 20–23.
4. Machiavelli, 22. Ultimately, he says that long-term stability is impossible because of fortune. A state could be forced into war, so one should seek glory and opt for the Roman model of organization. In theory, though, one could choose the Spartan model.
5. Machiavelli, *Prince*, 91.
6. My discussion of Thomistic action theory follows Westberg, *Right Practical Reason*; and Jensen, *Good and Evil Actions*.
7. Anscombe, *Intention*; Vogler, *Reasonably Vicious*.
8. That is not to say that such an end is unchangeable, aside from certain basic ends like happiness. As the agent deliberates about the means to an end, she may discover that the end is unreachable or other goals are more important and thus redirect action. Thomistic practical reason is thus dialectical in a way decision theory's schedule of preferences is not.

9. Chapter 10 examines this process of prudential reasoning and its associated virtues.

10. Scherz, "Living Indefinitely"; Hadot, *Present Alone Is Our Happiness*; Hadot, *Philosophy*; Goldschmidt, *Le système stoïcien*.

11. Cicero, *On Moral Ends*, 3.22.

12. Kant, *Groundwork of the Metaphysics of Morals*.

13. Finnis, *Natural Law and Natural Rights*, 111–18.

14. Aristotle, *Nicomachean Ethics*, 1140b7–8.

15. Moore, *Principia ethica*, 149. See also Sidgwick, *Methods of Ethics*, 131, 477.

16. Rawls, *Theory of Justice*, 153ff.

17. Savulescu, "Procreative Beneficence"; Savulescu, "In Defence of Procreative Beneficence"; Bourne, Douglas, and Savulescu, "Procreative Beneficence."

18. Borges, "Garden of Forking Paths."

19. Savage, *Foundations of Statistics*, 15.

20. Savage, 16.

21. John of Damascus, "Exposition of the Orthodox Faith," 2.4, 21.

22. Savage, *Foundations of Statistics*, 17.

23. Savage, 102.

24. Gigerenzer et al., *Empire of Chance*, 203–34.

25. Peng, "We've Always Worked," chap. 5.

26. Danaher, Nyholm, and Earp, "Quantified Relationship."

27. Gigerenzer, *Rationality for Mortals*, 127.

28. Vogler, *Reasonably Vicious*, 169–70.

3

Anxiety and the Temporality of Risk

The bad player is the one who tries to calculate and play with
the odds, as if his game, his life, were one of a large number
of games. . . . The good player does not fool himself,
and accepts that there is exactly one chance.

—*Ian Hacking*

In the passage in which the epigraph to this chapter appears, Ian Hacking, perhaps the foremost contemporary scholar of the history and philosophy of probability, is discussing the question of whether chance, necessity, or design serves as the foundation of the universe. In the process, he refers to what is known as the gambler's fallacy. This is when, knowing the objective odds, the gambler thinks he will be able to predict the next flip of the coin based on recent results.[1] For example, if there has been a run of heads, he bets on tails, thinking that things have to even out in the next flip. But chance does not work this way; each coin flip is independent, so there is an equal chance of heads or tails despite what happened on previous tosses. This lesson applies to all areas of life: just because the stock market has been going down does not mean that it is due for a rally; just because it has rained for the last few days does not mean we are due for sun. Historical odds are not necessarily a good predictor for an individual occurrence, a point to which we return in chapter 10.

There is a deeper lesson in this fallacy, however—one that has an impact on the understanding of time, which is the focus of this chapter. As chapter 2 discussed, probability theory envisions all future events as spread out in a problem space, as if all future combinations were in existence. The time series that is actually experienced is one of a large number of possible time series. Risk-based decision theory thus spatializes and multiplies time, a shift that is reflected in other areas of philosophy and popular culture. This shift changes aspects of our understanding of action by suppressing the possibility of novelty, attempting to ensure predictability, and allowing us a statistically rational way to govern our lives.

Yet the Hacking quotation suggests that this idea of time, this form of temporality, is conceptually mistaken. A person cannot approach the future as if choosing from a large number of options, because there is only one time. From a Christian perspective, this one time series is governed by divine providence. But this is not just an abstract, conceptual shift. As this new understanding of time has become more widespread through its embedding in technology, institutions, and education, it is engendering greater existential concerns and anxiety over choosing between these possible futures, leading to fears over missing out. As Søren Kierkegaard explored, a focus on the multitude of possibilities rather than seeking the actualization of God's providential will, as described in the introduction, creates an existential instability, a lack of grounding in current reality. This chapter explores this new temporality and how it leads to these dangers. Understanding this temporality will set the stage for discussions in later chapters of the other problems arising from risk-based decision theory.

THE TIME OF RISK

Decision theory requires one to foresee as many alternative possibilities as one can, as well as calculate the probability of these alternatives. In this way, the agent makes the alternative futures real to herself when making a decision, imagining herself in such possible futures. The strange thing is that, phenomenologically, the other alternatives do not cease to exist after the moment of choice. Once a decision is made, once one acts, committing oneself to one of the forking paths that represent the future, the traces of the other paths remain in the memory. They still seem like they exist. In some cases, one can even see them, almost feel their presence.

Two of the examples from the last chapter illustrate this experience of time. Take the financial example. A few years ago, one of my friends purchased Amazon stock, selling it once it reached around $200 in order to put the money into what she considered safer investments. In this way, she gained a good profit. However, given the ease of accessing stock prices, she has frequently been made aware of the fact that the stock price continued to rise and rise. She kicks herself over her decision to sell. She regrets that she does not inhabit that alternative temporal path in which she still owned the Amazon stock.

A similar experience could occur in the decision about what to do on a Friday night. In this case, the person was choosing between a number of options: staying in, going to dinner with friends, attending a party, and so on. Suppose he decides to stay in and has a very relaxing evening. He reaches the end of the evening feeling refreshed from his hard week. That is, until he checks his Instagram feed and sees pictures from the party that he decided not to attend. Social media shows his friends at the party and how much fun they seem to be having. This presentation of the unchosen alternative causes him to regret that he has missed out. The alternative becomes present to him, precisely in his absence from it, leading him to long for the alternative time series. It is important to note that both these examples depend on the mediation of contemporary technology to give information about alternatives. Although such experience of alternatives was possible in prior times, technology now makes it much more common and direct.

The axiomatization of probability theory requires such a new vision of future events. The actor envisions all possible events as if they were lying together in the same plane, giving a synoptic vision of future possibilities. This plane of possibilities leads to a spatialized, totalized vision of future times. This totalizing vision gives a peculiar sense to these different possibilities. They are not just potentialities, some of which may be actualized through decision. Instead, all of them are there before the agent, as if they were actualized in some possible world, just not the one where she exists.[2] As Henri Bergson notes in regard to future prediction, "We shall then be present in imagination at the phenomenon we wish to foretell," and after considering them "we shall thrust the event again into the future and say that we have *foreseen* it, when in reality we have *seen* it" (emphasis added).[3] In prediction, even in the prediction of one of an array of possibilities, one makes the future present. Further, in ideal theory there is no future possibility that is not contained in the plane; it is a closed system with no outside influence or novelty to disturb its unfolding. Of course, this is not the case in practice in any personal or policy arena. This description only seeks to illuminate the formal structure of this way of approaching the world, not how it has to be modified to fit real conditions. In these theoretical structures, all possible futures exist for the agent, present to vision.

Moreover, as decision theory requires the agent to look ahead to future decisions that arise as a result of the actor's first decision, the vision of time is further specified. Older conceptions of time included the river, an arrow, a cycle, or even a narrative unfolding. Now, it becomes the decision tree, tracing out all future possibilities as governed by ramifying checkpoints of decisions. The twentieth-century author Jorge Luis Borges understood time as a garden of forking paths ramifying and intersecting indefinitely, leading to many possible time series.[4] This vision becomes instantiated in the technology of managerial charts, in which possible futures lie in a plane organized as a flowchart. If one combines the idea that all possibilities in the plane appear to be actual, before one's sight, with this arboreal organization, then one understands that as one goes down one path of the flowchart / decision tree, the other branches do not cease to exist. They continue, present to consciousness as actualized in alternative futures not chosen. Time becomes an infinite, forking series of possibilities, all of which seem realized in some way.

What these examples illustrate is that a new experience of time has become available for our contemporaries, in part due to the development and application of probability theory. Long-developing ideas act to shape public consciousness. As the economist Friedrich Hayek (and John Maynard Keynes) argued,

> Public opinion on these matters is the work of men like ourselves, the economists and political philosophers of the past few generations. . . . I do not find myself often agreeing with the late Lord Keynes, but he has never said a truer thing than when he wrote, on a subject on which his own experience has singularly qualified him to speak, that "the ideas of economists and political philosophers, both when they are right and when they are wrong, are more powerful than is commonly understood. Indeed the world is ruled by little else. Madmen in authority, who hear voices in the air, are distilling their frenzy from some academic scribbler of a few years back."[5]

These ideas, in turn, shape how people understand the world and their resources for action. Probability theory clearly has this kind of influence on contemporary society. This model of decision-making has become normative in the intellectual sphere, so failures to adhere to it are termed biases by behavioral economists.[6] We are almost forced to operate in this temporality, at least in some spheres.

However, I am not claiming that these shifting temporalities are due wholly to theories of human action. Do not mistake this as misplaced idealism, thinking that the world is transformed only by intellectual shifts. Instead, what Hayek means and in part practically effected was that ideas shape the world by becoming popularized and embodied in policies, practices, institutions, technology, and education. Though decision theory has filtered into everyday consciousness, these shifts are also driven by other cultural forces, especially new technologies. The key driver here is the internet. Older forms of media (television, radio, newspapers) certainly gave access to other forms of life and to information about unfolding events, but the internet makes such information more immediate. My friend could constantly and instantaneously access the price of the stock she sold. An acquaintance's fun night out at the party automatically appears in Instagram and Facebook feeds. The forgone alternative futures (now presents) do not just lie passively in mind. They press themselves into attention. The absent becomes aggressively present. Although many of these developments were completely independent of probabilistic understandings of the world, merely fitting nicely with it, others, like the technologies that are discussed in chapters 7 and 8, were explicitly developed using it.

This model of understanding time also has entered the conceptual mainstream in certain areas of philosophy, science, and popular culture. One sees it in many fields. In philosophy, some interpretations of the modal logic of multiple worlds see these alternative possible worlds as concrete.[7] In cosmology, the idea of an infinite number of worlds in which all possible different values of the basic physical constants can be fulfilled serves as an explanatory defense against things like the Anthropic Principle, sheer contingency, or ugly Fine Tuning, ideas that might direct one to search for God as a principle for why the physical constants of our universe fall within the narrow range for intelligent life. Certain interpretations of quantum mechanics suggest the simultaneous existence of alternative solutions to all the possible quantum wave functions.[8] Finally, alternative futures and histories are widespread in science fiction, most famously in Borges's "The Garden of Forking Paths," but also in *Star Trek*, the writing of Philip K. Dick, the Avengers movies, and other popular entertainment. Our society is obsessed with alternative paths that haunt our actual present. Perhaps it is also this phenomenological experience of everyday decisions that makes the idea of multiple worlds so popular with our contemporaries.

It is not that the idea of alternative worlds is new. It is not; the possibility was already imagined in Antiquity. Epicurean philosophers postulated countless other worlds that arose beyond the bounds of our own due to the random swerves of the atoms that they conceived as the fundamental particles.[9] To them, this meant that there was no fundamental rational order to the world, no providence. The gods take no account of human action, so the philosopher need not concern himself with anything but his happiness found in *ataraxia*. Medieval Scholastic voluntarists postulated the many possible worlds that God could have created to emphasize His omnipotence, the power of His will to choose what the world would be, or even whether one could gain any true grasp of the world through the senses. This emphasis undermined aspects of teleology, because God could always have made things differently.[10] Today, however, multiple worlds arise in part because of how contemporary practical reason pictures choice in human action. What is different is what drives current discussions. Although different, it is important to note that all these uses of multiple worlds (to argue for the gods' indifference, God's power, or our choice) are tied to the denial of a teleological conception of nature or the idea of a providential wisdom guiding the affairs of the world.[11] Epicureans and contemporary atheists deny any governance by wisdom, while voluntarists prioritize will over wisdom. It is a picture of time that is thus amenable to contemporary society, where unfettered autonomy is among the highest values.

DURATION AND THE EXPERIENCE OF TIME

As may have become obvious in this description of risky temporality, this conception of time is not without its problems. Indeed, it involves many of the same mistakes about temporal experience that Henri Bergson identified in scientific models of time nearly one hundred and fifty years ago. At the turn of the twentieth century, Bergson was recognized as one of France's most important philosophers, influencing diverse intellectual movements, such as phenomenology, pragmatism, vitalism, and evolutionary thought. Time is a theme that runs throughout his work. His basic concern was that—in philosophy, science, and even in everyday experience—moderns have understood time in terms of space, primarily because they have sought to understand time in terms of number: "But as soon as we wish to picture *number* to ourselves, and not merely figures or words, we are compelled to have recourse to an extended image" (emphasis in the original).[12] To concretely think of a quantity of things, one pictures a number of those things lying together. In counting time, people do not keep its temporal nature in our mind. Instead, "we involuntarily fix at a point in space each of the moments which we count, and it is only on this condition that the abstract units come to form a sum."[13] This need for spatial representation arises because time is fundamentally a state of consciousness, "which cannot be regarded as numerical without the help of some symbolical representation, in which a necessary element is *space*."[14] For an image of this, one can think of a timeline, with each moment laid out linearly as occupying a distinct moment of space.

This is not a new or particularly modern experience of time, of course. Throughout much of Western history, time has been conceptualized in terms of arrows or circles.[15] Aristotle, who provided perhaps the first detailed engagement with time, already thought of it in terms of lines and points.[16] The high point of this way of thinking occurs in Kant, who made the intuition of time arise out of arithmetic as the linear addition of new points to the line of history. Space, in contrast, arose from geometry. But as geometry has been arithmetized in modern science, the two became interchangeable. Bergson argues that this mode of representing time in terms of space has shaped modern perception so that people now think of time in terms of space.[17]

This view is accentuated by technological tools that allow people to better conceptualize their own lives in such a spatial fashion, such as Facebook's timeline function, which is very different from narrative forms such as a diary. Yet this view is also supported by conceptual advances. Most important, relativistic physics theorizes time and space as merely different dimensions of the same manifold, similarly warping and changing due to gravity, speed, and other physical parameters. This mathematization of time allows for the utmost reduction of time to space. Decision theory and the axiomatization of probability, however, drive their own reduction of time to space. Probability theory places all events, and thus all times, onto a single plane. Decision theory transforms future action into a decision tree, again a linear branching graph of the future dependent on human choice. Time and space are thus interchangeable in much of contemporary thought.

Bergson rejects this interconvertibility of time and space.[18] In an insight upon which much of the phenomenological tradition builds, he says that humans do not experience time in such a spatialized way. A spatial temporality would require experience to consist of something like discrete moments that could in some way be isolated from all others: "We set our states of consciousness side by side in such a way as to perceive them simultaneously."[19] For Bergson, this isolation of the instant is completely wrong. It ignores the fact that moments flow into one another. Each moment retains aspects of the immediate past in the present and is continually projecting from the current moment into adjacent future moments.[20] The instantaneous present can only be isolated abstractly because the moment one fixes on it, it is already gone. Instead, the mind forms "both the past and the present states into an organic whole, as happens when we recall the notes of a tune, melting, so to speak, into one another."[21] The past is always shaping the present, and we project from the present into the future: "We can thus conceive of succession without distinction, and think of it as a mutual penetration, an interconnexion and organization of elements, each one of which represents the whole, and cannot be distinguished or isolated from it except by abstract thought."[22] He termed this "lived time duration," a term that highlights the interconnected nature of time, the continuing influence of the past upon the future, and the flowing nature of time. Times are not discrete.

Bergson's theorization of time first arose in his discussion of the question of free will, which shows how the question of temporality intersects with the concerns of decision theory. According to Bergson, the spatialization of time creates pseudo-problems. Because people envision time as discrete points, they think of decisions as occurring at a single instant of time. Therefore, they envision distinct possibilities arising at certain forks in time. The flowing time of the self is transformed into a geometric picture of spatial paths that confront people as independently existing realities: "In short, the continuous and living activity of this self, in which we have distinguished, by abstraction only, two opposite directions, is replaced by these directions themselves, transformed into indifferent inert things awaiting our choice."[23] The questions then become, Why did they take one fork rather than the other? Was this path determined or not? Could they have freely chosen the other path? The determinist, looking back from the endpoint, says that because he can reconstruct a chain of causes leading to that outcome, it must have been determined in advance by the universe's causal network. The believer in free will, taking the vantage point of the origin, sees multiple pathways that are open, so she thinks that there must be a freedom that allows the sovereign individual to impose her choice on the situation.[24] Bergson objects that this whole framework is wrong because it demands using a spatialized perspective either before or after the action has been performed. It fails to look at the action in process, as "a dynamic progress in which the self and its motives, like real living beings, are in a constant state of becoming."[25] The person is constantly growing, influenced by her surroundings, creating new opportunities as duration continues. She is neither determined nor do all the opportunities lie precalculated for her from the beginning. Time is not a garden of forking paths, but a lived, intersubjective experience. For the Christian, as the introduction discussed and chapter 9 further explores, it is lived in relation to God's will realized in the providential unfolding of history.

NOVELTY

Bergson's most serious objection to the spatial, decision theoretical concept of time and choice is that it denies any true novelty in the world. Nothing new can occur because all possibilities are given from the very beginning, charted on the decision tree. In such a deterministic view, matter "repeats the past unceasingly, because, subject to necessity, it unfolds a series of moments of which each is the equivalent of the preceding moment and may be deduced from it: thus its past is truly given in its present. But a being which evolves more or less freely creates something new every moment."[26] For the materialist or decision theorist, all lies already present in potentiality, waiting to unfold. It is predetermined by the physical causal nexus.

In one of her last works, Hannah Arendt, an émigré political philosopher who had been a student of Heidegger, builds on Bergson's discussion of time and free will. Echoing, though departing from, Augustine's distinction between free choice and free will (or Pinckaers's freedom for excellence or freedom of indifference), she argues that the linear view allows for free choice between preexistent alternatives but not for truly free will, which for her involves the ability to make a new beginning, what she calls natality:[27] "The *liberum arbitrium* decides between things equally possible and given to us, as it were, in *statu nascendi* as mere potentialities, whereas a power to begin something really new could not very well be preceded by any potentiality, which then would figure as one of the causes of the accomplished act."[28] For Arendt, the idea of the capacity for the new arises from Hebrew and Christian understandings of the *creatio ex nihilo*, the bringing forth of creation completely anew out of nothing. Even in salvation history, God's action is not determined by the past. As Isaiah prophesied, "I am about to do a new thing; now it springs forth, do you not perceive it?"[29] God acts unpredictably: making a covenant with a nomad, bringing Israel out of Egypt, raising a shepherd to the throne. God frequently acts by bringing something new into existence rather than merely continuing the effects of past events.

Arendt thinks that humans image this divine ability to act in novel ways, arguing that God created man so that there would be true beginnings. In support of this argument, she cites Augustine: "[*Initium*] *ergo ut esset, creatus est homo, ante quem nullus fuit* ('that there be a beginning, man was created before whom there was nobody')."[30] This quotation takes Augustine out of context; really, he is talking about God beginning salvation history, continuing his emphatic focus on God's creative activity. Even so, Arendt's idea of natality, of the ability for novelty to inhere in human action, is extremely important. In theological terms, it is in this willing of the new that we image God: "In this respect, he was the image of a Creator-God; but since he was temporal and not eternal, the capacity was entirely directed toward the future."[31] Humans image the Creator not through divine creation itself, although Arendt was interested in how humans make a shared world through craft production, but through action, most importantly through political action in which the person reveals herself by engaging with others.[32] Without these possibilities to freely will, action becomes merely the calculative choice of the machine, as in decision theory, doomed to proceed along the paths laid down by history, a point to which we return in chapter 7.

The importance of her insights becomes much clearer when one takes Arendt's primary example of the novel action, forgiveness.[33] Reflecting on the horrors that could arise in politics and war, especially the tragedies that engulfed Europe in the first half of the twentieth century, she asked how European civilization could escape the continuing aftershocks of this legacy. If left simply to the working out of historical causality, the future would merely hold a continual series of acts of vengeance as actors react to their adversaries' past crimes. All would consider themselves as victims owed vengeance, leading to a future of continued atrocity. Her answer to this politics of *ressentiment* was forgiveness, the novel act that breaks with history to allow a new peace to emerge in society: "Forgiving . . . is the only reaction which does not merely re-act but acts anew and unexpectedly, unconditioned by the act which provoked it and therefore freeing from its consequences both the one who forgives and the one who is forgiven."[34] Such action could not be calculated from the past. Because Christian forgiveness takes place under the guidance of God's grace, it not only images but also participates in God's creative action.

In his later appreciation of Bergson's thought, the twentieth-century Thomist philosopher Jacques Maritain develops Bergson's insight on novelty. Maritain affirms Bergson's "desire to safeguard the unforeseeableness of becoming, . . . the 'radical unforeseeableness' of every moment of the universe," against anyone who would attempt to predict future possibilities entirely from current conditions.[35] Bergson errs only in rejecting Thomistic categories in favor of a vitalist doctrine of becoming. The true Aristotelian understanding of potentiality, rather than one degraded by modern mechanistic thinking, entails a need for radical unpredictability. "In change, what happens at a certain moment did not exist at all in the preceding stage an already-happened-not-yet-manifested. . . . Potentiality, being nothing of what one can enunciate, for all one can enunciate is in act, being purely *ad actum*, is knowable only through act."[36] Unknowable until actually enacted, the concept of potentiality protects the radical novelty found in history. Persons, too, in Arendt's thought are unknowable until they reveal themselves in action.

This problem of conceptualizing novelty in decision theory's model of temporality is not merely a conceptual mistake but also leads to practical problems because it leaves people unprepared to confront catastrophes. To turn once more to Bergson, he described the shock of the start of World War I as suggesting that this world-altering event, before the fact, seemed impossible, almost inconceivable. Yet once it appeared, it seemed obvious, and one could clearly trace the lines of historical causation.[37] Similarly, great works of art, before they appear, are inconceivable, but after they occur, they seem necessary. Artists make the possible and the actual at the same time.[38] Again and again in recent years, we have had this experience; what was unconceived, perhaps seemingly impossible, became actualized. The French scientist and philosopher Jean-Pierre Dupuy developed such reflections in response to the September 11, 2001, terrorist attacks on the United States, for which many investigations have shown that evidence existed that would have allowed intelligence agencies to predict the attack. It was a failure of imagination almost more than one of coordination. Even pandemic planners had dismissed the possibility of locking down the entire society over a new illness like the coronavirus before it happened.[39] Unpredictability creates great problems for practical rationality.

ANXIETY AND REGRET

Philosophical and theological errors do not remain confined to the realm of intellectuals. When they become widespread and embedded in institutions, they also lead to problems in daily lived experience. At its most basic level, the sheer number of options that one can visualize before making a decision can be paralyzing.[40] Anyone who has seriously attempted to make investment decisions for retirement has experienced the overwhelming number of choices available. Even choosing a deodorant at the grocery store can be too much. The attempt to map out all possible outcomes for all possible scenarios exceeds the capacity of our finite minds.

This decision fatigue is made worse by the sense that the roads not taken will not disappear into the void of unreality. Instead, the alternative futures may remain ever present in their absence, unrealized in our timestream but remaining on the edge of consciousness. Lurking just out of view, these options remain primed to spring back into consciousness, bringing the alternate history into awareness. It happens when one catches the price of the stock that you sold or when friends' pictures from a party appear in an Instagram feed. At these moments, regret will appear, regret for the alternative path that still exists but is not actualized in one's own life.[41] It will be too late, and pangs of regret may be overwhelming. As Bergson noted, "The future . . . appears to us at the same time under a multitude of forms, equally attractive and equally possible. Even if the most coveted of these becomes realized, it will be necessary to give up the others, and we shall have lost a great deal. The idea of the future, pregnant with an infinity of possibilities, is thus more fruitful than the future itself."[42] Even if the best option is realized, one still regrets the plenitude left behind.

Psychologists and economists have suggested that this fear of regret is an important consideration in decision-making.[43] Regret is a frequent emotion today. People have a tendency to think of the goods that have been forgone through a choice rather than the goods obtained. It arises from counterfactual thinking of what might have been, the very mode in which decision theory trains people to engage.[44] Yet much of prospect theory, which is the psychological model of human prediction related to decision theory, fails to properly account for regret in decision-making.[45]

Regret plays a major role. It is this state of potential regret that characterizes the fear of missing out that so many young people experience. Though intensified by social media technologies, these are not solely to blame, despite what many commentators say. The real culprit is the sense of temporality that has become embedded in these technologies and that they support; it is the mode of deliberation that makes these futures ever present, forcing a person to generate a sense of alternative futures. I would suggest that temporality is at the heart of the paralyzing anxiety that now stalks young adults.[46]

The nineteenth-century Danish philosopher Søren Kierkegaard and the twentieth-century existentialist Martin Heidegger both explored how anxiety, taken in an existential rather than a clinical sense, is engendered by possibility. For Heidegger, the human "understands itself in terms of possibilities."[47] However, possibility is not an unalloyed good, because "it always stands in one possibility or another: it constantly is *not* other possibilities, and it has waived these in its existential projection."[48] Living requires choosing one possibility over another and thus foreclosing possibilities: "Freedom, however, is only in the choice of one possibility—that is, in tolerating one's not having chosen the others and one's not being able to choose them."[49] It is in this necessity to foreclose possibilities that problems arise. Though Heidegger's analysis of anxiety is rightly understood primarily in relation to his discussion of finitude as revealed in death, it is even more deeply tied to this inability to realize multiple futures. This foreclosure occurs not only through death. Death just brings these limitations more clearly into the foreground. Even if the transhumanist could extend life indefinitely through new biotechnologies, still numerous unrealized possibilities would occur at each moment.[50]

Because a person's actions lead to the nonexistence of certain possibilities through her choices, the person becomes the origin of a nullity, of nonexistence. This responsibility for forgoing possibilities leads to guilt.[51] The goods those unchosen possibilities contain will be forever lost when they are foreclosed by choice. Every action limits and forgoes possibilities and realized goods, causing a limitation of our being to one stream of time. This realiza-tion, or rather sense resting on the edge of consciousness, causes guilt and regret over that which can never be realized due to finitude. This guilt and regret lead one to flee into distraction and the common opinion, the popular media that ignores this fundamental finitude. The only way to avoid this fall into illusion is to come to grips with the reality of finitude, recogniz-ing with Hacking's good player in the epigraph that there is only one chance. That is why, for Heidegger, authenticity only comes through accepting death, the ultimate foreclosure of possibility: "When, by anticipation, one becomes free *for* one's own death, one is liberated from one's lostness in those possi-bilities which may accidentally thrust themselves upon one; and one is lib-erated in such a way that for the first time one can authentically understand and choose among the factical possibilities lying ahead of that possibility which is not to be outstripped."[52] Such freedom allows one to resolutely live through the choice of life one has made rather than constantly looking else-where in fear, desiring to live many possible lives. That latter way of being only feeds anxiety.

Kierkegaard's analysis is similar, although more theological. For him, anxiety is the basic mode of human existence: "Anxiety is freedom's actu-ality as the possibility of possibility."[53] It is not only despair at not realizing possibilities but also becomes a motivation in reaction to possibilities: It "is *a sympathetic* antipathy and *an antipathetic* sympathy."[54] One is simultane-ously both drawn to and repelled from some future possibility, in part due to the inevitable foreclosure of other possibilities. For this reason, Kierke-gaard compares it with the vertigo experienced upon looking into an abyss: "Anxiety is the dizziness of freedom, which emerges when the spirit wants to posit the synthesis and freedom looks down into its own possibility, laying hold of finiteness to support itself. Freedom succumbs in this dizziness."[55] For Kierkegaard, the fundamental arena of this possibility is sin: the choice of God's will or the turn away. In the Fall, human freedom succumbed to sin.

Using the parable of the lilies that is discussed more fully in chapter 4, Kierkegaard argues that a major source of anxiety lies in comparison. It is through comparison that a person becomes aware of other possibilities that he is not now living.[56] He seeks to put himself in another's place and thus becomes disappointed by his current calling. Once turned from the neces-sity of obedience and the call of the present, the self becomes lost in possi-bility. With the infinite possibilities of decision analysis open to one, "the self becomes an abstract possibility; it exhausts itself floundering about in pos-sibility, yet it never moves from where it is nor gets anywhere, for necessity is just that 'where.'"[57] Comparison drives him to live in other possibilities, other possible futures, which themselves give rise to worry and anxiety. It is only by embracing God's providence that people can find peace.

Key for my analysis, Kierkegaard's discussion of anxiety occurs in the context of an analysis of original sin. For Kierkegaard, the only distinction between Adam's sin and our own is that the possibility of sin has taken on an objective form and has become concrete in the world around us.[58] For Adam, sin was only a theoretical possibility. In contrast, we see sin all around us, and we are reared in sin: "Now if we consider the subsequent individual, every such individual has an historical environment in which it may become apparent that sensuousness can signify sinfulness."[59] The different possibilities of sin have become concrete alternative pathways open to the agent's imagination, different paths that lie before him, different ways to flee from God's call. This concretization of different possible paths makes the anxiety all the more intense and renders it even more difficult to avoid sin. The tie between concretization and increased anxiety is significant for my argument. Probability theory requires the agent to make possible futures concrete in a way that older theories of practical reason did not. Similarly, it enlarges the scope of comparison between the present in which the agent finds herself and the alternative presents she could have chosen. For Kierkegaard, this concretization cannot help but increase anxiety.

CONCLUSION

As these discussions suggest, anxiety over the future is not new. That is why the Stoics demanded a focus on the present, the only time that exists and in which one can act.[60] Only by focusing on the present can one resist being swept away in concern over the future. As chapter 4 explores, Jesus tells us in the Sermon on the Mount to not worry about tomorrow, even though the present itself may be troubled.[61] Similarly, Edith Stein sees in the present a care that can sustain us in the fight against anxiety over the future portrayed by Heidegger.[62] Chapter 9 pursues these insights toward an alternative engagement with time, one founded on resting in God's providential care.

Yet it does seem that the dangers revealed in these analyses have only become worse in our time. The foreclosure of possibilities is even more terrifying after one goes through the trouble of laying them all out before one's vision. It becomes more difficult to live resolutely when one realizes that the intended goals of action may not even be realized because your deliberation explicitly dwells on probabilities of success. The contemporary agent also knows that the guilt will be all the more certain as alternatives spontaneously appear on social media. These thinkers already could sense the playing out of this new modern sense of time and choice, which has only become more apparent since they wrote.

The concept of time embedded in decision theory presents theoretical, practical, and existential concerns. Theoretically, it betrays our actual experience of time, confusing time with space. Practically, the assumption of predictive power at the heart of risk analysis leaves us unprepared for future novelty. Decision-makers thus make society increasingly vulnerable to the unknown unknowns. Finally, individuals become increasingly anxious over the unrealized possibilities that they have made concrete in their decision analysis. Guilt arises over the responsibility for that which has been inevitably forgone. These last two considerations raise the question of responsibility: responsibility for diverse outcomes, for goods forgone, and for catastrophes. These considerations are addressed in later chapters. First, however, it is necessary to investigate what ends are encouraged by contemporary risk analysis.

NOTES

Hacking, *Taming of Chance*, 148.

1. Hacking, *Introduction to Probability*, 28.
2. For possible worlds, see Lewis, *On the Plurality of Worlds*.
3. Bergson, *Time and Free Will*, 195.
4. Borges, "Garden of Forking Paths."
5. Hayek, *Individualism and Economic Order*, 108.
6. Kahneman, *Thinking, Fast and Slow*.
7. Lewis, *On the Plurality of Worlds*.
8. For a recent argument in this vein, see Carroll, *Something Deeply Hidden*.
9. Long and Sedley, *Hellenistic Philosophers*, 49–50, 104–7.
10. For this narrative, see Blumenberg, *Legitimacy*, 181–203.
11. Thomas Aquinas discusses the tie between the idea of multiple worlds and chance in Aquinas, *Summa theologica*, I.47a3. For a broader genealogy relating these modes of thinking to technological modernity, see Blumenberg, *Legitimacy*, 125–226.
12. Bergson, *Time and Free Will*, 78.
13. Bergson, 79.
14. Bergson, 87.
15. Gould, *Time's Arrow, Time's Cycle*.
16. Aristotle, *Physics*, 220a4–a24; Sorabji, *Time*.
17. Bergson, *Time and Free Will*, 90–91.
18. He is not alone of course. Much of modernist literature, in part inspired by him, was dedicated to recovering a different grasp of time, as in Thomas Mann's *Magic Mountain*, Proust's *In Search of Lost Time*, and T. S. Eliot's *Four Quartets*. Certain strands of religious studies and philosophy have similarly attempted to sketch out a sacred time (Eliade, *Myth of Eternal Return*) or an epiphanic sense of time (Taylor, *Sources of the Self*, 419–93).

Theologically, Pope Francis seems to reject the spatialization of time, arguing that "time is greater than space"; Francis, *Evangelii gaudium*, 222–25.

19. Bergson, *Time and Free Will*, 101.

20. This projection is the essence of the later phenomenological understanding of time given by Edmund Husserl, Martin Heidegger, and Maurice Merleau-Ponty. This concern with how the moment is discrete distinguishes this discussion from analytical debates over A time vs. B time.

21. Bergson, *Time and Free Will*, 100. This recalls Augustine's use of the example of verse in *Confessions*, 11.27.

22. Bergson, *Time and Free Will*, 101.

23. Bergson, 176–77.

24. Bergson, 182.

25. Bergson, 183.

26. Bergson, *Matter and Memory*, 297. I do not embrace Bergson's full ontology because, as Maritain has shown, it is highly problematic; Maritain, *Bergsonian Philosophy*. Bergson's criticisms of standard understandings of time are very insightful, and Maritain continued to recognize the fruitfulness of Bergson's thought even after he broke with this philosophy: "Read Bergson. I have criticized him a lot, but read Bergson!" Quoted in the introduction of Maritain, 7.

27. For Arendt on natality, see O'Byrne, *Natality and Finitude*, 78–106.

28. Arendt, *Life of the Mind: Willing*, 29.

29. Is. 43:19. Aspects of my argument might suggest Jürgen Moltmann's discussions of the eschatological *novum* in his *Theology of Hope*. My use is slightly different as it focuses on all the different processes that God and humans can initiate in the moral life rather than primarily on eschatology. Oliver O'Donovan develops a similar point in his distinction between human anticipation based in the past and hope in God's future that destabilizes human anticipation. See O'Donovan, *Finding and Seeking*, 151–59.

30. Arendt, *Human Condition*, 177, citing Augustine, *City of God*, 12.21. See also Arendt, *Love and Saint Augustine*.

31. Arendt, *Life of the Mind: Willing*, 109.

32. Arendt, *Human Condition*, 7–16.

33. Arendt, 236–43.

34. Arendt, 241.

35. Maritain, *Bergsonian Philosophy*, 323.

36. Maritain, 57.

37. Dupuy, *Pour un catastrophisme eclaire*, 11.

38. Dupuy, 12.

39. Caduff, "What Went Wrong"; Stavrianakis and Tessier, "Go Suppress Yourself."

40. For the psychological research on such problems, see Schwartz, *Paradox of Choice*.

41. Jean-Pierre Dupuy argues that this fear of regret is at the basis of both the Rawlsian veil of ignorance as well as Hans Jonas's precaution, discussed in chapters 6 and 10, in Dupuy, *Pour un catastrophisme eclaire*, 127. Though such a perspective can be a valuable way of staving off environmental catastrophe, it has more destructive effects when applied to daily life.

42. Bergson, *Time and Free Will*, 9–10.

43. This literature is vast, but for a recent overview of work in psychology, see Zeelenberg, "Anticipated Regret"; and Schwartz, *Paradox of Choice*. The classic paper on regret in economics is Loomes and Sugden, "Regret Theory."

44. Epstude, "Counterfactual Thinking," 121–22.

45. Zeelenberg, "Anticipated Regret," 286.

46. For data on anxiety, risk aversion, and their relation to technology in younger generations, see Twenge, *IGen*.

47. Heidegger, *Being and Time*, 331.

48. Heidegger, 331.

49. Heidegger, 331.

50. Scherz, "Living Indefinitely."

51. Heidegger, *Being and Time*, 331–33.

52. Heidegger, 308.

53. Kierkegaard, *Concept of Anxiety*, 42. My interpretation is indebted to Beabout, *Freedom and Its Misuses*. There are of course many problems with his theology of anxiety, especially in its relationship to human nature. For example, the anxiety felt before the Fall already marked an alienation from God for Kierkegaard. See von Balthasar, *Christian and Anxiety*, 138–42. However, these problems do not negate its descriptive adequacy for fallen human nature.

54. Kierkegaard, *Concept of Anxiety*, 42.

55. Kierkegaard, 61.

56. Kierkegaard, *Consider the Lilies*, 22–23.

57. Kierkegaard, *Sickness unto Death*, 66.

58. Beabout, *Freedom and Its Misuses*, 55. Of course, Kierkegaard's framework requires a problematic denial of Adam's original grace that I would reject.

59. Kierkegaard, *Concept of Anxiety*, 73.

60. Scherz, "Living Indefinitely"; Hadot, *Present Alone*; Hadot, *Philosophy*; Goldschmidt, *Le système stoïcien*.

61. Mt. 6:34.

62. Stein, *Finite and Eternal Being*, 58.

4

The Hunger for Security

A new trinity is at work: traditional European values of liberty,
equality, and fraternity have been replaced in the 21st century by
comfort, security, and sustainability. They are now the dominant
values of our culture, a revolution that has barely been registered.

—*Rem Koolhaas*

Security is mortals' chiefest enemy.

—*Hecate,* Macbeth

One of the arguments for using risk-based decision theory is that it provides
security, minimizing dangers to human life. As chapter 10 discusses, protecting people from danger is one of the great benefits of this rationality when
it is done well and balanced by other goods. All people, Christians included,
have a stake in protecting themselves and others from reasonably foreseeable
dangers, as Thomistic models of practical reason also recognize. Yet we can
question the primacy of this goal in contemporary decision theory, the way
that security tends to become the main aim of the exercise of balancing ends.
Security was not always held in such high esteem. Indeed, the sentiment of
security was viewed quite negatively until the modern period. In contrast,
now freedom from fear is viewed as a psychological and political necessity.[1]

This chapter's two epigraphs show this shift. The witches' predictions at
the start of Act 4 in *Macbeth* serve to make the usurper overconfident, leading
to disastrous actions. Security and the lust for security in power lead Macbeth
to crime and folly, massacring potential threats to his rule in a way that alien-
ates his subjects. Today, the drive to control the future, to enact an immanent
providence, has transformed politics. As the architect Rem Koolhaas notes,
liberty, especially free speech, now seems dangerous; economic inequality
has increased; and deep internal political divisions are only widening, undermining fraternity. These values have been subordinated to the ultimate end of

immanent comfort encouraged by consumerism. Such comfort is stabilized by managerially ensured sustainability and security, which protects it from current and future dangers. Politics becomes an attempt at predictive control, a control ensured through the tools of risk analysis.

There is much that is good in this because these efforts allow predictability and regularity in contemporary lives. Wealthier citizens can afford insurance to protect themselves against most financial disasters. For those who lack resources, social insurance programs in many countries provide protection against unemployment, disability, and prolonged illness, as chapter 6 discusses. Moreover, probabilistic prediction allows preparation for the dangers of the natural world, such as weather forecasts enabling communities to evacuate before a hurricane strikes. Similarly, most people in the industrialized world are not buffeted by famines. These are good things. It is in these ways that risk analysis enables the control over the natural world promised in our creation in the image of God,[2] giving the knowledge that medieval and early modern scholars hoped would enable a return to prelapsarian conditions.[3] There is much in Scripture that would support such preparation for the future, especially insofar as it aids the disadvantaged, as part III will discuss.

Yet there is also a significant strand of Christian thought that is skeptical of such attempts to control the future, especially when higher goods are ignored. The sources of this skepticism lie throughout the Old Testament, in both the historical books and the Psalms, in the Gospels, and in the later tradition. Seen through these sources, the quest to attain security through the management of risk has many problems. First, it can lead to the delusion that people can ensure their own security through precautionary action, a delusion belied by practical experience. Further, if one's faith for future security lies in one's own efforts rather than in God's love, then it will lead only to further anxiety. Ultimately, this anxiety for security can become a desperate quest to assure one's own continued existence, undermining solidarity. Precisely because humans ultimately cannot ensure their own future, this anxious quest for security manifests in greed.[4] There is never enough money in the bank to face any possible contingency, so the greedy and anxious must always acquire more. Control is never thorough enough to ensure security, so the endangered politician strives for more. Instead of aiding those in present need, a risk calculus leads one to always think of the possible suffering of one's future self. Christian economic thinkers before the rise of commercial modernity were therefore suspicious of economic action that insulates people against risk. Finally, as part II of the book explores, the call to steward the world through reason can swiftly become a perverted form of dominion as we transform the world and others into material for use. This is the danger heralded by Pope Francis's denunciation of the technocratic paradigm, a concern shared by the Heideggerian tradition of the critique of technology, as well as other theological and philosophical voices.[5] This chapter develops an argument prefigured in earlier chapters that the way to counteract these problems is a renewed focus on trust in God's providential care.

FORTUNE AND POLITICS

In Antiquity in works such as Boethius's *Consolations of Philosophy* or in Stoics such as Seneca, Fortuna was seen as ultimately untrustworthy, so that one could only ever find peace and security in the eternal truth of philosophy, be it pagan or Christian. In contrast to the ancient recognition of the elemental wildness of Fortuna, modernity has seen chance as something that the right techniques could control or tame.[6] Already in the Renaissance, this shift is apparent. Machiavelli, in the twenty-fifth chapter of *The Prince*, likened Fortuna to "one of these violent rivers which, when they become enraged, flood the plains, ruin the trees and the buildings, lift Earth from this part, drop in another; each person flees before them, everyone yields to their impetus without being able to hinder them in any regard."[7] The prince is not completely powerless against her, however, with Machiavelli recommending two strategies. He favored the strategy of the bold adventurer, the entrepreneur, who attempted to overpower Fortuna, in a disturbing section of the book that echoes other early modern texts that compare nature to a woman.[8] She is to be overcome, held down, beaten, because "she lets herself be won more by the impetuous than by those who proceed coldly."[9] Yet he recognized another, less violent, approach. The wise prince could prevent the destructive effects of the flood of chance by building "dikes and dams so that when they rise later, either they go by a canal or their impetus is neither so wanton nor so damaging."[10] These dams and dikes would arise through technique. It is this technique of controlling chance that early modern science sought.[11]

Joseph Ratzinger, later Pope Benedict XVI, agreed that all our technological power is aimed at providing security against the forces of nature: "Technology originally arose as the means for assuring man's security, that it wanted to be and should be liberation as the guarantee of security: man need no longer fear the cosmos because he knows it, and, in knowing it, he understands how to control it."[12] Probability theory is perhaps the most important of these tools for controlling Fortuna. Foreseeing the future allows control over it, or at least the creation of safeguards against risks. The decision theory and tools that probability theory enables aim to provide control over the future and thus ensure security.

Yet, as chapters 6 and 10 will explore in more detail, ultimately this security is impossible to ensure. Mortals cannot foresee all future consequences. The unthought always threatens. Exaggerated attempts to grasp such control almost inevitably lead to absurd effects. For example, much of the funding for the development of decision theory came from the US military, which thought such techniques might help to provide security against the ultimate nightmare, a nuclear war between the United States and the Soviet Union.[13] At the same time, planners sought to prevent an outcome that they considered nearly as bad, the elimination of freedom by communist victory. The "rational" way to prevent both negative outcomes was the balance of terror, whereby any overreach by either side would result in complete destruction through nuclear war. The problem with this solution, which was recognized by game theorists themselves, was the instability that resulted from minor conflicts growing out of control.

Game theorists therefore sought for flexible responses short of an all-out nuclear exchange.[14] They developed plans for gradually escalating less serious nuclear strikes. At the lowest level, there were strikes on military units. If that did not stop the threatening behavior, then the United States might strike a small city. If that did not warn off the adversary, then larger cities might be hit, all in an effort to signal growing willingness to expand the scope of nuclear war. It was assumed that there would be a tit-for-tat response to each of the strikes as a way to maintain reciprocity in losses. Through these strategies, military theorists thought they could use nuclear weapons to control the international situation. These systems of rational control led to many potential disasters that had to be averted by the moral sense of even low-level actors, such as Stanislav Petrov, a Soviet lieutenant colonel who ignored indications of a seeming US missile launch at a time of increased tension in 1983.[15] His was only one of many examples of potential mishaps tied to the complexity of these systems.[16] Although some might say that the successful conclusion of the Cold War with no nuclear exchange indicates that the cost/benefit analysis worked, the sheer number of close calls that occurred over the thirty years of these systems' full activation shows how dangerous this form of reasoning is.

This attempt at control is also self-defeating when transferred to the individual level. No matter how much security a person may gain over his temporal future, inevitably, he will lose all in death. It was this final absurdity that Qoheleth lamented. People work all their lives to gather treasure that will eventually be enjoyed by others.[17] There is no way to know who these others will be or what character they will have. These reflections shed light on the interest of technology billionaires in transhumanist dreams of life extension. Such technologies promise them a chance to secure themselves and their health against the only certainty in life, death. Even before death, there is no way to secure ourselves against unforeseen disasters that may ruin all our plans: "The race is not to the swift, nor the battle to the strong, nor bread to the wise, nor riches to the intelligent, nor favor to the skillful; but time and chance happen to them all."[18] Such struggles for security must fail.

THE TURN TO IMMANENT GOODS

The problem with this quest for security is not only that it leads to counter-productive practical results. The deeper issue is that it distracts us from the ultimate ends that truly matter. Note that in the contrast between Aquinas and Machiavelli described in chapter 2, Aquinas's prince ordered his action toward the final end of eternal salvation for his citizens. In contrast, Machiavelli's politics is ordered toward the mere endurance of the prince's regime. Similarly, Max Weber contrasted his politics of responsibility for the effects of action with a politics aimed at an ultimate end.[19] Thus, risk management is tied to a political turn toward the immanent, reflecting a broader cultural focus on everyday life.[20]

This shift has also occurred at the personal level. When Cyprian talks about dangers in his treatise on jealousy and envy, it is with regard to solicitude against the introduction of vices.[21] The risks the Christian must guard against are evil thoughts. In contrast, probabilistic prediction encourages the person to become anxious about the temporal future. In so doing, the person begins to ignore God, succumbing to the vice of worldliness.[22] This focus on the immanent consequences of action is what Kierkegaard saw as one of the primary forms of modern despair: "For the petty bourgeois thinks he is in control of possibility, has lured this tremendous elasticity into the snare, or madhouse, of probabilities, thinks he holds it prisoner."[23] According to Kierkegaard, this confidence in the intellectual grasp of future probability loses sight of the possibility that God provides.[24] Accumulating goods against uncertainty, the bourgeois also ignores his neighbor, succumbing to injustice. As he attempts to ensure the conditions of total security, sins against justice become more and more serious.

Sollicitudo saeculi

Ultimately, solicitude for worldly security makes people miserable in their daily life. As it does so, it distracts them from the true happiness to which Jesus calls them. Kierkegaard's exegesis of Jesus's sayings on the birds of the air and the lilies of the field helps to demonstrate the problems with such desires.[25] The Christian need not have anxious concern over where she will find her food or how she shall be clothed. As discussed in chapter 3, Kierkegaard draws on the parable of the lilies of the field to trace these anxieties in part to improper comparison with others. The anxious person compares herself to others who have more or better goods and thus becomes enslaved to ambition and greed. She ceases to be happy living the life to which God has called her. Instead, she wants to define her own position of honor. The high dignity of being a human destined for God is not enough for her.

With regard to the birds' need for food, the comparison is slightly different, again involving temporal comparison but this time a comparison to the future with regard to security rather than a comparison with an alternative present enjoyed by others. The problem is that a person looks not just to current material needs but also thinks of tomorrow's. Birds cannot concern themselves with future need because "they live without temporal anticipation, with no sense of time, simply in the moment."[26] Solicitude over the future arises in a person when he improperly compares the present with the future and seeks to control that future. Kierkegaard analyzed this situation through a fable of a wood pigeon that compared itself with domestic pigeons who knew that a farmer would feed them. The wood pigeon became worried over whether the food that it found everyday would continue to be available to it: "It had conjured up an *anticipation* of need in its mind, and its peace had gone—it had discovered *material need*."[27] Here we see the tie between the concrete conjuring of future possibilities that is inherent in probabilistic decision theory and the problem of misplaced solicitude. It is anticipation rather than actual need that Kierkegaard is concerned about, because he recognizes that a person "in poverty is already placed in a difficult position," although he still may trust in God for his needs.[28] For one currently secure, however, obsessive care over tomorrow's material needs can enslave him. He seeks to acquire ever more, because no amount of material goods is ever enough to insure against all future contingencies: "Instead of *working* for the daily bread . . . to *slave* for it—and yet not be satisfied by it, because the care is to become rich."[29] This is ultimately a failure of vision; the person anxious for security is torn from the present and its enjoyment to gaze upon others and the future. He never truly lives because he is torn between times: "How rare is the person who actually is contemporary with himself; ordinarily most people are . . . several generations ahead of themselves in feelings, in delusions, in intentions, in resolutions, in wishes, in longings. But the believer (the one present) is in the highest sense contemporary with himself."[30] This comparison with the future and concern over it are accentuated in the risk-based model of action, which requires charting the future as a set of branching arrays and then comparing all these different possibilities.

The bird and the lily do live contentedly in the present, but this is because they lack the capacity to anticipate the future. The Christian cannot be like these nonrational beings, because he has the ability to anticipate the future. Yet he can transcend the temptation to cast himself into the future. He does this when his eyes do not focus on the comparison between the present and the future but look only to God, trusting in Him. The Christian is "content with what it is to be a man, to be content with what it is to be dependent, the creature as little capable of sustaining himself as of creating himself."[31] The fool seeks "to be himself his own Providence, whether for his whole life or only for to-morrow."[32] Focusing on God allows the Christian to dwell in eternity in a way. This eternal presence with God means that he does truly live in each moment, not as an isolated now but as united to God's plan across all times.[33] Solicitude is so deleterious because it makes a person avert his gaze from God, to give up this contact with the eternal. It is for these reasons that Jesus teaches the Christian to seek first the kingdom of God, to keep his intention centered on God's will. Such a focus will allow him to enjoy the things that he has and enable him to trust in God to provide for the future.

Of course, there are material cares that are proper. For example, not everyone has enough to eat; there are grievous cases of famine even today, as almost all theologians commenting upon these Gospel passages recognize.[34] To this end, Aquinas enjoins a proper solicitude.[35] Kierkegaard himself recognizes a proper concern for material things, especially with regard to those entrusted to one's care. This proper solicitude and its relation to using probabilistic rationality are taken up in more depth in part III. One response to this worry, which is surely correct, is to interrogate the attitude whereby a person goes about providing for these material needs. Is he anxious, ambitious, distracted from God? This attitude will be tied to how he goes about engaging the future, whether he uses the distracting temporality of risk.

Greed

Aquinas, though allowing for a proper solicitude for the needs of oneself and those in one's care, denounced improper solicitude over temporal goods and the future.[36] Such tendencies, even though resembling prudence, really spring from vice, from greed: "The undue use of reason appears chiefly in the vices opposed to justice, the chief of which is covetousness."[37] Proper solicitude seeks to ensure a limited range of bodily or charitable needs at a due time. Primarily, however, proper solicitude should aim at spiritual goods and duties. The danger is that excess concern over future needs or temporal goods may distract a person in such a way that she puts her end in them or at least is drawn away from spiritual goods.[38] As Aquinas notes, citing the parable of the sower, the thorns of temporal goods can choke the Word of God from having its proper effects in the human heart.

This problem is illustrated by the parable of the rich fool that Luke adjoins to the discourse on the birds of the air and lilies of the field.[39] The rich landowner has a bumper crop, so he decides to construct larger barns to store the crop and secure himself against any future needs. Satisfied that he is now secure, he goes to bed, only to find himself denounced by God and destined to die that very night. The landowner's folly is threefold. First, he places his trust in his own preparations for the future rather than God's care. This shows that he fundamentally misunderstands his relationship to the future and his control over it. Second, he goes about his plan for the wrong end, the wrong intention. He does not seek to serve God and others, instead aiming at pleasure. He will use his wealth to "relax, eat, drink, be merry!"[40] He has placed his end in earthly pleasure. Finally, he demonstrates greed, *pleonexia*, the unlimited desire for more, which is an improper use of God's gifts. Instead of sharing his bountiful harvest with the less fortunate, he keeps it all for himself. It is this aspect of fear for future security, its tendency to promote greed and the withholding of goods from the less fortunate in the name of prudence, that gives the most cause for concern.

Such improper solicitude turns one from justice toward one's neighbors. One covets the goods they own. Again, this care springs from comparison with others. But one can also see covetousness as aimed at possible future situations. For Aquinas, too, a reasonable desire for security can swiftly become improper greed. For example, most policymakers recognize that famine does not result from failures of supply but from failures of distribution. If the goods of the Earth were more equitably distributed, then the basic needs of all could be met. Catholic Social Teaching has termed this the universal destination of all goods, with *Gaudium et spes* arguing that "God intended the Earth with everything contained in it for the use of all human beings and peoples. . . . In using them, therefore, man should regard the external things that he legitimately possesses not only as his own but also as common in the sense that they should be able to benefit not only him but also others."[41] Property is not just for oneself but is to be used to serve the common good. Greed enters when a person seeks to use property for ambition or to secure her own future in an absolute way. Instead of trusting that others and God will be there for her in her need, she aims at self-sufficiency. Ultimately, this quest is self-defeating. No one can be self-sufficient, nor can anyone secure herself against all the insults of fortune. Even possessions become a solicitous concern. Boethius criticizes those who attempt "to banish need with plenty. But yet you achieve exactly the opposite. For you need a good many aids to help you guard your many kinds of precious furniture!"[42] The attempt to do so drives the miser to always desire more, not so much out of love for money or pleasure but out of fear: fear of future disaster and a desire to secure himself against it.[43]

David Cloutier discusses this contemporary relationship between security and acquisitiveness in his examination of luxury. One of the chief drivers of the quest for greater income and the failure to use that income to care for the poor is the felt need for retirement savings. People are constantly bombarded with the message that they are not saving enough, that they will be destitute in old age. For many people, this is true. For a good portion of society, it is because they are currently failing to make ends meet, frequently due to unjust economic circumstances. For others, it is due to foolish spending on consumer goods. Many households in the upper and upper middle classes, however, amass vast fortunes in retirement savings. Cloutier suggests that much of this perceived need is due not to the amount necessary to meet basic needs but to a desire for luxuries or from a misperception of needs. Retirement savings plans are pitched "in terms of the 'retirement of your dreams' in which yearning is 'unlimited' to the extent that the possible pleasures they could purchase in our economy are unlimited."[44] Security shifts from meeting needs to ensuring the availability of consumer goods.

Security and Usury

Turning to the longer history of Christian economic ethics, one discovers deeper suspicions of the desire to free oneself from risk, to be absolutely secure in acquisitions, in medieval and early modern discussions of usury.[45] Concerns about usury arose from scriptural exegesis. Canon law also rejected usury, leading to detailed discussions of what kinds of exchanges might be usurious, especially given the approval of certain kinds of usury in Roman law. Philosophical sources also had concerns, arising from the metaphysical conception of money as a substance that is sterile, not serving to produce anything but meant only for exchange.[46] Thus, there were many sources for condemning this practice.

There are two aspects of Scholastic discussions that bear directly on the topic of this book. The first is the idea that, in charging interest or higher prices for sales on credit, the usurer sold time. Money—being sterile, unlike land or livestock—should not be able to bring about an increase in goods. Thus, what the usurer is actually charging for is the time in which he goes without the possession of the money given in loan or on credit. As William of Auxerre argues with regard to the usurer, "He also acts against the universal natural law, because he sells time. . . . Nothing, however so *naturally* gives itself as time: willy-nilly things have time."[47] Scholastics recognized the close tie between financial developments and the transformation of time from lived experience into a commodity. This transformation of time is tied to injustice and greed. Time gives itself to all, but the usurer commodifies it in order to appropriate it. Such practices then alienate others from their time.

This denial of the ability to sell time was later qualified, through an acceptance of the idea of *lucrum cessans*, which is "profit lost as a result of lending."[48] The idea is that money is a tool that the skill of the merchant can use to generate profit. When the merchant forgoes the use of the money, he forgoes a certain amount of profit. Originally, the idea was tied to a delayed payment of a loan, in which case the lender could charge damages for the amount of profit that was forgone because he did not have access in a timely manner to the capital represented by the loan. Later Scholastics made it a more general principle that allowed for the payment of interest on loans. What is important for my argument is that here we start to see a focus on alternative, counterfactual futures. The merchant is not selling time but is rather accepting reimbursement for a possible future that is forgone. Usury and the temporality of risk are deeply related.

Second, and more important for the current chapter, the Scholastics had a deep suspicion of trying to gain money without any labor, effort, or risk of loss. Robert of Courçon wrote, "Any merchant making a contract with another for trading must, if he wishes to be a participant of the profit, show himself a participant of the danger and expenses which attend all buying and selling."[49] Risk was intimately tied to the justification of profit. The problem with the usurer is that he seeks to profit from a transaction with no risk. He attempts to maintain total security, offloading all danger onto the person who takes the loan. This is unjust. The usurer was distinguished from the partner, who may not be the person actually conducting the business but who shares in its risks.[50] In the late medieval period, risk became understood as a separate aspect of business, one that took on its own concrete quality. The danger of loss itself became understood as a something that could be sold.[51] It was understood as a service on the part of the insurer to bear the possibility of risk. Thus, risk became productive.

Yet this skepticism of contracts that shielded a person from risk is an important indication of Christian stances toward a desire by the wealthy and powerful for security. These desires were understood as inspired by greed and injustice. Already there was a recognition that the entrepreneur earned his pay through bearing uncertainty, an understanding discussed in more detail in chapter 6. If the reward does not come from labor, it must come from entrepreneurial risk. Thus, Patristic and medieval theologians would have great skepticism about our economy based on insurance mechanisms and about our financial system based on corporations offloading as much risk as possible onto others. It was only once people began to think in terms of opportunity costs, the risk of losing alternative futures, that insurance and interest became licit. Of course, viewing forgone alternative futures in terms of the risk of loss is deeply tied to the temporality of probability. Risk and insurance are thus in part born from the attempt to escape the Church's regulation of usury.

PROVIDENCE

What is the alternative to attempting to secure one's own future? In Christian tradition, it is trust in providence, as becomes clear when looking at a historical controversy over practices of security. At least in the United States, life insurance was viewed as morally suspect in the early nineteenth century.[52] It was seen as akin to gambling, trying to bet on whether a person would die or not within a certain period. The first life insurance policies could be taken out on anyone's life, even people in whom one had no personal interest. People gambled on how soon someone, frequently a public figure like a king or pope, would die. This practice seemed to raise threats against public order; there was always the temptation to kill the insured person in order to collect on the policy. People naturally recoiled at this morbid sport or business venture. This problem was largely eliminated through legal regulations that required an interest in the person upon whose life the policy was taken (i.e., a spouse, employee, or child).[53] There were also concerns over insurance's requirement to put a price on a human life. These concerns over equating human life with money continue even today in discussions of cost/benefit analysis because these analyses require providing a monetary price for lives lost or saved due to policy decisions so that the cost of death can be compared with the possibilities for economic growth.[54]

Beyond these disreputable aspects of life insurance, however, there was a more fundamental theological concern. Life insurance seemed to usurp God's providence. As the economic historian Viviana Zelizer describes it, "By insuring his life a man was not only 'betting against his God,' but, even worse, usurping His divine functions of protection. Life insurance misled men into

taking 'future consequences or results in their hands, which is God's preroga-
tive.'"[55] According to these critics, it is God whom the individual should trust
to care for his life and his surviving kin. Life insurance (but not other kinds
of insurance, like fire or marine insurance, curiously enough, which did not
depend on actuarial risk assessment until the twentieth century) seemed to
show a distrust in God.

Not all theologians opposed insurance. Rather, it depended on the denomi-
nation or theological outlook: "The conflict was set between the fundamen-
talist supporters of a deterministic ethos that held Providence responsible
for a man's family after his death, and spokesmen for a developing volunta-
ristic religious outlook to whom 'Providence helps he who helps himself.'"[56]
For these more liberal theologians, technologies like insurance could be seen
as part of God's providence. Such an argument hearkened back to the general
early modern program of trying to recapture man's prelapsarian control over
nature. Such theological support and the general reframing of insurance as
part of the duties of prudence gradually shifted the balance of opinion, making it broadly acceptable to the American populace.

Even though these concerns were overcome, such a position served as a
point of resistance to the onrushing push for greater control over contingency,
so it seems important to trace its sources in Christian theology. Although I
reject the position itself, the concerns expressed by it, or at least the insights
contained in the sources that inspired it, provide resources for interrogating
contemporary strategies for containing risk. They may reveal where a paradigm of probability-based decision theory can go astray, or what harmful for-
mative effects it might hide.

There are many inspirations for such concerns. In the first place, one can
find sources in Scripture for this fear that attempts at control over the future
insult God's providence. The Psalms constantly remind the reader that one
should trust in God alone rather than human contrivances: "It is better to
take refuge in the LORD than to put confidence in mortals. It is better to take
refuge in the LORD than to put confidence in princes."[57] No matter what contrivances one creates to deal with Fortuna, they will be successful only if they
align with God's will: "Unless the LORD builds the house, those who build
it labor in vain. Unless the LORD guards the city, the guard keeps watch in
vain."[58] No dams or dikes built through human planning alone can withstand
the power of the future. Any predictive planning will ultimately be overcome
by the unforeseen unless it is upheld by God.

The same lesson is found in the historical and prophetic writings. Beyond
the basic form of the Exodus, in which God delivers Israel from Egypt
through His power, He constantly attempts to show Israel that it is in Him

alone that they should trust. In the course of delivering Israel from domination by Midian, He reduced Gideon's army to the bare minimum, first from 32,000 to 10,000 men by requesting the departure of those who were afraid. Then, He winnowed it still further to only 300 in order to show that the victory over the Midianites belongs to Him alone. He said to Gideon, "The troops with you are too many for me to give the Midianites into their hand. Israel would only take the credit away from me, saying, 'My own hand has delivered me.'"[59] When the combined forces of the Moabites and Ammonites marched against King Jehoshaphat, God led the invaders to destroy themselves before the army of Judah could engage them, after Jehoshaphat admitted his powerlessness to defeat them.[60] Conversely, the attempts by the kings of Judah to gain security from the threat of Assyria and Babylon through alliances with neighbors like Egypt all came to naught.[61] The Old Testament seems to suggest that attempts at rational control over the future through human means can be folly rather than true prudence. Security lies in God's hands. It was this insight that was essential to the doctrine of providence. At the same time, Scripture also counsels prudent concern over common future risks, as in the Wisdom Literature discussed in chapter 11.

This doctrine of providence was not unique to Scripture, however, because it was central to many ancient philosophical systems and civic religions, such as Stoicism.[62] As rational beings, the gods should have the virtue of beneficence, involving themselves in human lives to aim at the good and ensure justice. The Stoics' unconcern about the future is due to their trust in and identification with the natural providence governing the world. How much more so should it be for Christians, for whom God is characterized as love, for whom Creation itself demonstrates God's overflowing goodness. It is this care for Creation to which Jesus points in arguing that Christians should give up their anxious solicitude for the future. God cares even for the lives of sparrows.[63] All Creation falls under God's care, so Christians should especially trust in His care for them. The Church has always put great store in Jesus's promise that God counts every hair on our heads, using it as a fundamental text for understanding the Resurrection of the body.[64]

It is important to note distinctions between different uses of the doctrine of providence in theology. One use that I am not advocating here is to use providence as an explanation from a third-person point of view for suffering in the world, to try to find reasons for disasters and sorrows in God's will. Such a theodicy is not my project here because God's reasons in history are generally hidden from human knowledge, such appeals are almost always unhelpful when there is a need for pastorally comforting those who are suffering, and the relationship between God's providential design and instances of suffering is theologically contested. Nor does such a doctrine entail a qui etist trust that all will be well in the end. As chapter 9 will emphasize, God calls each of us to act as an instrument of His will in the world, to further the kingdom of God through love of one another. Instead, I am focusing on the transformation that can occur when the moral agent embraces the doctrine of providence as an underlying interpretive perspective by which to approach action in the world. This perspective pushes back on the quest for security underlying much of the thought on risk. It requires that the Christian first seek the kingdom of God, despite the risks that might be entailed, secure in the knowledge that God governs the ultimate outcome of history. Such a stance does not simplistically believe that temporal existence will be untroubled, as God may call the Christian to bear a Cross. Yet even amid suffering, the Christian can trust in God. In so doing, the Christian participates in Jesus's Cross and God's salvific plan, putting ultimate goods above temporal security.

OBJECTIONS TO PROVIDENCE

Since the Enlightenment, scholars have challenged these notions of God's providential care, primarily using arguments from suffering. Many theologians have used other aspects of Scripture to challenge this classical picture of God's providence understood as the control and oversight of all things. In this classical understanding, drawing on a broader framework of the relationship between time and eternity, God's providential plan has been unchanging, with God guiding every particular action to a preordained end. The theologian David Fergusson is the most recent critic of what he calls the "Latin Default Setting" of providence.[65] Although recognizing that this understanding of providence can be found in Scripture and is predominant in the tradition, he points out that other aspects of God's action do not seem to fit this vision. God allows the existence and action of unruly forces, like Satan or Leviathan, that seem to threaten the fulfilment of His will.[66] There are indications that God changes His will in response to human action such as repentance, as in the example of Jonah's preaching to Nineveh.[67] God exists in relation to humans and other parts of Creation, so must react to their initiative.[68] Further, God's providential action is incomplete; in the face of suffering and evil, Scripture points to an eschatological fulfillment to come.[69] Beyond the problem of reconciling it with Scripture, the classical doctrine of providence also seems too constrained. Fergusson argues that theological works largely exclusively address providence under the subject of the doctrine of God, specifically in relation to Creation.[70] Such an understanding of providence does not allow for the recent recovery of the Trinitarian framework of theology, especially the economic Trinity. An adequate account of providence must take into account the role of the Son and the Holy Spirit as they act in Creation and salvation history. It must also take into account the role that providence can play in spirituality. For all these reasons, Fergusson calls for a polyphonic account, one that takes multiple perspectives on God's action and does not depend on the omnipotent Creator of the classical doctrine who oversees all actions.

These are formidable objections to the classical account of providence on which I rely, but there are answers to these questions in the tradition. To take seemingly the most serious objections first, many Patristic texts address exactly these questions of how to relate seemingly conflicting scriptural texts to the classical attributes of God, such as omnipotence, simplicity, providence, and eternity. Patristic exegetes recognized that many texts seem to run contrary to this picture of providence. They addressed these issues in terms of genre, typology, placing God's action in human terms, and so forth. Even today, such classical reflections on the meaning of prophecies that aim to change behavior are tremendously generative philosophically and theologically.[71] There is thus a massive set of resources that one could draw on to rebut these concerns. Fergusson, of course, recognizes these efforts, but his "argument is that the reading of Scripture in the Church's theology of providence has been generally inadequate to the diversity of biblical materials."[72] Every scriptural reading demands an interpretive key to make sense of the diversity of materials, so Fergusson is within his scholarly rights to develop his own and judge others' interpretations. But it is unclear that he provides enough of an argument to overthrow such an important hermeneutic tradition.

Partly, this is because such a shift would have important implications for the doctrine of God, implications that would reverberate throughout the rest of the structure of Christian theology. Providence is closely connected to the other classical attributes of God.[73] For example, providential action is enabled by divine omnipotence. Omniscience is interrelated with God's causal role in the providential governance of Creation. The lack of causal effects of creation on God is tied to divine simplicity, which is the reason for the interconnection of the divine attributes.

Divine simplicity is perhaps the most important attribute for these questions. This simplicity is beyond human comprehension. There is no extension or division in God. Even God's attributes—His goodness, love, wisdom, and so forth—are part of His essence rather than mere accidents. This has two important corollaries for providence. God's will is a single whole; God wills the world at once and creates it through His Word. As Augustine notes, "The will of God belongs to the very substance of God. Now if something arose in the substance of God which was not there before, that substance could not rightly be called eternal."[74] Further, God is not extended in time but exists in eternity. He is beyond time because He is the source of time. "In eternity nothing passes but all is present, whereas time cannot be present all at once. . . . Who shall lay hold upon the mind of man, that it may stand and see that time with its past and future must be determined by eternity, which stands and does not pass, which has in itself no past or future."[75] All times are present for Him in a *nunc stans*, an eternal present. This eternal unity contrasts with the temporal realm in which beings are extended through time and are modified by change: "You have given them to be parts of a whole: they are not all existent at once, but in their departures and successions constitute the whole of which they are parts."[76] This process of generation and corruption allows for the alteration of the world but is also the source of much of our suffering, for it leads to loss.

Many texts affirm that God created the world with a providential plan. God created through wisdom and with an end in mind, even if that end is not fathomable to us due to the limitations of human reason. A plan denotes a unity. Given that this plan unfolds through salvation history, that too must be a unity, tied to the unity of the Word, through whom time came to be. As Augustine argues, "For this is not an utterance in which what has been said passes away that the next thing may be said and so finally the whole utterance be complete: but all in one act, yet abiding eternally; otherwise it would be but time and change and no true eternity. . . . Thus it is by a Word co-eternal with Yourself that in one eternal act You say all that You say, and all things are made that You say are to be made."[77]

The Word is eternal and is spoken eternally rather than successively because the Word is the Second Person of the Trinity. If the Word were not eternal and unextended, one would have an Arian understanding of the Son. Fergusson does not provide a way to restructure these relations once providence is lost; nor do other critics.

If one wants to transform the classical understanding of providence, then one must also restructure the relationship between time and eternity. Most essentially, God can govern Creation providentially because He stands outside time. It is this existence outside time that in part gives God complete foresight and the ability to govern the world. In the classical conception, He created time and thus cannot be subject to it. If God is responding, shifting His engagements, if He has a real relationship with temporal creatures in Thomistic terms, then He would need to be subject to time. This would seem to necessitate positing that time is greater than God. Such a position would be at variance with monotheism of most varieties.[78] Even if one could evade these theological difficulties, one would still need to explain what time is. That was the essential problem with which Augustine wrestled, providing the Western tradition with its best conception of time. Fergusson rejects time-bound theologies like process theology or open theism for just these kinds of reasons, and at least Whitehead's and Bergson's ideas of time can be further criticized for aspects of vitalism.[79] Yet he does not provide his own conception of time. Without this, it is hard to subscribe to his polyphonic approach. Instead, it would seem to necessitate falling back upon problematic contemporary understandings of time.

Moreover, some of his criticisms do not seem to accurately reflect the tradition's understanding of providence, or at least the resources available in the tradition. To take two related examples, he argues that Stoic views of providence play too much of a role in the Christian tradition and that the doctrine of providence as it exists in current theology has little place for the Son or the Spirit. Stoicism, of course, played a major role in many aspects of Patristic thought, including providence.[80] The early Christians even found a similar language to Scripture in Stoic teaching on providence. For the Stoics, the divine Logos provided the providential, rational order exhibited in the world. Similarly, the constructive fire of the Stoic divine Pneuma ran through the world, binding things together and enabling activity. Finding these resonances to Christ as Logos and the Holy Spirit as Pneuma, the early Church Fathers cited Zeno and Cleanthes on the Word and Spirit creating the universe.[81] They drew on the idea of the Holy Spirit as that which holds the world together, vivifying it, thereby enabling the unfolding of providence.[82] Thus, the Stoic-influenced doctrine of providence, properly developed, has tremendous resources for supporting a classical Trinitarian theology.

Ultimately, Fergusson's case rests on the trouble that the problem of theodicy causes for providence. How can one understand evil and suffering in a world governed by an all-powerful and good God? There is not room in this study to adequately address this complex issue. The only thing to add is that a vast amount of writing addresses the problem of suffering from the position of the classical understanding of providence.[83] As I noted above, I am not seeking to use providence to provide access to the reasons for specific experiences of suffering—that is an impossible and pastorally unhelpful quest. At the same time, I hope that this book shows that contemporary understandings of time and responsibility raise a host of their own concerns, ones that the classical understanding of providence avoids.

CONCLUSION

The quest for security, for sure profit and the risk-free maintenance of earthly goods, must fail. Ultimately, Christians are to trust in God and His providence to care for future consequences. If one does so, then one has no need to fear future unpredictability. The biblical narrative shows that unpredictable events are not external to God's plan but essential parts of it. As discussed in chapter 3, God is the one who makes things new. The unpredictability of God's care, the lack of knowledge of the full contours of His plan, means that one must give up the attempt to gain complete control over the future. Despite his calls to build dams and dikes against fortune, Machiavelli recognized that these could fail in the face of a deluge, much like our levee systems, like those around New Orleans, constructed to contain hundred-year floods, fail in the face of the increasingly frequent thousand-year flood. The only true security is in God. That is why Jesus calls us to put our treasure in Heaven rather than trying to save it on Earth. We can only trust in God's providence, although that does not rule out human action of due solicitude that engages probabilistic risk analysis, as chapters 9 and 10 will discuss.

This turn to immanent security and worldly treasure has effects beyond our spiritual life. Mammon is a cruel master who will fail you in the end, but he also leads one to cruelty toward others. This can occur through a rejection of their needs, as this chapter describes. It can also occur through attempts to control them. Because others are major sources of unpredictability, the use of probability to predict and influence others' behavior seems to be a great aid toward security. Part II will illustrate how this turn from trust in God leads to the objectification and control of others, ultimately resulting in dangerous shifts in contemporary subjectivity.

NOTES

Koolhaas, "Rem Koolhaas Asks: Are Smart Cities Condemned to Be Stupid?"
Shakespeare, "Macbeth," Act 3, Scene 5, 1059.
1. Delumeau, *Rassurer et Proteger*, 9–29.
2. Gn. 1:26. Of course, this dominion can and has been grievously misused; White, "Historical Roots." But any justification of environmental devastation from these verses is a misinterpretation of their implications of stewardship; Francis, *Laudato si'*, 65–75; Northcott, *Environment and Christian Ethics*.
3. Harrison, *Fall of Man*.
4. O'Donovan, *Finding and Seeking*, 174.

5. Francis, *Laudato si'*; Heidegger, "Question Concerning Technology"; Husserl, *Crisis of European Sciences*; Grant, "Knowing and Making"; Borgmann, *Technology*; Ellul, *Technological Society*.

6. Hacking, *Taming of Chance*.

7. Machiavelli, *Prince*, 98.

8. Merchant, *Death of Nature*.

9. Machiavelli, *Prince*, 101.

10. Machiavelli, 98.

11. Doneson, "Conquest of Fortune."

12. Ratzinger, "Technological Security," 244–45.

13. Edwards, *Closed World*. My critique of game theory and its role in nuclear security draws on Welch, *Feminist Ethic*.

14. Edwards, *Closed World*, 119, 132.

15. Kishkovsky and Matsnev, "Stanislav Petrov."

16. For others, see Perrow, *Normal Accidents*, 282–93.

17. Eccl. 6:2.

18. Eccl. 9:11.

19. Weber, "Politics as a Vocation."

20. Taylor, *Sources of the Self*.

21. Cyprian, "On Jealousy and Envy," 1.

22. See Elliot, "Christian as Homo Viator."

23. Kierkegaard, *Sickness unto Death*, 72.

24. Kierkegaard, 71.

25. Mt. 6:25–34; Lk. 12:22–32.

26. Kierkegaard, *Consider the Lilies*, 27.

27. Kierkegaard, 30.

28. Kierkegaard, "Cares of the Pagans," 20.

29. Kierkegaard, 21.

30. Kierkegaard, 74.

31. Kierkegaard, *Consider the Lilies*, 32.

32. Kierkegaard, 32.

33. Scherz, "Living Indefinitely."

34. For commentary, see France, *Gospel of Matthew*, 263–72; and Luz, *Matthew 1–7*, 338–48. For an insightful engagement of biblical commentaries with Thomistic virtue, see Mattison, *Sermon on the Mount*.

35. Aquinas, *Summa theologica*, II-II 47a9.

36. Aquinas, II-II 55a6, a7.

37. Aquinas, II-II 55a8.

38. Aquinas, II-II 55a6. For a recent analysis of Aquinas's understanding of wealth, which focuses on the ideal of mendicant poverty, see Franks, *He Became Poor*.

39. Lk. 12:13–21.

40. Lk. 12:19.

41. Paul VI, *Gaudium et spes*, 69.

42. Boethius, "Consolation of Philosophy," 2.5.63–66.

43. For this dynamic of greed, see Aristotle, *Politics*, 1.9.

44. Cloutier, *Vice of Luxury*, 34.

45. The classic source for theological discussions of usury, which I follow here, is Noonan, *Scholastic Analysis of Usury*. I have also drawn on Dempsey, *Interest and Usury*; Daston, *Classical Probability*; Gigerenzer et al., *Empire of Chance*; Langholm, *Economics in the Medieval Schools*; Ceccarelli, "Risky Business"; and McCall, *Church and the Usurers*.

46. Noonan, *Scholastic Analysis of Usury*, 52.

47. Quoted by Noonan, 43.

48. Noonan, 115. For a broader discussion, see 107–33. For a theological critique, see Franks, *He Became Poor*. This concept is related to later economic ideas of opportunity cost.

49. Quoted by Noonan, *Scholastic Analysis of Usury*, 135.

50. Noonan, 134–53.

51. Noonan, 203; Ceccarelli, "Risky Business."

52. Zelizer, *Morals and Markets*.

53. The use of life insurance as a tool of speculation did not end in the early modern period. At the height of the HIV epidemic, before the successes of antiretroviral therapies, a speculative market in viaticals developed. Speculators would pay an AIDS patient a discounted amount of his life insurance policy to use for health care and living expenses in return for being made the beneficiary of the policy. The gamble on the part of investors was that the initial pay out and ongoing premiums would be significantly less than the policy was worth. During this period, there were even investment funds in viaticals; Mirowski, *Never Let a Serious Crisis Go to Waste*, 125–26. Such a practice is morally corrupting because it allows one to profit from an earlier death of another while making prolonged survival a disappointment.

54. Zelizer, *Morals and Markets*, 61–65; Sunstein, *Laws of Fear*, 132–48. Zelizer discusses other concerns, e.g., tempting fate and shaping the approach to death. These other concerns seem to have less connection to my argument, so I do not address them.

55. Zelizer, *Morals and Markets*, 73. She quotes Standen, *Ideal Protection*; and Albree, *Evils of Life Insurance*.

56. Zelizer, *Morals and Markets*, 75.

57. Ps. 118:8–9.

58. Ps. 127:1.

59. Jdg. 7:2.

60. 2 Chr. 20.

61. E.g., Is. 30–31.

62. Seneca, "De Providentia." For Patristic uses of Stoic ideas of providence, see Spanneut, *Le stoïcisme des Pères de l'église*, chap. 10; and Colish, *Stoic Tradition*.

63. Mt. 10:29.

64. Mt. 10:30.

65. Fergusson, *Providence of God*.

66. Fergusson, 22.

67. Fergusson, 27–32.

68. Fergusson, 32–36.

69. Fergusson, 37–41.

70. Fergusson, 9–11.

71. E.g., Dupuy, *Pour un catastrophisme eclaire*.

72. Fergusson, *Providence of God*, 30.

73. Though the literature is vast, for a discussion of some of these issues, see Leftow, *Time and Eternity*; Burrell, *Aquinas*; and Garrigou-Lagrange, *Providence*.

74. Augustine, *Confessions*, 11.10.

75. Augustine, 11.11. For a defense of God's eternity, see Leftow, *Time and Eternity*. For a phenomenological discussion of this point, see Stein, *Finite and Eternal Being*.

76. Augustine, *Confessions*, 4.10.

77. Augustine, 11.7.

78. Burrell, *Freedom and Creation*. For a similar argument in relation to preexisting matter, see Tertullian, "Against Hermogenes."

79. Fergusson, *Providence of God*, 252–71.

80. For examples and discussion of this influence on Patristic thought, see Spanneut, *Le stoïcisme des Pères de l'église*; Colish, *Stoic Tradition*; Thorsteinsson, *Roman Christianity*; and Byers, *Perception*. A contrary view is given by Rowe, *One True Life*.

81. Spanneut, *Le stoïcisme des Pères de l'église*, 298.

82. Spanneut, 332–41.

83. The most concise and comprehensive Catholic work on this topic is by John Paul II, *Salvifici doloris*.

PART II

The Governance of Others as Objects of Risk

5

The Shifting Meaning of Probability

Those who require to be guided by the counsel of others,
are able . . . to take counsel for themselves in this point
at least, that they require the counsel of others.

—*Thomas Aquinas*

Chapter 4 explored the search for a security independent of God or others through the means of controlling risk. Wealth is one way to achieve this partial security, providing resources that can be deployed to meet any new crisis. But wealth still leaves a person open to violence or disappointment by others because other people are far more difficult to predict and control than nature, a point that Alasdair MacIntyre emphasizes against the probabilistic tradition of thought.[1] If science and wealth are the ways to respond to natural risks, then politics and social science become the way to respond to the dangers posed by others. Machiavelli provided strategies and tactics that the prince could use to control these dangers. He was followed by much of early modern political thought, in which theorists such as Thomas Hobbes and Jean-Jacques Rousseau saw others as dangerous, with a person's social relations always threatening violence or domination. Much of this literature sought protection from the other through institutional frameworks, such as sovereignty or rights.

Today, we interpret the danger of the other in the language of risk. In an increasingly complex, interconnected society, political and economic systems, and thereby the rights of individuals, are threatened not merely by straightforward interpersonal violence or tyranny. Individual consumer habits, health decisions, laziness, and many other aspects of individual action also endanger contemporary systems of governance and individual prosperity in subtle ways. Insufficient consumer demand threatens economic growth; smoking raises health care costs; improper work habits decrease economic competitiveness; and insufficient retirement savings threaten the solvency of social insurance programs. A whole range of individual choices have implications for the security and prosperity of others. For these reasons, it is no longer adequate for politics merely to control violence. Individual action needs to be predicted and managed to mitigate these broader risks. Part II discusses how probability theory has shown itself to be an excellent tool to control others. Yet to succeed, it requires that those who govern treat people not as subjects with reason and free will but as objects of prediction and control. This loss of intersubjective engagement in favor of objectification results in a denial of the image of God in those so treated.

As this chapter argues, this use of probability for the management of others marks the end of a long process of change in the meaning of the word "probability." Tracing this process will illustrate the shifts that have occurred in mechanisms of power due to mathematical probability theory. Originally, probability marked a modality of trust in others, especially others' opinions. Probable opinions were those of people who were trustworthy. Probability was thus intersubjective, marking relationships of authority and interpersonal confidence. In contemporary social science and politics, however, probability is an abstract prediction of behavior. Individuals are treated as the objects of probabilistic analytics that use the same mathematical tools deployed to describe physical objects like gas molecules, a social physics such as the one dreamed of by Auguste Comte and more recently by technology researchers like Alexander Pentland, described in chapter 7. Therefore, society has moved from a system in which the person rested her hope for the future in trust in God's providence and communal solidarity, which are intersubjective relations, to one in which security is sought through the manipulation of mechanistic nature and other people envisioned as predictable objects through the lens of natural science.[2] This chapter traces this shift. As this section explores, the move from an intersubjective to a subject–object relationship has implications for the power exercised by those deploying probabilistic tools in the social sphere.

THE ORIGINS OF PROBABILITY AND PROBABILISM

The word "probability" derives from the Latin *probabilitas*, meaning credibility or plausibility.[3] This word in turn was derived from *probabilis*, which also has connotations of a person who is laudable or worthy of approval.[4] The term thus originates in an intersubjective context of praise and blame. Something that was probable was something that could be trusted, although it differed from conditions of certitude. In the intellectual sphere, probability referred to the realm of opinion and uncertainty rather than that of science and demonstration. Because almost all premodern scholars, following Aristotle, saw the realm of practical affairs and rhetoric as beset by uncertainty and governed only by general rules, it was obviously a realm of the probable.[5] Thought in these areas started from probable opinions, Aristotle's *endoxa*, opinions accepted by everyone or most of the wise.[6]

One sees this sense of probability in medieval thought in relation to legal evidence.[7] Unless the accused confessed, the judge could not be sure of his guilt.[8] Many cases relied on witnesses, and it became very difficult to decide on guilt when there were a number of witnesses on either side of a case. In such situations, judges were forced to weigh the probability of the evidence on each side, leading to complex systems for weighing various kinds of evidence, including the credibility of certain kinds of witnesses. Probability was divided between intrinsic probability, based on the inherent strength of the arguments, and extrinsic probability, referring to the trustworthiness of witnesses. Basically, the question of probability boiled down to how much the judge could trust witnesses and how many and of what kind were needed to outweigh countervailing evidence.

During the late medieval and early modern periods, as commentators have repeatedly noted, moral theology became more legalistic.[9] As Roman and canon law shaped theology more and more, moral theology began to adopt legal concepts like probability, especially because probability was also tied to ideas of uncertainty in action. The central arena where probability became important was situations of uncertain conscience.[10] The question was, What should the person do when she did not know if an action was morally correct or not? As legalism intensified, the question was usually framed as, What should she do when she was uncertain as to whether a moral law was binding in a certain situation? Or should she act on the side of freedom or of law? The classic understanding had been that if a person doubted the morality of an action in conscience, then she should not act. That position became less tenable over time, for a number of reasons. First, the sheer number of positive ecclesiastical and civil laws dramatically increased over the course of the Renaissance and early modern period, meaning that a person was always in danger of violating some law or another. As the historian Stefania Tutino argues, "It became increasingly more difficult for the individual penitents, confessors, and indeed subjects to navigate a larger and larger body of different and at times conflicting norms and authorities."[11] For these reasons, a pure tutiorism, or the path of safety of following the law, could by paralyzing.

The second major problem concerned those cases in which laws or rights conflicted because of the uncertainty of the concrete case. In such a case, there was no safest option. One classic example of this was a woman who remarried after her husband's death on a voyage, who then comes to doubt the accuracy of the report of her husband's death.[12] If she continued conjugal relations, she put herself in danger of adultery. But if she did not, then she would fail to pay the unfortunately named marriage debt, thus denying justice to her husband. Either way, she risked sin. This is not the best example to become a textbook case, but one could imagine similar cases of conflicting rights and duties.[13] For such reasons, along with its ties to Jansenism, the Magisterium ultimately condemned tutiorism as inimical to human moral freedom. Although these concerns arise in part from legalism, they also reflect the honest acceptance of moral uncertainty and the difficulty of prudential judgment. What was needed was some kind of method that could help the person decide in cases of moral uncertainty.

One mode of dealing with such a lack of assurance was through counsel. The morally perplexed could turn to those who were wise for guidance. Aquinas saw this as the solution to the objection that not all Christians in a state of grace possess the infused virtue of prudence, because some in the Church are not intelligent enough to provide counsel for themselves on action: "Those who require to be guided by the counsel of others, are able, if they have grace, to take counsel for themselves in this point at least, that they require the counsel of others and can discern good from evil counsel."[14] For later probabilists, like the seventeenth-century Cistercian scholar and moral theologian Juan Caramuel, the very act of seeking counsel from an authority changed the nature of moral choice in a case of a doubting conscience, showing the crucial good intention of seeking the right choice.[15] Most Catholics would seek such counsel from the local priest. Along with the requirement for yearly confession, this tendency drove a need to train priests in the arts of moral discernment. Moral theologians wrote books of detailed cases, to serve as references for priests when in doubt or to train them in seminaries after the Council of Trent. Through this process, moral theologians became the wise persons to whom others turned for guidance in cases of conscience.

Although this process was effective in many cases, questions arose when moral theologians disagreed about a case. Which opinion should one adopt? One generally accepted answer was that it was safe to follow a probable opinion, meaning that an opinion by a trustworthy authority was acceptable to follow even at the expense of being wrong or if there were other available opinions.[16] This seemingly simple device led to systems of great complexity. First, there was the question of how one knew whether an opinion was probable. How many learned authors support it? What kind of authority did such an author need to have? Second, was one bound to follow a different opinion if it was more probable? Strict probabilists said no because probability meant that an opinion was trustworthy enough. Probabiliorists held that a person was bound to follow a more probable opinion because it was more likely to be true. Laxists were those who seemed to make any opinion seem probable and held that only one authority was necessary in order to make an opinion probable. Finally, equiprobabilists held that one could accept an opinion only if it were equally as probable as the alternative options. This last stance seemed to become victorious after the Redemptorist moral theologian Alphonsus Ligouri's eighteenth-century advocacy of it. These were the complexities into which moral theology could descend when framed in terms of the law–freedom dialectic.

Two important assumptions lay behind these debates. First, it was acceptable to place one's trust in approved authorities for guidance in the moral life. Moral decision-making takes place in a context of interpersonal advice and thus a relation of trust. It also takes place in an ecclesial community that encompasses a tradition of moral discourse. No matter how abstruse this discourse could become, it was still an ongoing conversation between scholars governed by authoritative texts. The participants in this discourse were licensed and overseen by ecclesiastical authorities, as shown by the condemnations of particular positions that began to emerge in the latter half of the seventeenth century. Second, this debate relied on the mercy of God.[17] It was not a strict, mechanical legalism. Every participant recognized that intentions mattered to God. If the actor sincerely sought God's will by taking counsel with wiser heads, God would mercifully accept the subjective intention of the action, even if it turned out to be objectively sinful. The debate was over how one goes about sincerely seeking God's will. Thus, this understanding of probability was placed in an intersubjective context of trust in authoritative writers, trust in an ecclesial community, and trust in God's mercy.

THE REJECTION OF PROBABILISM

Although probabilism was never condemned and continued to operate in discussions and textbooks of moral theology up until Vatican II, its popularity as a theoretical framework declined in the late seventeenth century. In part, this was due to the popularity of Pascal's *Provincial Letters*. This work was part of the polemical war waged between Jesuits and Jansenists, a group centered on the Port Royal convent that adopted a stricter, late Augustinian position on issues of fallen human nature, grace, and free will that contrasted with much of Counter-Reformation Catholic thought. To their opponents, they seemed to deny true human freedom. Among their other concerns, the Jansenists found Catholic moral theology too lax. Although the *Pastoral Letters* as a whole take aim at Jesuit theology on a number of fronts, Letters 5 and 6 specifically and scathingly criticized probabilism and confessional practice.[18] These letters portrayed probabilism as a system of thought that could excuse anything. Moreover, Pascal described it as an almost consumerist model of spiritual guidance, telling the individual penitent what he wanted to hear, all in the interest of the Jesuit order's power and influence. The *Letters* were a success in Parisian salons, and in the next few decades, more and more theologians began to launch their own critiques of probabilism. Eventually, even the superior general of the Jesuits rejected probabilism to papal approval.

In *The Art of Conjecture*, the philosopher James Franklin describes this rejection of probabilism as a victory for a very modern form of moral practice. Given Pascal's criticism of the contemporary texts of moral theology, Franklin describes it as a turn away from moral authorities toward personal judgment of moral situations: "The real source of the disagreement is that Pascal believes there are no experts in morals and that anyone (or at least the saved) can work out his opinions in morals for himself. The modern world has followed Pascal in this."[19] In the case of the Jansenists, this personal judgment may have been stricter than that of many moral theologians, but Franklin argues that it set the stage for the subjective, relativistic morality of the contemporary world. Although there are aspects of Pascal's thought, especially as it follows Jansenist leanings toward Calvinism, that may reflect such an understanding, this seems to be a misreading of his argument. Pascal never advocates turning away from external moral authorities to personal judgment. Indeed, in his wager, he advocates engaging in external practices to reshape subjective beliefs and judgments, imitating those who already believe. He counsels the convert: "Follow the way by which they began; by acting as if they believed, taking the holy water, having masses said."[20] In numbers 268, 269, and 270 of his *Pensées*, he argues for the need for submission to authority in relation to religious truths. Rather, the argument was over which authorities to trust. Fundamental to probabilist method, at least after the sixteenth-century work of the Jesuit moral theologian Gabriel Vazquez, was that one should preferentially rely on more recent authorities.[21] They were thought to be more up-to-date, to have access to better arguments, new insights, and better acquaintance with conditions in society. Pascal, in contrast, preferred to turn to the guidance of Scripture, Patristic authors, and magisterial teaching: "It is easy to see that all are welcome that come your way, except the ancient fathers…. But I foresee three or four serious difficulties and powerful barriers which will oppose your career. They are the

Holy Scriptures, . . . the popes, and the councils, whom you cannot gainsay, and who are all in the way of the gospels."[22] He trusted what has remained constant and enduring and criticized the hermeneutic with which probabilists engaged these writers, one that attempted to explain away difficult commands.[23] It was an argument over how to read and engage the tradition, one that resonated with broader debates about the relative value of the ancients versus the moderns in seventeenth-century France.[24] It was an argument that was still situated within the boundaries of intersubjective trust.

Although this particular critique may not apply to Pascal himself, Franklin is marking a real shift to which Pascal contributed in a different way. Reliance on moral authority and the prudent counsel of others has eroded in modern moral thought, through such means as Hobbes's geometric method in morality and politics and Kant's critique of heteronomy. Probability theory also has contributed to this process, and in that Pascal did play a role. Modern decision theory shifts moral judgment out of an intersubjective context into one split between objective and subjective features, those depicted in the split between objectivist and subjectivist models of probability theory. Probability no longer refers to trustworthy opinions. On one hand, probability now involves objects in the world or the frequency of states of affairs. Judgments of probability are about objects rather than other subjects, or at least they are about subjects treated as objects. Everything is turned into an abstract object of mathematical analysis. This shift allows for more accurate prediction and control over the world. Yet at the same time, these probability judgments can also be considered subjective bets, especially in the Bayesian model. As these calculations are deployed in decision-making, they must be combined with subjective expert valuation of different outcomes and states of affairs. Probability embeds the subject/object divide in thought.

The originators of probability theory seemed unaware of this mixture of the subjective and objective interpretation of probability. According to Ian Hacking, this unacknowledged combination occurred due to two interrelated assumptions.[25] First, early theorists believed that probability theory sought to reproduce the judgments of an ideal rational man, one whose practical wisdom was approximated by the Enlightenment philosophes.[26] Unlike today, early probability theory did not seek to revise the contemporary framework of choice but to reflect prudential judgment. Given the right training, everyone would agree on estimates of probability and valuation of states of affairs. There was no conflict between subjective and objective probability but rather a harmony. This harmony was assured by a second background assumption, that the world was providentially ordered and that God had embedded comprehensible signs into the order of the universe.[27] Descending from Christian frameworks of the image of God, as modified by Deism, the assumption of providence allowed Enlightenment theorists to expect that the rational man had the capacity to recognize and follow the rational order of the universe.

This was all to change. Ideas of providence were lost, and with them the idea of an objective order open to rational human grasp. Without this undergirding feature, there was no assurance that everyone would agree on objective probabilities. With the rise of emotivist and noncognitive interpretations of value, rational expectations became radically subjective and thus ultimately dependent upon individual preference and desire.[28] In the older model of probability, the process of judgment involved consulting a trusted person who would help one discern the will of God, Who is also a person who undergirds the rational created order. Judgment was thoroughly intersubjective, based on faith in others. Once this interpretive framework is lost, the subject/object divide is enthroned. The actor ceases to act relationally but attempts to gain as much control as possible over the world of objects in order to realize her subjective values.

PERSONS AS OBJECTS OF PROBABILITY

Many of the objects over which individuals, but more usually governments and other large institutions, attempt to gain control are people. As part II of the book discusses, people and actions are modeled using the same statistical frameworks that physicists use to model physical systems. In a large enough population, statistical regularities appear, which can be predicted and used to guide action. Such regularities have been used to attempt to gain certainty and control over social life. For example, modern attempts to use probability in the legal sphere differ significantly from premodern ones. Instead of being used in relation to the trustworthiness of witnesses, it was used in relation to jurors. Scholars raised questions of how many jurors were needed in order to ensure a just verdict in the case, regardless of who the jurors were.[29] This was the question for which the nineteenth-century mathematician Siméon Denis Poisson devised his law of large numbers. How many jurors does one need before their individual differences disappear in a sure decision? Probability becomes an attempt to erase the individual, to erase the particular free subject and submerge him in a predictable population. Although these attempts to ensure juror accuracy failed, one sees here the modern attempt to gain as much objective control and certainty over a situation as possible, regardless of the personal characteristics of the people involved.

This points to a broader use of statistics to gain predictive control over others who are no longer treated as persons to trust or with whom to reason but as objects or abstract representations. Such procedures are surely appropriate in many areas, but it will also become apparent that, when misused, such a way of perceiving others can be dangerous. It threatens subtle forms of tyranny while reshaping people's subjective understanding so that they no longer understand themselves as being in the image of God. Part I looked at the modern subject/object divide of probability in terms of the way subjective judgments of probabilistic futures affect the moral character of the actor. In part II, which comprises chapters 5 through 8, I look at the object side of the divide, to see what are the effects of being treated as the object of another's risk calculation. Ironically, however, such attempts at control frequently arise out of good motivations to protect others' security. Chapter 6 bridges the divide between the subjective and objective aspects of this question by looking at the frameworks of responsibility that drive objectification in social policy, showing the benefits and limitations of these techniques. Then, in chapter 7, I look in detail at these modes of objectification before turning to their problems of reason and free will in chapter 8.

NOTES

Aquinas, *Summa theologica*, II-II 47.14ad2.

1. MacIntyre, *After Virtue*, 88–108.
2. This framework relates to the technocratic paradigm discussed by Francis, *Laudato si'*.
3. "Probability"; Lewis, "Probabilitas."
4. Lewis, "Probabilis."
5. Aristotle, *Nicomachean Ethics*, 1094b14.
6. Aristotle, "Topics," 100b20.
7. Franklin, *Art of Conjecture*, 12–39.
8. This fact explains the importance of torture as a means to secure evidence. Judges and inquisitors did not want to unjustly convict the accused.
9. Mahoney, *Making of Moral Theology*, 1–36, 224–58; Pinckaers, *Sources of Christian Ethics*, 240–79.
10. The following account of probabilism draws on Tutino, *Uncertainty in Post-Reformation Catholicism*; Fleming, *Defending Probabilism*; Franklin, *Art of Conjecture*; Mahoney, *Making of Moral Theology*, 135–43; and Jonsen and Toulmin, *Abuse of Casuistry*.
11. Tutino, *Uncertainty in Post-Reformation Catholicism*, 20.
12. Tutino, 40; Franklin, *Art of Conjecture*, 73.
13. For a recent example of such arguments, Cathleen Kaveny questioned rules for Catholic hospitals surrounding cooperation with evil because of the duty to serve the health needs of the poor; Kaveny, "Tax Lawyers, Prophets, and Pilgrims."

14. Aquinas, *Summa theologica*, II-II 47.14 ad2.
15. Cited by Fleming, *Defending Probabilism*, 116.
16. For the practical presentation of these issues, see any of the pre–Vatican II manuals of moral theology, such as Koch, *Handbook of Moral Theology*, 1:203–35.
17. Fleming, *Defending Probabilism*.
18. Pascal, *Pensées and the Provincial Letters*, 372–401. For a critique of his arguments, see Jonsen and Toulmin, *Abuse of Casuistry*, 231–49.
19. Franklin, *Art of Conjecture*, 98.
20. Pascal, *Pensées and the Provincial Letters*, 83.
21. Tutino, *Uncertainty in Post-Reformation Catholicism*, 80.
22. Pascal, *Pensées and the Provincial Letters*, 386.
23. Pascal, 388–91.
24. For this dispute and its relation to modern ideas of progress, see Sorel, *Illusions of Progress*.
25. Hacking, *Emergence of Probability*. This interpretation is challenged by many, such as Garber and Zabell, "On the Emergence of Probability."
26. Gigerenzer et al., *Empire of Chance*, 14–18.
27. Hacking, *Emergence of Probability*, 39–48.
28. For this narrative, see MacIntyre, *After Virtue*.
29. Hacking, *Taming of Chance*, 95–104.

6

Responsibility for Risk

The great political event of the last two centuries has
been without doubt the application of the calculus
of probabilities to the government of society.

—*François Ewald*

The changed experience of temporality that engenders feelings of anxiety
over future possibilities is tied to a demand for security at the individual
level. These issues are also at the heart of the problem of responsibility, but
at the level of social relations. The question of responsibility is, For what can
a person be called to account by others, and especially what are the kinds
of consequences to which he or she must attend?[1] These concerns do not
extend merely to persons' own security but also to their duties toward others.
Responsibility can take the form of care for others' lives. Because of this connection to others under one's care, this chapter moves to a consideration of
collective action, to the care of policymakers, those concerned with either all
society in terms of government or with collective enterprises like corporations. One hundred years ago, Max Weber put the question of responsibility
at the center of political ethics.[2] He contrasted an ethics of ultimate ends,
tied to the Sermon on the Mount's singular commitment to the kingdom of
God discussed in chapters 3 and 4, with an ethic of responsibility. Whereas
the former is uncompromising, sticking to its ideals no matter what the consequences, the latter is concerned about the results of action. This does not
mean that it is purely utilitarian, but it does make the concern for those in
its care central. It is this ethic and this concern that Weber thinks proper for
the politician. Chapter 9 will explore how to interweave the Sermon on the
Mount with an ethics of responsibility, but this chapter examines the concrete embodiment of this concern for others in contemporary politics.

This concern can also shift to private life. Today, as chapter 3 explored,
many people feel called to account for unrealized possibilities, for not living

up to their potential. They feel guilt because they could not actualize all the beneficial forking paths of time, limited as each person is to one timestream. Those unrealized possibilities that nevertheless remain present in their absence haunt them both before and after choice. This situation represents a relatively new framing of guilt. Even in the public arena, the idea of responsibility is relatively new. In most languages, the word did not appear until the end of the eighteenth century, marking an emergent post-Enlightenment and postrevolutionary concept of politics, ethics, and subjectivity.[3] It was tied to a new feeling of technological power to control the future. Older experiences of guilt were more deontological. Guilt focused on past immoral or imprudent actions, so a major goal of the moral life was abstaining from sin. Of course, a person had to meet moral obligations like providing the necessities of life for kin. Similarly, there were clear sins of omission. However, there was no need to think of every eventuality or to optimize life's possibilities.

A new model of guilt emerges with utilitarianism. With the aim of maximizing the good across society, each person, especially the policymaker, can be called to account for actions not taken, for possibilities not realized. One becomes responsible for the entire future that could come into existence. The site of evaluation shifts from sins of commission to sins of omission, a shift that correlatively allows ethicists to justify many actions that would previously have been forbidden; many actions that previously would have counted as sins seem to allow for better future possibilities. At the same time, the weight of the future rests more heavily on the individual as forgone possibilities impinge on conscience. This model sets up the agent for almost inevitable failure because possible outcomes are diverse, incommensurable, and mutually exclusive. Some cannot be realized at the same time, and their incommensurability makes any ordering almost impossible.

This new model of responsibility could only be actualized because probability theory changed the broader understanding of society, first at the level of policymakers and social theorists before gradually transforming the broader social imaginary. Statistics and actuarial technologies allowed governments and corporations like insurance companies to better predict risk throughout the population. The distribution of different risks became much better known. As risks became more predictable, there arose a new duty to insure against them. When risks became too great for individuals, governments took upon themselves the responsibility to intervene. It thus fell to the state to prevent or at least compensate for risk through insurance systems but also regulatory frameworks for environmental and national security risks.[4]

This chapter outlines the two most prominent models of contemporary responsibility.[5] The first, what I call managerial responsibility, draws on the decision theoretical framework, assisted by actuarial technologies to help the policymaker maximize future goods, allowing her to take responsibility for both actualized and unrealized possibilities. However, by attempting to control so much, she makes herself vulnerable to novel risks. This problem gives rise to an alternative perspective within this managerial model, one that aims less at maximizing future goods than at preventing future disasters. Although many regard this precautionary framework as an alternative to managerial responsibility, I suggest that it serves merely as a check and variation on this larger model. However, it has a similar problem because of dangers that remain unthought as well as a tendency to focus on conspicuous dangers, becoming ultimately self-defeating. Under both these modes, managerial responsibility engaging probabilistic risk assessment has revolutionized governance, as Ewald notes in the chapter's epigraph.

The second, entrepreneurial model of responsibility also makes the individual bear responsibility for all the consequences of action. It relates differently to risk, however, seeing it as generative and failure as inevitable. "Fail fast, fail often," say the Silicon Valley elite. The *moral* stakes of failure are thus much less, if not nonexistent, as long as one is of a certain class. But the individual must endure the full *material* and *economic* weight of failure. Managerial and entrepreneurial responsibility take different attitudes toward prediction, risk, and temporality. The moral judgments and existential posture stemming from these positions are very different. Both, however, focus on immanent security and rely on ideas of individuals as subject to forces beyond their knowledge: the market and distributions of risk. To grasp the contemporary role of risk and the existential response to it, we must understand these modes of responsibility.

MANAGERIAL RESPONSIBILITY

Managerial responsibility emerged from the practical elaboration of utilitarianism, or, rather, it is the practical form of governance that utilitarianism was developed to support. It is the essence of Weber's idea of responsibility. Managers and policymakers seek to know all possible costs and benefits of the available policy options in order to maximize profit while minimizing the risk of loss (the minimax or maximin framework).[6] Achieving this goal requires intense efforts at prediction, calculation, and control. After these efforts, the decision-maker is held responsible for all consequences, both those actual-ized and those forgone. After all, the consequences all result from the care he took in his efforts at calculation and prediction. The manager thus takes on total ownership over his part of the world.

This framework has a long history. Beginning in the early modern period, both state and private actors used statistical conceptions of risk to control their future.[7] Governments thought they could use the power of mathemat-ical analysis to shape their societies, while businesses sought to bring insur-ance to the masses, thereby giving people a hedge against the future. In both forms, control of risk could bring security, a security seemingly underwritten by scientific analysis. Understanding this history helps to give a sense of the full range of effects of this framework on the world.

Risk and the Social

The early modern state, engaged as it was in competition with its neighbors, sought to increase all its available resources. In order to do this, it needed knowledge of what its resources were. States thus gathered data on as many aspects of life as possible, hence the term "statistics": the mathematical analy-sis of the state.[8] States gathered information on population, agricultural pro-duction, trade, and manufacturing. The idea was to use this information to develop systems of precise control over all aspects of life and production. Information would allow a police state.

Such attempts at control were less successful than governments hoped. Yet, as analysts pored over these statistics, they developed important insights. They discovered regularities in the data, seemingly law-like natural consisten-cies of agricultural production, population, and trade. New social scientists, like Adolphe Quetelet, a Belgian who redirected his application of statistics in correcting astronomical measurements to using them to determine social averages, discovered regularities in categories like suicide, crime, and even misaddressed letters. Year in and year out, the rates would stay nearly the same within the same society, although differing between them. This reg-ularity led people like Quetelet to ascribe these pattens to a force beyond individual free choice. Society became understood as an entity existing on a separate plane from individuals, with its own characteristics revealed by sta-tistical distributions. Common life was revealed by probabilistic techniques; and the individual could be understood, in part, by the ways he or she fit into these different distributions.

This new understanding of society required new methods of governance and control over the future. One major technique that served this end was insurance, especially the statistical and actuarial techniques created primarily by the life insurance industry. It was only with the development of better government data, better actuarial tables, and better statistical tools in the beginning to the mid-nineteenth century that life insurance became a stable business.[9] Before that period, miscalculations of mortality risk, small customer pools, and undercapitalization frequently caused these businesses to collapse. There were major technical changes needed for life insurance to become successful. In contrast, other forms of insurance, such as maritime or fire insurance, existed for a long period, successfully relying on the individual prudence of the underwriter to price risks. Some of these industries did not adopt actuarial techniques until the mid-twentieth century.[10] Statistical models for things like hurricanes in relation to property insurance were not used until the 1980s.[11] Much of reinsurance still depends more on prudential judgment than actuarial techniques. It was thus a very specific development of insurance in relation to life that created the grounds for a changed mode of governance.

As chapter 4 described, through intensive marketing by insurers as well as through broader societal shifts in conceptions of life and religion, purchasing life insurance came to be seen as a responsible action. It was a way for the head of a household to be provident for his family. Life insurance would provide a measure of economic security in the event of the breadwinner's death so that his children could continue their education and his wife would not need to work. It thus appealed to the well off as a way to gain some kind of control over their future and be responsible for the family.

This same impetus also spread among the working classes at about the same time, even though they could not afford the relatively high prices of private life insurance. Instead, they turned to a different organizational form, mutual aid societies, consisting of members of certain occupations or ethnic groups.[12] The actual aid provided by such societies might be small: enough to cover the costs of a funeral or perhaps provide support through a few weeks of illness or disability. But it was an essential support for families on the margins of poverty.

From the late nineteenth to the early twentieth century, insurance companies began to offer policies aimed at these groups lower down in the socioeconomic hierarchy, targeted to such societies, to employers, to unions, or even to individuals. These plans might offer life insurance, disability coverage, burial benefits, or even health insurance. In some cases, these expansions were resisted by workers who feared the loss of control over their pooled economic resources.[13] This expansion of insurance to the working class was eventually taken up by government, especially in relation to the growing problem of workers' compensation for industrial accidents. Though most of Europe eventually followed the lead of Bismarck in Germany in providing broad programs of social insurance, this movement met greater opposition in the United States, however, from a variety of interests.[14] Life insurers, among the largest companies of the time, feared that the death benefits that were part of early plans for national health insurance would erode their business. Doctors feared greater regulation. More surprisingly, even labor unions opposed the first attempts at national health insurance because they saw union-provided insurance as one of the greatest incentives for workers to join a union. Government programs could impede organizing efforts. Gradually, however, through both private and public mechanisms, insurance coverage of various kinds spread over the majority of society. It thus provided individuals with security against disaster through the collective management of risk.

Insurance was not the only form of the governance of risk that was possible. Especially as costs of social insurance increased, governments sought to prevent risks by acting on social conditions and individual behavior. As Foucault's concept of biopolitics describes, the system of power used by states moved away from a disciplinary strategy of determining a norm of behavior or performance and then forcing society and individuals to meet that norm. Instead, governments recognized that statistical indicators tended to fall into normal distributions, with regular curves. Rather than totally remaking the curve, governments sought to use regulations to shift the curve ever so slightly.[15] The policymaker could look for mild deviations or outliers in the distribution and address these. This information allowed the government to take action against any source of deviance. For example, eugenics sought to shift the characteristics of the population shown in the normal distribution by sterilizing the lower end of that distribution.[16] By looking for particular regulations and policies that shift statistical distributions, a government can take control over the future of a population.

Like government, insurance companies also attempted to control risks by adjusting normalized distributions of death and ill health. The only way to control costs was to work to manage the distribution of risks. The most basic mechanism for managing risk is to simply reject people who are at high risk from insurance coverage—those with preexisting conditions, for example. However, insurers soon followed the state in attempting to use statistical knowledge of risk to alter behavior. Already in the 1910s, the Metropolitan Life Insurance Company was trying to adapt to what Irving Fisher called the "modern conception of death" by using its vast actuarial knowledge of the causes of death to shape the occurrence of death.[17] It sent nurses out for what would today be called wellness visits, it advocated for weight loss, and so on. Insurance companies produced detailed guides for healthy living.[18] They encouraged consumer safety through research labs performing product safety testing, results that were then disseminated through public service announcements. More recently, insurance companies have joined with employers to pioneer wellness programs that encourage healthy living among policy holders. Thus, insurance companies followed government in controlling future risk through the management of individual behavior.

Statistical analyses of historical data enabled the state to determine not only which aspects of society to target but also the possible future consequences of any intervention. Past data can predict future effects, or at least one can generate different scenarios with weighted probabilities. Such predictions and scenarios interpreted through decision theory allow the policymaker to compare the possible benefits and possible types of harm of different proposed courses of action. This cost/benefit analysis is invaluable.

This quantitative assessment of future action has the benefit of supporting two goals of modern governance: democratic equality and objectivity. Cost/benefit analysis did not come into prominence primarily because of its accuracy or effectiveness.[19] It became widespread, first in the United States and then in other countries, because of a distrust of authority. Before cost/benefit analysis, policy decisions were made through the prudential judgments of experts, administrators, or politicians. Such a mode of action struck many as inequitable and undemocratic. It relied on the authority of experts, which could seem like the dominance of an unaccountable ruling class. Prudential judgments by experts are based on experience, tacit knowledge, long deliberation, and weighing of reasons, much of which is noncommunicable. Such prudential judgments are not really public reasons, open to all. Nor are they objective, because they depend on subjectively gained and held experience.

Numbers, conversely, seem objective. A comparison between the net benefits of one course of action and the net benefits of another course of action, all specified in dollar amounts, is accessible to everyone. Cost/benefit analysis thus opens decision-making to public scrutiny. There are, as discussed below, problems with this optimistic description of cost/benefit analysis. Yet cost/benefit analysis has undermined domains of expert prudential judgment throughout public life. In this way, statistical reasoning about risk has allowed for new modes of government action: the adjustment of normalized distributions through democratically accessible quantitative decision-making. At the same time, it transforms politics based on intersubjective trust in others' judgment to a politics of objective, impersonal control.

Because they *can* intervene, governments are seen as having an *obligation* to intervene to prevent risk, to shift the distribution of risk, or at least to

make reparations for risks that eventuate in harm. As we will see, this obligation for prevention is at the core of Hans Jonas's imperative of responsibility.
It is also part of regular managerial responsibility. Somebody will be held to
blame if there is a disaster or an increase in the incidence of a disease, even
if the mechanisms of accountability leave much to be desired. Policymakers
and individuals are now responsible for managing their risks and those of
people in their care.

The Problems of Risk Assessment

This mode of responsibility for the population is perhaps the dominant form
in both public and private life today. As the history discussed above shows, it
has long ruled the affairs of government and many corporations. These practices cannot stay restricted to the public sphere though. As people engage
them day in and day out at work, it shapes their practical reasoning, becoming
a habitual way to confront any problem. Moreover, in efforts to make people
better workers, these tools are promoted in private life. Just as corporate time
management, with its array of calendars and task lists, shapes private life, so
too does corporate decision-making begin to transform that of the family, as
chapter 2 discussed. Management theorists become life coaches.

This is the dominant relationship to responsibility today, but it is not un-
challenged. In part, this is because of some obvious flaws in accurately predicting and calculating the odds and utilities of the future.[20] Performing a risk
assessment is central to contemporary policy decision-making. Risk assessments take a particular problem or decision, look at past data and current conditions, and decide on certain parameters to analyze. They use information
about the past and present to determine the types of harm and benefits that
may arise from possible future scenarios.[21] Most risk assessment methodologies then perform a cost/benefit analysis, attempting to provide monetary
values for the harm and benefits that may arise from the decision or technology. They also try to determine mitigation strategies and compare the cost
of mitigation with the possible benefits of preventing harm. These cost comparisons and mitigation strategies are then used by decision-makers.

It is not my purpose to denounce risk assessment techniques. As I discuss
in chapter 10, they can serve a vital role in many aspects of life and society.
At the same time, there are a number of valid criticisms of these methods.[22]
First, they tend to be bureaucratic in nature, depending on set procedures for
performing the assessment and using set evidentiary guidelines that may not
be ideal for every situation. For example, the conflicting sides in the debate
over whether nicotinamide-based pesticides are in part responsible for the

collapse of bee populations in the United States have relied on two different evidentiary bases.[23] Those denying the impact of pesticides on bees cite
highly controlled field studies. Those blaming pesticides in part for the death
of bees argue that such highly controlled studies do not adequately reflect the
real situation in American agriculture, where bees are stressed on multiple
fronts, including from these pesticides. These advocates rely instead on more
observational studies and the experience of those engaged in agriculture and
apiculture. These latter studies are inevitably less statistically rigorous, however, because they are less highly controlled. This lack of control may better
reflect the complexity of the real world, a complexity difficult to capture in
bureaucratic knowledge procedures. These debates over evidence are widespread in risk/benefit analyses.[24] The critique of bureaucracy extends to a
critique of the role of expertise in these decisions, leading to arguments that
important community stakeholders are frequently left out of these decisions,
which rely on committees of scientific experts, economists, and other professional policymakers.

The second major class of critiques addresses how these analyses deal
with harm. First, in order to make the risks and benefits commensurable,
these studies claim to be able to provide monetary values for harm. As chapter 2 discussed, modern decision-making forces the actor to balance a host of
goods at play in an array of scenarios. Such a comparison would be impossible in an objective manner, unless these goods were translated into a quantitative, commensurable scale. Our society's favorite tool for commensuration
is money. The best studies are cautious in their claims, recognizing the limitations of their quite sophisticated economic methodology to price harm.[25]
Still, some critics are understandably concerned about any efforts to put economic prices on human life, disability, beauty, or ecological diversity.[26] These
critics argue that any such effort is both demeaning to important noneco-
nomic values and destined to undervalue the things that are most important
to human flourishing because of these techniques' fundamentally economic
focus. In other words, human life is priceless.

A related critique focuses on the way that these analyses discount future
harm. Because of inflation and expectations of return on investment, economic analyses always discount future costs and problems.[27] These efforts at
discounting become even more complicated once one takes into account concerns that affect future generations, like population-level disasters caused by
genetics or environmental damage from human activities. For example, early
reports on climate change by the National Academy of Sciences contained
economic analyses that exploited the uncertainty of climate prediction to suggest "that serious changes were so far off as to be essentially discountable."[28]

Critics argue that economic analyses tend to overly discount future harm, thereby undervaluing responsibility to future generations. Thus, the calculation of the monetary values of harm tends to demean and undervalue essential aspects of human flourishing.

However, some such seemingly objective methodology is necessary if society is to take into account the repercussions of policies, especially in a democratic society that values transparent decision-making. As chapter 10 argues, risk assessment can be an extremely valuable tool when it is understood as an aid for counsel rather than as a calculation that dictates decisions. The most circumspect in this field are aware of the limitations of their methods: "To say that forecasting is prone to error is not only a commonplace, but also an understatement. Nonetheless, it is an essential aspect of the human condition that we attempt to foresee the future in an effort to shape it. . . . The assessor suggests a range of possible policy options; the decision-maker decides which of these to . . . implement."[29] Problems arise when policymakers fail to take these cautions on the limitations of foresight into account.

The Problem of Uncertainty

Despite these issues with costing risks, this methodology works fairly well for well-known risks. The problem is that not all risks are well known and calculable. Some are novel, rare, or erratic in their occurrence. Such limitations have long been known to utilitarians and decision theorists. Though demanding that one choose the action that will bring about the most good, theorists recognize limitations in both the knowledge of long-range consequences and the knowledge of options. Leonard Savage, for example, knew that the application of pure decision theory "is utterly ridiculous . . . because the task implied in making such a decision is not even remotely resembled by human possibility. It is even utterly beyond our power to plan a picnic or to play a game of chess in accordance with the principle, even when the world of states and set of available acts . . . are artificially reduced to the narrowest reasonable limits." For the theory to work, the actor must "artificially confin[e] attention to so small a world that the . . . principle can be applied there."[30] Similarly, Sidgwick and Moore noted the problem of the complexity of utilitarian calculation and argued for neglecting less probable contingencies, focusing only on the most likely effects in the immediate future that will occur to anyone.[31] However, Savage saw how unsatisfactory this approach is: "I find it difficult to say with any completeness how such isolated situations are actually arrived at and justified."[32] Despite this limited knowledge of consequences and the admittedly restricted applicability to only closed situations, decision theory has expanded to address all forms of practical reasoning.

To illuminate these theoretical problems, it is helpful to use a distinction developed by the early-twentieth-century economist Frank Knight between calculable dangers, which he called risks, and those that are incalculable, which he called uncertainty.[33] Calculable risks are represented by those kinds of risks that can be insured against because actuaries have gathered enough data to accurately calculate their frequency, like death, fire, and flood. These categories are ones for which the actuary can calculate von Mises' long-run frequency, which requires large amounts of data. Uncertainty, however, occurs in decisions that happen once, when confronting new situations for which risks are unknown, or in situations where risks are emergent. There is no way to calculate or apply long-run frequencies of risk in such cases, so one is basically gambling, relying on extremely unreliable subjective probabilities.[34] For Knight, *all* single decisions are made under uncertainty, because all these decisions have novel properties. Yet if one is making many decisions of a similar sort, their risks can be averaged through a consistent policy. Risks can then be insured or mitigated. The great danger lies in mistaking situations of uncertainty for situations of risk. Such an error gives false confidence, allowing one to think that all dangers are accounted for when they are not.

The method of probabilistic decision theory can enhance this danger of overconfidence, of believing that the model captures all contingencies. Although the goal should be to know the limits of an analysis, this conflicts with the other goal of capturing everything possible or everything meaningful to the analysis. The trader and philosopher Nassim Taleb argues that policymakers and economists have far too great a belief in the regularity of the world. They make decisions relying on calculable risks, forgetting the insight of Bergson and Arendt that novel dangers may always appear. Taleb has criticized risk assessment methodologies in many areas, especially in finance, specifically because of their dependence on past and present data, which blinds them to novel events.[35] In complex systems—like markets or nature—rare, novel events can have an outsize effect, leading to bankruptcies and extinctions. Such events will not be captured by risk assessments, so these will be blind to absolutely crucial considerations. Taleb calls these Black Swan risks.[36] Too much confidence in extrapolative calculations from past data can lead to future disaster.

These catastrophic dangers are almost impossible to capture in contemporary risk analysis. Analysts demand evidence as to the frequency of the occurrence of a danger. However, that evidence will either not exist or be extremely weak for rare, catastrophic risks. Moreover, because their likelihood is low, it is possible that their inclusion will not affect the outcome. Yet, as in Pascal's wager, it does not really matter what their probability is, because if they do occur, their damage will be unimaginable, far beyond any calculable benefits. Managerial risk is thus caught in a bind. It promises to bear the responsibility for all future consequences. Yet this is impossible because some risks will remain unthought. Therefore, by attempting to assure maximal good, it opens itself to huge damage. At the same time, it blinds itself to these risks because they are from the first excluded from the analysis.

Precaution

Two responses have emerged to these problems of managerial responsibility. The first, the precautionary principle, remains within the sphere of managerial policymaking. Philosophically developed by Hans Jonas, it has entered into national laws, UN declarations, and the general policymaking toolkit. Jonas argued that, given the unprecedented powers of contemporary technology to make an impact on the future through nuclear war, genetic modification gone awry, or human-made ecological damage, people must focus on their responsibilities to ensure the continuation of humankind. Jonas argued that policymaking must take account of these potential catastrophes. His imperative of responsibility was to "act so that the effects of your action are compatible with the permanence of genuine human life."[37] We must make an effort to imagine possible dangers. Once imagined, they cannot be dismissed in calculations as low-likelihood events but must be prevented at almost any cost. We have a duty to care for the world and for human existence. This principle has entered the sphere of policymaking in terms set by Principle 15 of the Rio Declaration on the Environment and Development: "In order to protect the environment, the precautionary approach shall be widely applied by States according to their capabilities. Where there are threats of serious or irreversible damage, lack of full scientific certainty shall not be used as a reason for postponing cost-effective measures to prevent environmental degradation."[38] Even if the existence of a danger is not completely proven or seems unlikely, it must be addressed. This principle, which attempts to address the imbalance between our increased power to cause harm and our decreased predictive knowledge of the future, has been embraced by governments, international agencies, environmental ethicists, and religious leaders, most recently Pope Francis in the encyclical *Laudato si'*: "If objective information suggests that serious and irreversible damage may result, a project should be halted or modified, even in the absence of indisputable proof."[39]

Though adopted in principle, the precautionary principle has had less impact in practice, due to conceptual difficulties.[40] First, one must actually have an inkling that a danger exists. If a danger is truly novel and unthought of, however, it will not even occur to one. Taken to its logical extremes, the precautionary principle would seem to demand quietism and stasis because all new developments may harbor unknown risks. Second, the use of this principle frequently just leads to calls for more research, which may or may not clarify the situation. Third, the threatened catastrophe must be weighed against the forgone benefits. Critics point out that, frequently, a course of action opposed by precaution itself promises to prevent great dangers: genetic modification aims to combat genetic disease; fragile levee systems that constrain rivers prevent regular flooding; economic development seeks to save people from starving. These are themselves great goods endangered by precaution. The precautionary principle is in danger of becoming self-canceling; precaution toward one intervention itself generates dangers of other catastrophes. The specification of "cost-effective" measures in the Rio Declaration already limits its scope.

Another problem is that people tend to focus on particularly feared dangers, a category called dread risks. Frequently, dread risks are ones that have occurred recently and thus are more available to a person's memory. This is a problem called availability bias by behavioral economists. People focus on conspicuous dangers. This focus blinds them to other benefits and types of harm. For example, after the September 11, 2001, terrorist attacks on the United States, many people stopped flying out of fear of the catastrophic risk of a terrorist attack. Instead, they drove to their destinations. Unfortunately, driving is much riskier than air travel, leading to a greater number of excess deaths from road accidents in the year after the attacks than died on the hijacked flights themselves (1,595 road deaths in excess of the number of road deaths in prior years vs. 296 deaths on the hijacked flights).[41] Policymakers can err in two directions, by either leaving catastrophic risks unaddressed or by overly focusing on a particular dread risk to the exclusion of control over other possible risks. These are the disquieting results of making oneself responsible for all outcomes.

The Lack of Managerial Guilt

Before moving on to the next paradigm, it is worth noting what guilt means for this managerial risk paradigm. The managerial paradigm seeks to foster goods of economic development and population health while, in its precautionary form, preventing the devastation of human and other kinds of life. As William Schweiker, who has integrated many of these aspects into his Christian ethics of responsibility, puts it: "In all actions and relations we are to respect and enhance the integrity of life before God," with integrity of life meaning "the integration of the vitalities, needs, and interests of life into some coherent and identifiable whole."[42] The agent looks to maximize and protect the powers of life while also respecting the rights of others.

Under this framework, guilt comes from not foreseeing appropriately, not calculating risks properly, and not insuring. Guilt appears after a failed policy or choice. That is how it appears when this framework is internalized in personal life. Things look a bit different once one turns to larger spheres of corporate or public decision-making. There, guilt takes the form of an unforeseen disaster for which there is no response. Unfortunately, once these problems appear, the policymakers in question have usually left office. The CEO who led the corporation to ruin has retired and liquidated his stock options. The politician who initiated the disastrous chain of events through her policies will have retired to private life by the time the danger comes to fruition. Given the complexity of catastrophes, it is easy enough to point to some other cause or some circumstance that made foresight impossible. Because the full weight of environmental and systemic financial problems usually falls on the poor, decision-makers may not even notice the catastrophe. Thus, few of the powerful are ever truly called to account for their actions under the managerial paradigm.

For the common person, those who do not make government or corporate policy, evil becomes tied to thoughtlessness, not foreseeing the greater systemic problems that individual actions exacerbate. As Dupuy argues, "The apocalypse that looms before us will be less the result of our malignity, or even our stupidity, than of our thoughtlessness."[43] A person adds her little bit to pollution, buys the sweat-shop produced good, or forgets to get vaccinated. Guilt takes the form of a banality of evil as each person exacerbates structures of sin leading to the oppression of the weak, heedless of the broader consequences of her actions.[44] Thus, though the managerial paradigm can be a useful tool, it is not an effective form of responsibility in its social form because it never truly provides accountability. Yet, in its individual form, it can lay a heavy burden of guilt and regret.

ENTREPRENEURIAL RISK

The managerial approach to risk had more effects than merely failing to predict a few dangers. As it developed, policymakers discovered that more and more intervention in society and individuals' lives was necessary if risks were to be kept at bay. The mid-twentieth-century dream of government control over the future through regulations and policies shaping the normal curve of risks eventually ran into a concerted opposition holding a very different attitude toward risk. For many, risk was not primarily a danger to be held at bay through the direction of human behavior. Instead of a danger, risk and uncertainty became the source of productive opportunity, a source of innovation and freedom. This position led to changes in two primary spheres, the economic and the social. These positive conceptions of risk have had a profound impact on policy and society since the 1970s.

The Reaction to the Managerial State

For a long time, the fields of business and economics have seen risk as a source of profit. In his discussion of risk and uncertainty, Frank Knight argued that all entrepreneurial profit arises from the personal assumption of the burdens of uncertain decisions by the entrepreneur.[45] His argument was that if there were perfect knowledge of market conditions, if all the consequences of a particular business decision were knowable and thus uncertainty did not exist, then there would be a perfectly competitive market.[46] Everyone would know every business opportunity and every cost and thus would only pay the minimal price possible. Under such perfect competition, no one is able to make a profit because all prices decrease to the minimal level in order to attract consumer demand. It is only by undertaking programs whose outcomes are not certain, such as research into innovative technologies or the development of a new product, that a company is able to profit. Yet such investments may not succeed; the research may lead to a dead end or the product may not find a market, leading to loss instead of profit. All these potentially profitable decisions are risky. Although Knight did recognize that some risks are quantifiable, and thus insurable, he believed that the most important business decisions involve unquantifiable uncertainty.[47] It was this uncertainty that was crucial for business growth and technological innovation.

Neoliberal economists after Friedrich Hayek and Milton Friedman feared that the growing regulation and state control that sought to manage risks threatened to stifle the individual freedom necessary to drive economic growth.[48] Even John Maynard Keynes, the neoliberals' bête noir, wrote about the importance of the animal spirits that drive the market.[49] An increasingly influential group of economists argued (and continue to argue) that government regulations crush these animal spirits, ultimately harming society. This theoretical position gained political strength due to the experience of the stagflation of the 1970s. Rising costs combined with widespread unemployment created a picture of a stagnant, overly managed society. Economic failure and, more important, the inability of the dominant Keynesian economic theory of the time to account for this economic failure brought into doubt the ability of government to control and manage risk and future outcomes. In this atmosphere, a movement gained strength to decrease regulations that cushioned people from risk in order to unleash entrepreneurial innovation and economic growth. This movement embracing entrepreneurial risk led to the Reagan and Thatcher revolutions that still fundamentally shape the contemporary political imagination.

As the sociologists Luc Boltanski and Eve Chiapello have argued, this economic critique of mid-century risk-reducing *regulations* was joined by a social and cultural critique of risk-reducing *institutions*.[50] Government regulatory systems supported and were supported by a network of social institutions, some preexisting modernity, some newborn with the Industrial Revolution, that constrained risk for most individuals. The family assured education of children, support for women, care for the elderly, and so forth. Class institutions like mutual aid societies, clubs, the pub, and the labor union provided networks of social support. The lifelong career at the same company ensured stable, predictable advancement and a pension in retirement. There were predefined educational pathways tied to certain classes and leading to certain jobs. Thus, social institutions allowed a person to rely on a predictable life course and buffered the person against suffering from dramatic risks.

However, such institutions also constrained action. Family life requires a certain form of sexuality; a lifelong career can shape a person into the man in the gray flannel suit; fitting into working-class institutions requires certain interests and habits. A growing number of cultural critics lambasted the resulting enforced conformity. This framework of social support also excluded groups that did not fit into the dominant pattern, such as racial minorities.[51] The movement Boltanski and Chiapello term the "artistic critique," which was embodied in the growing counterculture of the 1960s, demanded more behavioral freedom. Members of the counterculture wanted the freedom to live more creatively, undertaking lifestyles that entailed more risk. This freedom required them to deconstruct the social institutions that served to constrain risk. Thus, people could live as creative individuals, undertaking the risks that could lead to beautiful, fulfilling lives. It is this framework that the counterculture thought would lead to greater social flourishing.

Through these intertwined forces of market neoliberalism and lifestyle revolution, a new ethical ideal came into being. A person was now to be a risk taker. The counterculturalist turned Silicon Valley ideologue John Perry

Barlow described the difference between the entrepreneurial vision and older forms of managerial risk regulation as the distinction between "the people who crave certainty and the people who trust chance. . . . Large organizations and their drones huddle on one end of my scale, busily trying to impose predictable homogeneity on messy circumstance. On the other end, freelancers and ne'er-do-wells cavort about, getting by on luck if they get by at all."[52] These latter ideals are now central to our culture as individuals seek jobs and a lifestyle that fulfills their desires, challenges them to continually innovate, and thrills them with ever new risks leading to ever greater rewards.[53] The moral exemplar of this new culture is the technology entrepreneur or the freelance graphic designer. It is the digital nomad, unbound by home, community, or office. It is a lifetime of continuous creativity and productive risk, lived flexibly, without a net.

Managing Risks through the Market

This entrepreneurial paradigm rejects the idea that any single actor or organization can have a grasp of society or the market adequate to managing it in the way managerial theory wants. This critique is basically epistemological and bears some relation to the criticism of risk analysis discussed above. There is no way that anyone can grasp all the different factors and risks confronting something like an economy. Moreover, any such predictive system will fail to foresee truly novel developments and thus will not respond to them appropriately. Such failures in the face of current or future risks will lead to inefficiencies that will themselves harm the economy, creating new risks. In the attempt to control or prevent unforeseen developments, the managerial system runs the risk of stagnation.

In the absence of the possibility of central planning, how can society direct itself? The genius of neoliberal theorists shows itself in their vision of a tool for processing the vast amounts of information necessary: the market. In a shift from former economic theories, the market was no longer understood as a site of exchange but instead as an information processor operating through competition.[54] It gathers all the information about consumer preferences, supplies of resources, production costs, and so on, and integrates them through the price mechanism. It can even integrate predictions about the future through insurance policies, stock sales, commodities contracts, derivatives, and other financial instruments. None of this requires the totalizing vision of one person or organization. Instead, it relies on the distributed knowledge of individuals, crowd learning, and self-organizing systems. It is what Hayek called *kosmos*, spontaneous order, as opposed to *taxis*, an order that has been created and organized through technique.[55] Even individual firms can take advantage of these tools by reorganizing themselves on the model of internal markets: outsourcing their production, subcontracting nonessential features, and hiring more freelancers.

It is important to note that this understanding of the market is not antigovernment. These economists understand that frequently there will be barriers to a properly functioning market, requiring government intervention. Markets may not properly price some negative externalities, like pollution, requiring government intervention to appropriately shift prices through things like a carbon tax or a sulfur cap-and-trade market. Moreover, some resources may not currently fall under the market, so, according to neoliberal theorists, they will not be efficiently managed and will degrade due to the tragedy of the commons. Thus, these resources, like water in some developing countries or public lands, should be privatized so that individual owners can appropriately manage and care for them. Government undertakes this privatization of public resources. It is important for everyone to have health insurance to manage health risks, but such health insurance should be provided through subsidized, market-like exchanges. These theorists even allow for safety net programs of straightforward redistribution, like the negative income tax or basic income, as long as these are delivered in a market-neutral way, one that does not shape the determination of prices. In these ways, government does have important roles in foreseeing potential risks and also manipulating institutions and individuals in how they relate to these risks, but its response must be through market mechanisms.

Such markets do not have the same problems with novelty as managerial systems. Instead, they drive novelty and change. The engine of both creativity and efficiency in the market is the figure of the entrepreneur. Fundamentally, the entrepreneur is the person who discovers new information and introduces it into the market system.[56] This information could be just basic knowledge of arbitrage opportunities, the knowledge of how to pay a little more for a resource and sell it for a little less to consumers, and thus outcompete one's competitors. In this way, the entrepreneur introduces efficiency into the market. Alternatively, the entrepreneur could introduce new products, modes of production, or combinations of factors that fundamentally change the shape of the market, things like the iPhone or the assembly line.[57] Through these mechanisms, old jobs are lost and new ones are created. The entrepreneur is the agent of novelty, driving unpredictable changes throughout society—Silicon Valley's creative destruction.

To engage in these activities, the entrepreneur must take risks. Knight understood the fundamental function of the entrepreneur as bearing the dangers of uncertainty.[58] Managers try to predict all risks and eliminate them through contingency planning and insurance. Entrepreneurs cannot. New techniques have no track record that would allow her to establish predictive methods. Each business decision is an individual one. It is through risk-bearing that entrepreneurs earn their often outsize profits, but profits that are never assured.

Here we see the entrepreneurial paradigm's fundamentally different relationship to future dangers. As Jackson Lears puts it in his history of luck in the United States, "The gamblers' moral economy existed beyond the managerial quest for systematic control."[59] This mode accepts the unpredictability of human affairs. It embraces it and sees it as the engine for growth, efficiency, and creativity. Every person is in some way an entrepreneur, a risk-bearer in their life, making career decisions, investment choices, and so forth. On the individual level, any entrepreneur can fail, can be defeated by uncertainty, overwhelmed by the impossible to predict changes in circumstances. Every entrepreneur faces disaster. Yet, on a societal level, these individual risks are productive, leading to economic growth, technological development, and the fulfillment of individual desires. The epistemological limitations of managerial systems do not allow them to deliver such benefits. Thus, there is a management of risk at the social level but a more precarious or exciting (depending on one's level of risk aversion) existence for the individual.

Responsibility in the Market

In this framework, each individual bears the responsibility for the outcome of his or her confrontation with uncertainty. As Hayek argued, "If the individual is to be free to choose, it is inevitable that he should bear the risk attaching to that choice and that in consequence he be rewarded, not according to the goodness or badness of his intentions, but solely on the basis of the value of the results to others."[60] If an entrepreneur's guess on the future turns out to be wrong, her business will fail. She will be left with indebtedness and the waste of time that cannot be recovered. Yet, in theory, this responsibility is not moral. In the moral economy of the gambler and speculator described by Lears, "net worth may have nothing to do with moral worth."[61] No ethical opprobrium should adhere to the failure, just the temporal losses. Everyone knows it was a gamble, so the entrepreneur should take it as a loss in poker—shrug her shoulders and play again. The game requires losers, with losing even becoming an aspect of redemption. In an earlier period, "the figure of 'the loser' became an oddly powerful specter in a society that deified winning and denied defeat."[62] There is a way that this nonmoral approach is instantiated in Silicon Valley with its easy acceptance of business failures.

Yet even though failure among multimillionaire entrepreneurs may bear no stigma, it is unclear that the same holds true for society as a whole. It is difficult to distinguish between economic and moral responsibility, even in Hayek's thought. Elsewhere, he notes that "the morality of individual responsibility of the able adult for the welfare of himself and his family is still the basis for most moral judgments of action."[63] Given US society's historical commitment to a Protestant work ethic, economic failure has always been morally freighted.[64] In the earlier liberal tradition, failures in economic life or bankruptcy brought on by illness were attributed to a vice, lack of foresight, or lack of proper predictive ability.[65] It seems this moral stigma may be becoming worse for those who are left behind by the new economy. With everyone's financial stability increasingly uncertain, the economist and historian of neoliberalism Philip Mirowski suggests that one of the ways that people who still have stable jobs have adjusted has been to take on "a set of attitudes reminiscent of Nietzsche's creditor psychology," which he calls "everyday sadism."[66] Rhetoric on both the left and right shows disdain for both individuals and whole regions that have not succeeded in the entrepreneurial, market-based system. Even in popular culture, talk shows display failed lives for mockery or reality television humiliates its victims. As Mirowski argues, "The complement to a culture of celebrity has become therefore the unabashed theater of cruelty, the public spaces where we gaze upon the half-speed car wrecks of the lives of others in the throes of failure."[67] This is all the more problematic because the system ignores the problem of inequality. For those with fewer resources, a single failure can trap them in a lifetime of economic misfortune. Hayek was clear-eyed with regard to this aspect of his preferred system: "To suffer disappointment, adversity and hardship is a discipline to which in any society most must submit, and it is a discipline by which it is desirable that all able persons ought to have to submit."[68] Risk can be exhilarating and productive, but, without adequate buffers, it can also be terrifyingly destructive.

Furthermore, this model fails to deal with broader consequences and catastrophes at the level of society. Although externalities can be priced and regulated by market-based government action, there will always be opposition to such policies from interested parties, as we see with pollution and climate change. Moreover, sometimes the interventions will come too late. An unforeseen event can be catastrophic, as was the 2008 financial collapse leading to widespread suffering in a system without appropriate support for individuals. Although accounting for some risks, a market leaves many threats in place. It does not fully answer the epistemological problem of novel dangers.

From a theological perspective, the faith in the market is troubling. As many have noted, the market can become endowed with many of the features of providence, as had Adam Smith's original Invisible Hand.[69] In neoliberal ideology, the market makes all things work for the good, weaving disparate events together to produce universal prosperity. At its worst, this can veer toward an idolatry of the market. For Hayek, Fortuna in the form of market results becomes ultimately responsible for a person's failures at the hands of the market: "What mitigates these hardships in a free society is that no arbitrary human will imposes them, but that their incidence is determined by an impersonal process and unforeseeable chance."[70] The market and fortune become the source of hope and fate. Even at a more moderate level, it leads people to place their trust in a process that cannot truly confront risk. God's providence is replaced by the market's.

CONCLUSION

These two systems show both extremes of a society based on risk and responsibility. In both these dominant systems, there is an attempt to provide a technological solution to the uncertainty of human life. For managerial responsibility, it is a paternalistic, human providence, the attempt to foresee and plan for all future scenarios, in line with the framework of decision theory. For entrepreneurial responsibility, it is the potentially cruel providence of the market. Both fail in their aims. The first fails in the task of total foresight, instead myopically focusing on common or conspicuous dangers. The second fails the task of justice, burdening society, especially the weakest in society, with the failures of its false god.

Although I explore a form of Christian responsibility in chapter 9, at this point it is necessary to examine some of the specific technologies used by both these systems. Recently, these rationalities have begun to merge. As we saw, both states and insurance companies have long sought to shape probability distributions by influencing human behavior. In doing so, they begin to treat individuals less as persons and more as predictable components of the population. With the development of tools to gather and manipulate Big Data, more and more companies are using these tools to shape the behavior of populations. This pattern leads to concerns over ethical subjectivity and objective injustice. Instead of subjects to be respected, individuals become objects in the vision of those in power.

NOTES

"Le grand événement politique des deux derniers siécles a sans doute été l'application du calcul des probabilités au gouvernement de la société." Ewald, *L'etat providence*, 143.

1. For a review of responsibility in Christian ethics, see Jonsen, *Responsibility*; and McKenny, "Responsibility."
2. Weber, "Politics as a Vocation."
3. Haskell, *Objectivity Is Not Neutrality*, 282.
4. For this history, see Ewald, *L'etat providence*; Witt, *Accidental Republic*; Moses, *First Modern Risk*; and Beck, *Risk Society*.
5. This typology of responsibility is not exhaustive, and many other theories can be thought of as variations of these three. My primary focus is on the actor's relationship with future risks and consequences rather than past actions, especially past actions of collective guilt, such as the Holocaust or slavery.

   My typology draws loosely on the discussion of risk by Douglas and Wildavsky, *Risk and Culture*, 90–125. They highlighted a commercial and governmental form of risk management congruent with the managerial form I describe and a sectarian one that is tied to the precautionary approach. However, all three of their ideal types largely relate to issues raised by the managerial form of risk, although their entrepreneurial form is somewhat related to the entrepreneurial form discussed here.
6. Savage, *Foundations of Statistics*, 164ff. Its most famous use is in Rawls, *Theory of Justice*, 152ff.
7. Hacking, *Taming of Chance*; Bernstein, *Against the Gods*; Desrosieres, *Politics of Large Numbers*; Bouk, *How Our Days Became Numbered*.
8. Foucault, *Security, Territory, Population*, 255–332; Hacking, *Taming of Chance*, 16–35.
9. Hacking, *Taming of Chance*, 47–55; Bernstein, *Against the Gods*, 73–88; Bouk, *How Our Days Became Numbered*.
10. Haueter and Jones, *Managing Risk*, 19.
11. Jarzabkowski, Bednarek, and Spee, *Making a Market*, 68.
12. Starr, *Social Transformation*, 240–43; Witt, *Accidental Republic*, 71–102. These societies were diverse. Though many of them did not embrace actuarial rationality, some did, sliding toward becoming insurance companies with rituals of solidarity to prevent moral hazard.
13. Defert, "Popular Life."
14. For this history in the United States, see Starr, *Social Transformation*, 235–89; and Witt, *Accidental Republic*. For the comparative case, see Moses, *First Modern Risk*. These different approaches to insurance were tied to different understandings of statistical analysis. See Porter, *Rise of Statistical Thinking*; Hacking, *Taming of Chance*; and Desrosieres, *Politics of Large Numbers*.
15. Foucault, *Security, Territory, Population*, 62; Foucault, *Society Must Be Defended*, 239–64; Foucault, *History of Sexuality, Volume 1*, 133–60.
16. Kevles, *In the Name of Eugenics*; Carlson, *Unfit*.

17. Bouk, *How Our Days Became Numbered*, 115, 128–35.
18. E.g., Fisher and Fisk, *How to Live*.
19. Porter, *Trust in Numbers*.
20. This section draws on Scherz, "Prudence, Precaution, and Uncertainty."
21. There are many methods of performing a risk analysis. See Shrader-Frechette, *Science Policy*; HM Treasury, "Orange Book"; Braun, *Technology in Context*.
22. Shrader-Frechette, *Science Policy*; Brock, *Christian Ethics*.
23. Kleinman and Suryanarayanan, "Dying Bees."
24. E.g., Wynne, "Seasick"; and Jasanoff, "Breaking the Waves."
25. For methods of pricing values, see Sunstein, *Laws of Fear*.
26. Braun, *Technology in Context*, 125; Shrader-Frechette, *Science Policy*.
27. Braun, *Technology in Context*, 127. For a recent philosophical discussion of problems in our relation to the future, see Sullivan, *Time Biases*.
28. Oreskes and Conway, *Merchants of Doubt*, 179; see 174–85 for a full discussion of this report.
29. Braun, *Technology in Context*, 32–33.
30. Savage, *Foundations of Statistics*, 16. Note the requirement for a simplified, closed world, as described by Edwards, *Closed World*.
31. Sidgwick, *Methods of Ethics*, 131; Moore, *Principia ethica*, 149–52.
32. Savage, *Foundations of Statistics*, 83.
33. Knight, *Risk, Uncertainty, and Profit*, 20.
34. Knight, 282.
35. Taleb, *Antifragile*, 8–9.
36. Taleb, *Black Swan*.
37. Jonas, *Imperative of Responsibility*, 11.
38. United Nations, "Rio Declaration."
39. Francis, *Laudato si'*, 186.
40. Sunstein, *Laws of Fear*; Sunstein, *Worst-Case Scenarios*.
41. Gigerenzer, *Rationality for Mortals*, 92.
42. Schweiker, *Responsibility and Christian Ethics*, 125, 128.
43. Dupuy, *Short Treatise on the Metaphysics of Tsunamis*, 58.
44. Arendt, *Eichmann in Jerusalem*.
45. Knight, *Risk, Uncertainty, and Profit*, 232.
46. Knight, 197–98.
47. Knight, 5.
48. Although there is an unfortunate tendency in the academy to use neoliberalism merely as a term of abuse for contemporary capitalism, I use it to describe a group of theorists who saw the market as an ideal information processor and encouraged the deployment of markets and corresponding entrepreneurial characteristics in many areas of society. In this, I follow the analyses given by Foucault, *Birth of Biopolitics*; Mirowski and Plehwe, *Road from Mont Pelerin*; Payne, *Consumer, Credit, and Neoliberalism*; Mirowski, *Never Let a Serious Crisis Go to Waste*; and Brown, *Undoing the Demos*.
49. For a broader discussion of this topic in early twentieth-century history and its possible relevance for today, see Lears, "Animal Spirits."
50. Boltanski and Chiapello, *New Spirit of Capitalism*, 167–202.
51. For discussions of these problems in these earlier systems, see Harvey, *Brief History of Neoliberalism*; and Harvey, *Condition of Postmodernity*.

52. Barlow, "Crime and Puzzlement." For the connection between the counterculture, the computer industry, and the entrepreneurial ideal, see Turner, *From Counterculture to Cyberculture*.

53. Martin, *Flexible Bodies*; Binkley, *Happiness as Enterprise*. For a discussion of this new ethical ideal in science, see Scherz, *Science and Christian Ethics*.

54. Foucault, *Birth of Biopolitics*; Mirowski, *Science-Mart*.

55. Hayek, *Law, Legislation, and Liberty, Volume 1*, 35–54.

56. Kirzner, *Competition and Entrepreneurship*, 30–87.

57. Schumpeter, *Theory of Economic Development*, 78.

58. Knight, *Risk, Uncertainty, and Profit*, 244. Schumpeter rejects this interpretation, arguing that really the capitalist bears the loss if the decision is unsuccessful. See Schumpeter, *Theory of Economic Development*, 137.

59. Lears, *Something for Nothing*, 267.

60. Hayek, *Individualism and Economic Order*, 21–22. For a critique of the growth of this politics of personal responsibility and its effects on the welfare state as well as a good overview of analytic philosophies of responsibility, see Mounk, *Age of Responsibility*.

61. Lears, *Something for Nothing*, 3.

62. Lears, 270.

63. Hayek, *New Studies in Philosophy*, 299.

64. This tension between the morality of the Protestant work ethic and the morality of the gambler runs throughout Lears, *Something for Nothing*.

65. Ewald, *L'etat providence*, 64–73.

66. Mirowski, *Never Let a Serious Crisis Go to Waste*, 130.

67. Mirowski, 133.

68. Hayek, *New Studies in Philosophy*, 307.

69. Milbank, *Theology and Social Theory*, 37–42; Long, *Divine Economy*.

70. Hayek, *New Studies in Philosophy*, 307.

7

Probabilistic Mechanisms of Control

Technological simulation no longer simply displaces reality,
it claims to unveil its essence. Cybernetic constructs no
longer imitate living things, they claim to explain to us
what life is. Life is nothing other than this simulation.

—*Robert Spaemann*

Probabilistic analysis promises actors, especially states and corporations, that it can make others more predictable, allowing greater control over the future. Older philosophical models of the person are not amenable to such claims of predictability.[1] In Aristotelian or Stoic philosophy, action emerges out of the matrix of one's past personal experience, from which arises ideas of the good that inspire actions seeking to attain specific ends. In such models, actions are a free statement of character. Actions express the person and are ineliminably individual.[2] Because of these aspects of action, mathematical modeling becomes difficult. This mediation of the person's response to a situation through a conceptual framework regarding the good requires judgment, which is not entirely predictable because it is free. Conceptions of the good, the just, or the beautiful are also not easily analyzable in mathematical terms. For these reasons, the classical humanistic and Christian understanding of the person and human action are inhospitable to the idea that one can calculate future action through mathematical technique.

For predictability, what was needed was a new vision of the human that could better serve as a basis for modeling. The individual needed to be more like things that can be mathematically analyzed: the objects of physics, such as gas molecules, electrons, and asteroids. This shift required the elimination of the personal element of action, in that actions needed to be more objectively interchangeable. Nonmathematical concepts had to take up less of a role in this understanding of action because of the difficulty of modeling them. Complex forms of human judgment needed to be reduced to a more predictable, quantifiable form. There were two important paths to this new understanding. First, scholars started to create a picture of the human individual as a probabilistic calculating machine responding to stimuli. Action becomes behavior. Second, this model of individual action merged with ideas of population-level prediction arising from actuarial technologies. For both frameworks, free will and judgment serve little purpose. Although these paradigms might have started as abstractions meant to make simulations easier, soon powerful actors began seeking to reshape people in the image of this simulation. This chapter attempts to describe variants of this picture of the human individual, some of its history, and how it is deployed in today's social technologies.

THE NEW MODEL OF HUMAN NATURE

Thomas Hobbes sought two important goals.[3] First, he wanted to adjust anthropology to the new seventeenth-century mechanistic philosophy, in which everything is a body driven by force. He sought to make society explainable in terms of science.[4] For his geometric science of morality to succeed, immaterial and unpredictable individual thoughts had to be tamed. Brute desire seemed much more amenable to scientific analysis. Second, in response to the chaos of the English Civil War, he wanted to assure social stability. There needed to be predictive rules that could rationally ground the absolutist state described in *Leviathan*, rules that would control the violent enthusiasm and competition of the masses. In the resulting picture, humans become purely immanent, driven by desires for the impressions of things that strike their senses. The older understanding of happiness as a state of rest or summum bonum does not drive human action in Hobbes's vision.[5] Instead, individuals act for merely momentary satisfaction of desire while the next moment will find them desiring something else. As the literary theorist Thomas Pfau describes, starting with Hobbes, desires and passions no longer emerge out of a hermeneutic, cognitive process that itself has a long history in both the individual and a tradition.[6] In these older forms, desires would themselves be judged and become the target of reform based on their relationship to higher ends. For Hobbes, desires become merely efficient causes, forces that push the individual toward certain actions. Prudent deliberation in this model ceases to be wise judgment but becomes the chaos of alternating, opposed desires that eventually result in a decision.[7] The last desire in the sequence is translated into action. This picture of a war of ceaselessly alternating desires (internally mirroring the external war of all against all), brought to a conclusion by the arbitrary strength of a victorious desire, appeared in ancient understandings of action but generally as a description of defective action. It was the Stoic picture of vicious human reasoning or the Aristotelian understanding of the akratic man: an inner life of continuous turmoil because the actor is not coherent.[8] For Hobbes, this state describes all agents.

One can see how this picture is convenient both for post-Cartesian science and for political power. The scholar does not need to deal with the mysterious force of thought or the soul that fits poorly with naturalism and materialism. The human is moved only by surrounding forces like a machine, as the eighteenth-century philosophe La Mettrie theorized.[9] If moved purely by efficient causes, then human actors will be just as predictable as the solids of Newtonian mechanics.

The need to harmonize philosophical anthropology with reductionist science and for a politics of predictive control leads to an assault on interiority and rationality that appears in neuroscience and economics today. Many in the philosophy of neuroscience try to explain away consciousness as an epiphenomenon of underlying neural processes. In Daniel Dennett's vision, for example, conscious experiences, called qualia, are merely a Cartesian theater that the brain provides with no actual effect in the world. What we take to be deliberation is merely the struggle of memes that have infected our mental machinery like viruses, which fight among themselves to become actualized in behavior.[10] Other scholars dismiss our experienced mental world and ideas of the self as just so much folk psychology. For them, it is really the mechanisms of neural machinery driven by external stimuli and genetic programs that generate actions. Thus, there is a deep drive to eliminate interior experience and judgment in order to explain human action by reductionist science.

Noninstrumental conceptual thought also disappears. When a choice is rational in this vision of the human, it is driven by an unconscious utilitarian calculus.[11] The only rationality that is allowable is an instrumental calculative mode of thought that aligns with the rational expectations delivered by decision theory. If observed human behavior does not meet these predictions, it is irrational. In this line, behavioral economics has identified many different ways in which standard human judgment diverges from probabilistic modeling.[12] These are termed irrational biases and must be corrected. As discussed in an earlier chapter, this is a great change from early modern approaches to probability. In these earlier approaches, mathematical descriptions were made to align with the deliverances of prudence. The goal was to make the calculations match the judgment of the prudent person. Now, economists seek to make prudence align with calculation. This is despite the fact that alternative interpretive frameworks, even within psychology, can show the reasonableness of actions that differ from the results of decision theory in the context of daily life.[13]

In these works, contemporary theorists seek to remove much of the older anthropological framework. Their person is no longer a subject insofar as conscious experience is merely epiphenomenal, no longer mattering for most human action. Nor is the person rational, as reason is no longer even the slave of desire but merely the post hoc justification for desires. Alternatively, human reason, in its current biased form, no longer serves to meet human desires and so must be reshaped. The only rationality that counts is instrumental, quantitative, probabilistic reason. The human has been rethought as an object that is both describable by probabilistic analysis and that should itself perform probabilistic analysis.

THE ACTUARIAL SELF

This tendency to abstract from judgment and reason was aided by the advance of actuarial technologies. As discussed in the last chapter, nineteenth-century statisticians began noting a number of social regularities. Every year, the numbers of crimes, suicides, and misaddressed letters were similar. It seemed that the population had a reality and existence that transcended its individual members. As in the objectivist model of probability, social thought became focused on the collectivity because it seemed that the actions of individuals were in part determined by population effects. The social scientist could determine the risk of an individual falling victim to various social ills based on the population of which he or she was a part.

This population-level regularity raised questions of free will, ones that continue today in the structure-agency debates. If population-level statistics are so regular, then how could individuals be acting freely? They seemed obligated to engage in a certain number of each category of action covered by statistics. As Adolphe Quetelet described it, crime is a "budget that is paid with frightening regularity every year."[14] In the mid–nineteenth century, some, such as Henry Buckle, used these regularities to deny individual free will, sparking great debates.[15] Even those who did not deny free will, like Quetelet, disconnected free will and judgment from social phenomena. Free will may exist and may even allow for the various actions that create a risk profile, but it is unnecessary for social analysis.

This absence of humanistic ideas of the person in nascent social science became apparent in the fact that physicists adopted ideas from social statistics to describe physical objects.[16] James Clerk Maxwell and Ludwig Boltzmann described gas molecules as just such a population with regular probabilistic characteristics. Evolution describes the rise and fall of the genetics of populations of animals in such probabilistic terms. These concepts describing nonrational nature originally arose in descriptions of human society. Importantly, this model leads to certain implications about power. If free will is not essential to the analysis of social regularities, then the policymaker can, and indeed must, turn toward other mechanisms in order to shape society. These mechanisms of power are the subject of this chapter.

PHILOSOPHICAL ANTHROPOLOGY
IN BEHAVIORIST SOCIAL SCIENCE

First, however, it is necessary to note how probabilistic modeling of populations can be combined with the Hobbesian anthropology. The psychologist Barry Schwartz argues that this new anthropology has developed into sophisticated explanatory paradigms that address nearly every area of human life.[17] Although different fields can illustrate my point, Schwartz's chosen disciplines of economics, sociobiology, and behaviorism illustrate this emerging picture of human nature especially well and illuminate certain features important for the examples given later in the chapter and my overall argument. Population-level modeling plays a great role in these fields. These three dominant fields interconnect in such a way as to give a totalizing framework for describing the individual, society, and biology, a model of study that can obtain evidence objectively with no need for the subjective perspective.

Economics serves as the basic paradigm of rationality for this new model of human nature. Rationality is instrumental, the deployment of scarce resources to maximize the achievement of the goods contained in one's schedule of preferences. The actor uses the probabilistic decision theory described in chapter 2 as a tool to maximize expected value. For this model of reason, there is no need for a detailed theory of the mind. The mind is a black box, as seen by the fact that preferences are thought to be better inferred from market behavior than from discussions with individuals. This is the model of *homo economicus*.

This model of reason and action has been abstracted to the evolutionary level of the gene and species in a second discipline, a variant of evolutionary biology. Over the course of the last fifty years, an intellectual paradigm began with the evolutionary biologist E. O. Wilson's sociobiology in the 1970s, before becoming restructured as evolutionary psychology in the 1990s and then again changing to what today is called behavioral genetics.[18] Though there are differences between these three paradigms, they share intellectual characteristics, and behavioral geneticists admit their dependence on sociobiology. For sociobiology, the actors in the living world are genes rather than individual organisms. These genes seek to maximize their propagation. They influence behavior by shaping the neural circuitry that drives responses to various situations.

This evolutionary model focuses on populations. Probabilistic reasoning serves as the major framework because genes are probabilistically transferred to the next generation. Probabilistic reasoning also serves to explain otherwise baffling cooperative and altruistic actions among animals and humans.[19] For example, individuals will sacrifice themselves for close kin because they share a significant portion of DNA. Even though the individual organism will die, a portion of its genes will be propagated by the kin that survive due to its sacrifice. Reciprocal, cooperative behavior also can be explained through game theory, an offshoot of decision theory. In certain situations, an animal maximizes its expected present or at least its future rewards through cooperation, even if it runs the risk of betrayal. Unfortunately, according to these theorists, because these behaviors have been selected over a long period of time, the neural pathways and programmed behavior shaped by human evolution may no longer be optimal for the contemporary situation. Behaviors that helped one succeed on the Pleistocene savannah may not work as well in the modern office. Such maladaptive behavior must be addressed by science.

These arguments drive the emergence of a picture of human action arising from largely unseen forces: genes that have been shaped by millions of years of evolution. These forces use a probabilistic calculus to enact behaviors that will maximize the chances of propagation of genes. As E. O. Wilson puts it, "The mind will be more precisely explained as an epiphenomenon of the neuronal machinery of the brain. That machinery is in turn the product of genetic evolution by natural selection. . . . By a judicious extension of the methods and ideas of neurobiology, ethology, and sociobiology a proper foundation can be laid for the social sciences."[20] Reason has relatively little role to play here. The drivers of behavior, desires and motivations, emerge from the needs of genes rather than the individual. They are hidden from consciousness. Similarly, responses to stimuli are governed by neural pathways encoding a hidden utility calculus. Wilson suggests that this knowledge might allow us to gain control over our genes and the evolutionary process: "The human species can change its own nature. What will it choose? . . . Will it press on toward still higher intelligence and creativity, accompanied by a greater—or lesser—capacity for emotional response?"[21] Yet it is not clear how that would happen. As C. S. Lewis noted, those who make choices are individual agents, not the abstractions like "man" or "the human species" discussed by Wilson.[22] Who would be the agent who acts, if the human individual is a construct of genes? For these writers, the metaphor of the human most commonly used is the Cartesian one of animals as machines, although updated to the technology of robots and computers. People enact programming over which they have no control. There is no person, just the program.

There have been many critiques of the first two disciplines Schwartz discusses, with many books in theology, philosophy, and the social sciences detailing the problems of *homo economicus* and evolutionary psychology. These are not the focus of this part of the book. Instead, the focus is on the last discipline described by Schwartz, behaviorism. Though it has been criticized, it has been written about relatively less often than other reductionist frameworks. Its influence on today's world of thought, discourse, and practice is also more subtle. Here, behaviorism serves not only as a paradigmatic case of the new way of understanding the person but also as an influential source for contemporary technologies.[23]

Behaviorism is a psychological paradigm developed by J. B. Watson in the early twentieth century but popularized and perfected by B. F. Skinner.[24] Its goal, as stated by Watson, "is the prediction and control of behavior."[25] Its basic conceptual argument is the one described above in relation to mechanistic science. There cannot be any true science of mind, any actual psychology, as long as researchers are engaging things as subjective and unobservable as thoughts. Skinner argues, "One difficulty is that almost all of what is called behavioral science continues to trace behavior to states of mind, feelings, traits of character, human nature, and so on. Physics and biology once followed similar practices and advanced only when they discarded them. . . . [Behavioral science] will not solve our problems . . . until it replaces traditional prescientific views."[26] Therefore, Watson decided that "the time seems to have come when psychology must discard all reference to consciousness."[27] Introspection is just not a reliable source of scientific evidence for the behavioral technology required to govern society. The mind must be black-boxed and only external evidence admitted. Therefore, these scholars focused only on observable behavior.

The convenient corollary of this methodological turn is that one can easily study animal behavior in order to make inferences about human behavior. The behaviorist "recognizes no dividing line between man and brute."[28] In experiments, "The man and the animal should be placed as nearly as possible under the same experimental conditions."[29] More precisely, both humans and animals were treated as machines. Skinner's advances in the field occurred because he was able to gain total control over the environment of pigeons.[30] The pigeons were engaged as stimulus/response machines. Behaviorists think of animals as generating different behaviors initially in a stochastic fashion, much as genetic processes generate new mutations. In experiments, researchers would provide a stimulus. When the research subject responded to the stimulus with the randomly generated behavior that was sought, it would receive a reward (or punishment). For example, a light would come on in the pigeon's cage. After a while, the bird would peck the target under that light when it flashed. When it did so, a food pellet was dispensed. The pigeons were drastically underfed, so they quickly learned to associate pecking the target when the light came on as leading to food and would rapidly respond.

This procedure is called operant conditioning. Organisms learn to associate a reward with a stimulus/response pair, and thus repeat the desired behavior. Skinner thought that this is what happens with human learning as well. Initially, behavior is somewhat random or due to evolutionary programs/constructs. As certain of these behaviors are rewarded with pleasure, they are reinforced and thus occur more frequently. Ones that produce pain occur less frequently. The Darwinian natural selection of sociobiology is replicated at the level of the individual organism: "The environment not only prods or lashes, it *selects*. Its role is similar to that in natural selection, though on a very different time scale."[31] Natural selection of genetic variants and environmental selection of successful behaviors are two sides of the same coin. Only behaviors producing pleasure survive.

Importantly, behavior responds to stimuli in a probabilistic manner. On one hand, reward or punishment does not always need to follow the behavior to induce conditioning. Rewards must appear only a certain percentage of the time. Indeed, a variable rate of reward can be an even more powerful tool for encouraging a behavior, as we shall see in the next chapter with regard to gambling and social media. On the other hand, behaviorists do not need a 100 percent response rate in order to declare success: "In an experiment on operant behavior the important data are changes in the probability of a response, usually observed as changes in rate, but it is difficult if not impossible to follow a change in rate through casual observation."[32] Organisms will always display some variability in behavior, if only to provide the variation necessary for natural selection. Thus, one merely needs to see an increased probability of a behavior to declare the conditioning a success. Behaviorism provides a thorough, theoretical model of the organism as a biological machine operating under hidden motivations due to probabilistic reasoning in order to maximize expected value.

FIVE ASPECTS OF THIS MODEL OF POWER

Five aspects of these systems of thought, especially behaviorism, are important for my analysis. First are the ends of action enunciated in sociobiology, behaviorism, and many social sciences.[33] For sociobiology, the end is the bare propagation of genes. Similarly, when replying to the question of why a society should engage in behavioral modification, Skinner argues that using behaviorism will maximize group survival. As he argues, "The simple fact is that a culture which *for any reason* induces its members to work for its survival, or for the survival of some of its practices, is more likely to survive. Survival is the only value according to which a culture is eventually to be judged."[34] Although this was perhaps a sensible response coming out of World War II and in the face of the Soviet threat during the Cold War, there is no further justification for why survival should matter to us. The proximate ends, the one through which this ultimate end of survival is encouraged, are preference satisfaction or pleasure. These provide the motivation for all actions. Again, these are not rational ends but merely blind desires or drives. Because they are not tied to any deeper natural necessity, preferences and pleasures can be modified by whatever force is in control in the system: the behavioral programmer, the gene, or the evolutionary process. In any case, however, action and motivation are not ultimately rationally founded or defensible for anything other than self-preservation.

This ordering reflects a fundamental shift in the understanding of human motivation that occurred in the early modern period. As the German Catholic philosopher Robert Spaemann puts it, "In the place of the dynamic-teleological structure, by virtue of which everything that exists is ordered to an activity proper to it, an activity that in turn is ordered to the realization of a specific bonum, we now have an inversion of teleology: being does not rise up to activity, but activity instead has as its sole goal the preservation of that which already simply exists."[35] In premodern frameworks, ethics had aimed at transcending the self in the Platonic world of forms, the Aristotelian polis or contemplation, the Stoic sage at one with divine providence, or the Christian Beatific Vision. In the modern period, ethics becomes dully immanent, purely aimed at the survival of the individual as he is.[36] This shift contributes to the broader replacement of ends with outcomes in the theory of action. Pleasure or survival are the only ends, so the agent must merely evaluate all possible outcomes of action based on these two imperatives.

Second, behavior is altered primarily through environmental change. Behavior changes because what is rewarded by the surrounding world shifts. This is clear in evolution, in which environmental changes lead to differential survival of organisms. A shift in environment will lead to extinctions and the success of variants that better fit the new conditions. In economics, shifts in the market demand that companies, workers, and consumers change their behavior. Behaviorists need to control environmental stimuli and the resulting rewards in order to train their objects of research. In social and political power, what is desired is a change in the characteristics of the population, and that occurs seemingly only by adjusting social conditions. In none of these cases is behavior change explained or encouraged by engaging with the subject as a creature with reason and will, as in the image of God. There is little hope that rational argument will induce change. Neither can the subject of the behavioral intervention argue with another subject, the controller, about the changing circumstance. Dramatic changes are no one's fault, but the result of a brute physical surd: the market, nature, the environment. This makes it all the more dangerous because the subject can identify no will that opposes his own that in turn he can oppose. The subject may not even be aware of changes taking place. This modality makes it difficult to resist abuses, giving those in control greater power. As Jean-Jacques Rousseau argued in relation to education, "As long as children find resistance only in things and never in wills, they will become neither rebellious nor irascible."[37] One gains greater influence over someone if resistance to her will always seems to come merely from the nature of things.

Thus, in the third aspect, such tools are disempowering to those who are treated as their objects. It is commonly argued that neoliberal market imperatives disempower workers. The manager or policymaker just appeals to the brute fact of market demands; "there is no alternative," as Margaret Thatcher said. It is even more so when environments are shaped by experts but without the knowledge of those in the environment. It gives great power to behavioral programmers for eliminating resistance. Moreover, behavioral tools assume intensive surveillance and control to ensure outcomes and to know whether the designed behaviors are occurring. These features of expert empowerment through surveillance and environmental manipulation will become clear in the examples that follow.

Fourth, part of the reason for the need for massive amounts of information from surveillance is that the outcomes are probabilistic. There is no assurance that behavior will change all the time for all the objects of control. Indeed, that rarely happens. Instead, behavioral programmers seek to alter behavior a certain percentage of the time for a certain percentage of actors. Even a low amount of transformed behavior can be extremely profitable given a large enough population. Such shifts can shape the properties of the collectivity.

Fifth and finally, these frameworks are experimental. Evolution exper iments with new genetic variants through mating and mutation. Similarly, behaviorism does not embrace the classical utopia of Plato, where a perfect set of laws would be created once and for all. Instead, behavioral program- mers need to continually tinker with behavioristic systems. The reactions of the objects of behavioral modification are never certain. The behavioral programmers might always devise better variations, and rewards schedules could be made more efficient. A primary theme of Skinner's novel describing his utopian ideal, *Walden Two*, is the need to always run experiments.[38] Coin- cidentally, this gives experts even more power and aligns governance more closely with experimental science.

A last thing to note about these systems, though not a necessary feature, is that they generally have revolutionary intentions. Most obviously, free market economic theorists have reshaped society over the last forty years. The sociologist Howard Kaye describes sociobiologists as "cultural revo- lutionaries."[39] Skinner also wanted to transform society, to move it beyond hidebound notions of freedom and dignity into a more efficient future. His concern was that our evolutionarily and culturally developed repertoire of responses was no longer effective against contemporary threats. Behavioral conditioning works only with relatively short-term responses, so negative behaviors, such as addiction or pollution, may lead to short-term pleasure at the cost of long-term damage. In the past, cultural and religious norms had served to make up the difference between short- and long-term effects. With the loss of these resources in postmodernity, behavioral programming becomes necessary. Moreover, even those older traditions were not adjusted to new long-term threats like global warming. Thus, Skinner aimed at societal transformation.

THREE MODALITIES OF THE NEW ANTHROPOLOGY

These disciplines continue to have a significant effect on contemporary policy. Economics and behavioral genetics remain prominent research para- digms: economic analysis dominates politics, and behavioral genetics is simi- larly influential. However, behaviorism as a research program disappeared after the 1970s in the face of problems with its research results and the rise of cognitive neuroscience. Researchers began to focus on what went on inside the head, although not in terms of consciousness and subjective experience. Rather, the focus turned to neurons, brain localization, and internal biases. Yet even with its demise as an independent research program, many of behaviorism's basic ideas survived to influence psychology and other fields. As a past president of the Association for Psychological Science said, "In a very real sense, all psychologists today . . . are behaviorists."[40] The rest of this chapter surveys three areas where forms of power based on probabilistic technologies and elements of this new anthropology are deployed: nudging, workplace social physics, and surveillance capitalism. These three examples draw on the five aspects of power noted in economics, sociobiology, and behaviorism related to expert control and its anthropological presuppositions. The first, nudging, is the mildest form of this program, one that has possible overlaps with older models of the person. It perhaps shows how these technologies could be helpfully deployed. The other two examples, however, suggest the easy slide of this form of power into manipulation. Together, they begin to illustrate what it might mean to be an object of probabilistic, risk-based reasoning in contemporary society.

Biopolitical Nudging

As chapter 6 discussed, early modern states began using statistics to develop policies to foster the life of their citizens. By shaping the life, strength, and health of its population, a state could ensure military and industrial strength. In contrast to Machiavelli's emphasis on glory or Aquinas's focus on beatitude, both of which were visions of the good life, this new form of politics emphasized what the Italian philosopher Giorgio Agamben, building on Hannah Arendt, calls bare life, mere biological existence.[41] This is a form of power called, after Michel Foucault, biopower or, in its statistical instantiation, biopolitics.[42]

Biopolitics can operate through many forms, though fundamentally it is a regulatory politics, operating on statistical normal curves by shaping the distribution of traits in a population. In this, it contrasts with Foucault's concept of anatomopolitics or discipline, which imposes a norm on individual bodies through educational programs.[43] Biopolitics works through indirect means: financial incentives like taxes on sugary sodas, health insurance plans with regular checkups, or water quality monitoring. It also has taken on a number of different modalities: state-sponsored eugenics, Keynesian regulation, neoliberal economic incentives. Here, I examine the modality of biopolitical nudging.

Nudging arose from behavioral economics. Noting that people estimate probabilities poorly and that they do not make all their choices fully in line with expected value, behavioral economists have argued that individuals are not fully rational, if rationality is understood in terms of decision theory.

Instead, they are subject to common fallacies and biases in reasoning. These would include availability bias (overestimating the likelihood of events that have recently occurred), anchoring biases (misestimating a value in relation to a convenient reference value), loss aversion (overweighting the cost of losses in relation to gains), and many others.[44] Of course, other scholars, drawing from the tradition of Herbert Simon's satisficing, note that these are in fact rational heuristics with which to operate in most situations.[45] For the most part, information is incomplete, so an economic actor will not have the full read-out of probabilities of risks to draw on in decision-making. For this reason, these so-called fallacies and biases allow for the actor to make the most of limited information.

For example, the way a doctor frames statistics has a large effect on which treatment a patient chooses. Patients are much more likely to choose a treatment framed as having a 90 percent chance of survival versus one framed as having a 10 percent chance of death, even though these are statistically equivalent.[46] This example suggests to the behavioral economist the irrationality of framing effects. This phenomenon leads behavioral economists of the libertarian paternalist persuasion to not seek the explicit preferences of individuals, because they will be unreliable due to the ways that questions are framed.[47] Yet critics point out that this analysis ignores the intersubjective aspect of human communication, the way people pick up on nonexplicit clues in another's words.[48] In the medical example, people intuit that the doctor's framing encodes an implicit recommendation—that is, he mentions survival because he thinks the operation is a good idea or death because he is trying to discourage it. It is eminently rational for a patient to rely on the recommendation of an expert health professional. Thus, people are using an intersubjective form of rationality ignored by the probabilistic decision theory of economics. Despite this and other critiques, behavioral economists have succeeded in portraying people as fundamentally irrational, acting in ways that harm their well-being.

However, behavioral economics has a solution for this supposed problem of irrationality. Many of these biases come from how choices are presented. If policymakers can shift what is called the choice architecture of a situation, the environment in which the decision is made, then people can be nudged toward making better choices.[49] One of the most common examples regards retirement saving.[50] Even though it would improve one's future life to invest in a 401(k), not everyone does so. This is due to status quo bias and inertia. People simply fail to act to initiate the investments. Under a system of nudging, the employer simply changes investing in a retirement account from an opt-in choice that the employee actively makes to an opt-out choice. Upon hiring, money is automatically taken from her paycheck for retirement unless she actually chooses against it. This reverses the operation of the status quo bias to her benefit. The status quo is now saving for retirement. Much nudging, as in this example, is completely unobjectionable. For instance, setting up effective default options makes good sense, especially if those in power can explain how they came to the default option.[51] Other aspects of nudging would be clearly embraced by any ethics, such as providing clear information on alternatives. These make for good modifications to a purely economic rationality.

However, other modifications of choice architectures may be more problematic. Take the supermarket and other food displays that serve as a prime example for Thaler and Sunstein.[52] Marketers know that consumers will be more likely to buy whatever easily presents itself to them, so they pay extra for space on the endcaps of aisles. This takes advantage of availability bias; people are more likely to choose based on information straightforwardly available to their memory. Policymakers could improve people's health by taking advantage of this bias to push people to eat healthy food. Thus, school cafeterias could put fruit at eye level at an early place in line, or supermarkets could set the produce area at the entrance to the store. In this way, biases could be manipulated to improve well-being using a subconscious influence.

These tools exhibit many of the aspects seen earlier in the chapter in behaviorist models of action. Biopolitics, in its focus on bare life, reorients the person toward immanent goods of health. It shapes immediate choices by making certain ends available in the environment. It relies on expert judgment and control, with even its proponents claiming that it is a kind of soft paternalism. Experts create situations to lead persons to act for what they take to be their own good. These ends are generally ones of health and economic maximization, which are the basic survival goals of behaviorism and biopolitics. These may not be the individual's actual preferences, but they are thought of as what *should* be her preferences, so technologies are put in place that shift the chooser's preferences. Rather, they shift how she evaluates the probabilities of achieving certain preferences in a situation, thus directing her to the "right," rational choice. It is the environment that is changed in order to influence individual behavior rather than individual will or rationality. Agents are thought of as responding to the environment using a faulty probabilistic economic rationality, one that must be reshaped by nudges. They are seen as using instrumental rationality, but in a faulty way that experts can correct. It is the situation that is manipulated in order to redirect the object of policy rather than the subject being engaged by persuasion or dialogue.

The hiddenness of the manipulation increases the power of the expert archi-tect of the choice situation because there is no awareness of a policy decision that could be challenged. For such interventions to work, the nudgers must have increased control over social environments. Moreover, the expert must also have increased surveillance power because of the need for information in order to appropriately evaluate and modify the nudges. These are ongoing experiments, whose results can only be judged probabilistically. There is no thought that nudging will lead to a certain result in the case of every person upon whom it is deployed. Instead, it seeks to increase the frequency of the policymaker's approved choice. Even if it does this in only a percentage of cases, it is still a success. Thus, it is an ideal deployment of probabilistic rea-soning with regard to human behavior as a tool of power.

This kind of use can be justified as seeking genuine natural goods of health by arranging the supermarket space, which had to be arranged in some way or another in any case. But it does raise some major questions. The first is the pragmatic one of whether it actually works in practice outside spe-cial experimental setups in labs.[53] Although fundamentally pragmatic, this question also helps to indicate whether the underlying theory of the human person and human rationality is accurate. As many critics note, it seems to underrate the individual's ability to engage in an intersubjective rationality. The second, more normative concern involves the question of freedom, as choices are constrained by the architecture. The architecture may ideally be justified to the participants, but when used by private entities it may not be. This can have problematic effects, as the other modalities show.

Depositing the Will in the Environment

It would be a mistake to wholly condemn these tools. In the best interpreta-tion, some mechanisms of nudging can intersect with alternative models of the self, such as those coming from the virtue tradition. As many have noted, behavioral economics can serve to push back against a pure economic rational-ity. Nudging does not require the continual prediction and weighting of possi-bilities that I critiqued in part I of this book. Virtue ethicists should accept that deployment of conscious, rational thought is not necessary at all times.

First, people consciously make preemptive decisions that make later choices easier through various forms of cognitive offloading. The philosopher of technology and motorcycle mechanic Matthew Crawford, though critical of much technology, has contrasted automation with jigs.[54] When making a series of the same cuts, a carpenter, rather than measuring the board each time, will construct a jig to guide the cut. This investment of time and attention allows the carpenter to focus on more important aspects of his work. Some of his knowledge is deliberately placed into the structure of the spatial environment in order to guide future action. Similarly, people also create habits and routines that structure time in order to help them move through the day with a minimum of distraction from important goals: having a set time to exercise, a commitment to morning prayer, standard meal times. By committing themselves to a schedule, they ensure that they will meet important goals without having to deliberate each time they enact them.

Moreover, people can consciously bind themselves to a course of action when they fear future temptations. They set an alarm clock, turn on an internet blocker, or give their keys to the bartender. As Jon Elster describes it, binding oneself to a future action "seems to require that we temporarily deposit our will in some external structures; that we set up a causal process in the external world that after some time returns to its source and modifies our behavior."[55] All these strategies, however, flow from the prior conscious choice of the agent.[56] That is where they are different from exploiting psychic mechanisms and biases that lie outside the individual's knowledge.[57] These kinds of conscious depositions of will in the environment to achieve important goals are laudable uses of technology.

Another way that the agent can consciously give over responsibility is through intersubjective trust. One trusts an authority based on their knowledge and their responsibility. This is what happens in the case of the default retirement option or the doctor's recommendation. It recalls the earlier probabilism, in which people relied on the moral intuitions of expert theologians. Again, however, this offloading of rational choice occurs through a conscious relationship of trust. Presumably, the moral theologian, doctor, financial adviser, or other authority can also explain their decision to the actor. It is thus a rational, fiduciary relationship. As we will see, the problem is that the tools of behavioral governance can be used to manipulate people toward the ends of the programmer without the individual's knowledge or volition.

Social Physics

We see this manipulation in a second paradigm of governance, a form of workplace management that has been dubbed "social physics" by its main proponent, the computer scientist Alex Pentland. This is an old term, used by early social scientists to describe their dreams of doing for humanity what Newton did for natural philosophy. Auguste Comte, the founder of positivism, originally wanted to call his sociology social physics, although the term had already been taken by Quetelet to describe the statistical analysis of populations. Quetelet's probabilistic thought is probably closer to Pentland's usage than Comte's more deterministic sociological framework.[58]

This paradigm also derives from a long history of attempts to manage and control workers, especially those toiling in the factories of the Industrial Revolution.[59] At the turn of the twentieth century, Frederick Taylor created the discipline of scientific management by treating workers in factories as machines, taking what was once skilled artisanal labor, breaking it down into isolated movements, calculating the most efficient way to perform these tasks through time-motion studies, and then assigning only one of these tasks to each worker.[60] Historians question whether these techniques actually improved efficiency. What they did do, however, was to transfer power from skilled artisanal workers to managers, who could then hire a cheaper, unskilled workforce. Power was transferred with knowledge, leaving workers to perform repetitive, mind-numbing tasks all day long.

However, this technique led to the demoralization of the workforce, creating the need for human relations experts who could encourage productivity. In part, this development led to the human relations framework, which noted that workers are more productive when organized into teams, leading to a greater focus on morale and buy-in from the workforce.[61] Shaping worker motivation became the proximate goal. Yet it is much more difficult to encourage morale than to treat workers like mere machines. New theorizations were necessary to properly manipulate new knowledge workers.

Pentland's social physics fills this gap by combining the focus on the social nature of humans with a more machine-like understanding of the person—although, in this case, the machines are networked computers. This framework is social but largely a sociality of machines. The basic assumption is that most human behavior arises from copying our peers.[62] If one accepts this assumption, then the best way to influence an individual's behavior is to work on her friends. For example, Facebook ran an experiment on an election day showing that people were much more likely to vote if they saw that their friends had voted than if they merely had seen an encouragement to vote on their page with no information about their friends.[63] One acts on an individual by acting on her network.

Because peer connections are so important, altering network dynamics can change behavior. For example, experts can incentivize the recruitment of friends. Pentland describes his lab's solution to a DARPA challenge to find ten weather balloons distributed across the United States.[64] They did so by not only rewarding people who found a balloon with $2,000 but also by giving $1,000 to the person who invited the finder to join the network, $500 to whoever invited that person, and so forth. The goal is to use people to build as large a network as possible directed toward the outcome that the network designer wants. People have an incentive to recruit as many friends as possible. In this manner, relationships can be instrumentally deployed to generate a preferred outcome.

A second strategy that is more complex is tuning a network for optimal idea flow.[65] Because this strategy is largely aimed at the manipulation of knowledge workers, the goal is to get them to deploy and communicate the best ideas. For this to happen, the organization needs ideas to flow optimally through a network. Generally, the higher the rate of idea flow, the better, because productivity comes from applying an idea to a new situation or combining different ideas. Managers can optimize idea flow in many ways. A simple strategy is to provide time for informal communication. One call center improved performance simply by allowing whole teams to take coffee breaks together rather than one individual at a time.[66] This change allowed workers to share work strategies. At a more sophisticated level, badges can indicate who has been talking most at a meeting, preventing any one person from dominating the conversation and allowing other voices with alternative ideas to be heard.[67] At a higher level, organizations can identify those individuals who are especially active nodes for facilitating idea sharing. Their jobs can be modified to allow them to better fulfill this role. In this manner, workers are treated as nodes in a network.

Again, this paradigm demonstrates many of the features seen in behaviorist frameworks. First, it is probabilistic, shaping dynamics and improving the odds of certain behaviors occurring rather than determining them. For example, one of the premier uses of these tools is to predict flight risk by identifying those employees most likely to be recruited by competitors.[68] This is a risk rather than a certainty, one that management can shape through better compensation or by letting the at-risk people go before too many resources have been invested in them. Even more pointedly, for idea flow to work optimally, some workers need to be noncompliant with its dictates. As Pentland says, "contrarians are important."[69] In order to avoid groupthink, there need to be some stubborn contrarians. Moreover, for truly new ideas to arise (rather than the mere recombination of existing cultural resources so common in postmodernity), there need to be solitary, independent thinkers. Thus, this system must be primarily probabilistic.

Second, this mode of management acts by shaping the environment, in this case the social environment. Although depending on human relationality, this management style is not itself relational. It treats the relations and the humans who serve as the nodes of this relational network as objects for manipulation. People are assumed to act in a statistically predictable manner, responding to incentives, influences, and other stimuli. Behavior is not changed by engaging the reason and will of workers, but by assuming that they will imitate their peers. For the most part, the relational network is shaped indirectly through devices or break scheduling. Workers may not be aware of the ends to which the new policies are directed, and thus there is no clear managerial will to oppose. It is just the environment, the device, or peers that are influencing them in subtle ways.

This modality increases the power of managers and experts. The social physics expert must have a great deal of surveillance and control. Pentland describes collecting all the "data crumbs" that workers leave behind throughout the day: keystrokes, emails, call logs, website traffic, working hours. Corporations already have access to all these data. Pentland also encourages companies to gather even more information through badges (which he, conveniently enough, designs and sells) that collect biometric data like heart rate, tone of voice, and movement. With this information, companies can deduce contacts, relational networks, emotions, and personalities, allowing even greater levels of manipulation. All this information can be processed in order for the expert to manipulate workplace networks by running a series of experiments to test which new configurations optimize idea flow. All this greatly enhances experts' control of workers.

This is all put to the end of corporate profitability. Yet the business world also sees this kind of optimization as necessary. As the sociologist Joseph Davis notes, "For organizations, the promise to identify and reduce employees' 'wasted potential' is not merely a means of increasing efficiency and innovation. It is also a means of surviving in an ever-tougher competitive environment."[70] Corporate survival is at stake. This corporate end is served by manipulating and using the desires and motivations of workers.

Someone might object to this description. Because it is about ideas, must it not pay attention to human rationality and interiority? One might think so until the definition of idea that Pentland uses becomes clear: "An idea is a strategy (an action, outcome, and features that identify when to apply the action) for instrumental behavior."[71] Thus an idea is not really something held in the intellect; it is just a pragmatic tactic, a form of instrumental rationality. It is a response to a certain stimulus. Ultimately, it is just a behavior. Moreover, Pentland thinks of ideas in terms of cybernetic information. Famously, in Claude Shannon's information theory, the semantic content of information does not matter.[72] So here, the actual content of ideas, whether they are good or bad, does not matter, just as long as they optimally flow through the network. People are not treated as rational creatures but as cybernetic machines for processing and transmitting information.

Surveillance Capitalism

The most dramatic and expansive use of the probabilistic modeling of behavior arises in what the social psychologist Shoshana Zuboff has described as a new iteration of capitalism: surveillance capitalism.[73] Almost every corporate actor, but especially tech giants like Google and Facebook, are tracking people through the internet, collecting the massive amount of information that people leave behind. With the internet of things, the new technology paradigm that seeks to use internet connectivity to mine the data from most common household devices from fridges to TVs to lighting, this tracking emerges from merely the digital realm to encompass the entirety of contemporary life. These data are mined by sophisticated machine-learning algorithms to give a better picture of individual life and behavior.

These data and the profile generated by data mining are sold to others, such as advertisers that use them to better target ads. More important, via what Zuboff calls a behavioral surplus, information about behavior left in digital crumbs is sold and then mined to generate predictions of future behavior.[74] These behavioral futures are valuable because they can be used to attempt to change behavior. Programmers use strategies very similar to nudging, drawing on the user's specific profile to shift the choice architecture of the online environment or place a pitch at the moment that it is most effective, all based on a specific profile. The algorithm predicts that the user is hungry, so a fast food delivery ad appears. These predictions allow corporate and government actors to shift the internet environment in order to increase sales and usage. More interestingly, these behavioral predictions can be used in the offline world as well: maps that take a person by preferred stores or games like Pokemon Go that can herd people into certain locales.[75] These behavioral futures also allow for more traditional forms of risk management, such as highly individualized car insurance rates based on increasingly stratified risk profiles or intensive surveillance of individual driving.[76]

This paradigm again deploys the aspects of behaviorist power. The end is corporate profit, but it acts by meeting, exciting, and manipulating consumer preferences. It alters the environment in order to shape behavior. In this case, it is largely an online environment, but there are also ways to manipulate the environmental experience of those who are offline. This can be done by manipulating actual movements through mapping software or through augmented reality technologies that shape how the user experiences the world.[77] To be effective, the object of manipulation cannot know exactly what the manipulation is. Thus, there is no will to act against. It is just the way the device and program work. The object of manipulation is not engaged through reason and will but more covertly.

Because it needs to control the environment, this paradigm also demands massive amounts of data on personal behavior. It is for this reason that surveillance capacities are now integrated into almost every computer program and internet-connected device. Though many of the apps produced by these companies may be free, the companies make their money by commodifying these surveillance data or transforming them into actionable and marketable predictions. Because surveillance is so central to this paradigm, it is questionable whether regulatory and legal changes in favor of privacy will actually have their intended effects.

Companies need this volume of surveillance data because the effects of these kinds of manipulations are probabilistic. These companies do not seek a deterministic control of behavior, as that is out of reach of these methods. If they can shift consumer behavior even by only 1 or 2 percent, that can still lead to large profits when the target population numbers in the hundreds of millions. Such shifts can be detected only with large amounts of data. When dealing with such marginal shifts in behavior, the manipulations must be continually optimized. That is why the big tech companies are constantly running experiments on their users, testing which formats are more effective, shifting designs, tweaking algorithms. Every internet user is now an object of research. In these ways, surveillance capitalism embodies many of the most important characteristics of behaviorist models of power.

CONCLUSION

The new understanding of human nature described above has led to emergent forms of power based on probabilistic modeling. These are not the only forms it inspires, of course; nor do all these paradigms instantiate this vision to the same degree. Though these techniques can bring many benefits in their train in terms of efficiency, convenience, and even substantive goods like human life and health, they also raise numerous concerns. First, the ends of these projects are purely immanent, aimed largely at the survival of a community, population, corporation, or other body. They aim at bare life. This is an important consideration to which policymakers should be attentive. Yet it is ultimately a subordinate good—what Alasdair MacIntyre would call an

external good, external to the ends of important human practices.[78] The ultimate human good is eternal life, so moral theology must be suspicious of
anything that draws too much attention away from this higher end, setting an
immanent ultimate good. Political society must remain open to the supernatural and other higher goods. If it impedes these, then a social arrangement is
deficient. Even considered as a purely immanent project, the common good
must aim at the integral fulfillment of the human person, supporting relationships, virtue, participation, and the like.

That these forms of power can impede these higher goods is clear from the
way they operate. They proceed by manipulating individual goals, and thus
individual desires, but not by directing them to true goods. Instead, they warp
individual ends. They conceptualize goals as purely individual life plans and
desires as brute, efficient causes. They are not thought of as rationally shaped
desires or ends that must correspond to a substantive vision of reality. A different conception of ends is what is required for true integral fulfillment. These
programs do not support seeking richer ends but instead use concepts that
impede their attainment.

Second, behaviorist modes of governance disempower the objects of governance in relationship to experts, especially because these systems depend
on centralized systems of surveillance and control. The exercise of power
is opaque to those subjected to it, while the lives of citizens are laid bare to
analysts combing through every crumb of web history, movement data, voice
capture, and purchasing profile. Such data allow for exercises of power that
cannot be resisted, not because of their overwhelming force but because of
their subtlety and undetectability.[79] It is notable that many of these tools were
developed with investment funding by national security agencies. This infrastructure, though generally used by corporations, can be rapidly deployed for
security purposes. These tools centralize forms of power and manipulation.

Further, their fundamental mode of operation lies in transforming the
environment. In itself, this is fine; outlawing vicious, socially destructive
behaviors can remove temptations, form virtuous social practices, or help
reinforce a virtuous resolution, thus supporting an education in virtue. The
problem is that these forms of power do not engage the reason and will of
those subject to it but instead tend to operate out of public view. Insofar as
there is not rational engagement with those subject to power, one dimin-
ishes them, disrespecting their capacities. In the *Laws*, Plato describes the
importance of the rational justification of laws, comparing it with medical
care for the free versus that for slaves in classical Greece.[80] For slaves, phy-
sicians just tell them what to do without explanation. But free men, to be

respected, require reasons. To translate the insight behind this framework into contemporary terms, any intervention into a community first requires community outreach and involvement to determine what the community considers its problems to be and how issues arose. One must engage with others' lived experience and rational analysis. Only then are policymakers treating them as subjects rather than objects, treating them as made in the image of God.

The deeper concern for the theologian, however, is with the underlying anthropology driving these systems. Although these techniques can sometimes be used for reasonable purposes, the danger lies in the worldview and forms of power that lie behind them. As their use becomes more prevalent, society becomes more deeply engaged with this anthropology. So one must ask, does this anthropology properly reflect human dignity? How does it shape us to see ourselves and others? How does it shape action? Given its mechanistic conception of human action, its immanent ends, and its manipulative framework, this mode of power would seem to create deep problems. Indeed, chapter 8 examines how these tools, at their extreme, can transform human agency, denuding it of responsibility.

NOTES

Spaemann, "In Defense of Anthropomorphism," 78.
1. See the critique of social science by MacIntyre, *After Virtue*, 88–108.
2. For this understanding of action, see Arendt, *Human Condition*, 7–17.
3. This section draws on Schwartz, *Battle for Human Nature*, 41–48.
4. Hobbes, *Leviathan*, 19–26.
5. Hobbes, 57.
6. Pfau, *Minding the Modern*, 139.
7. Hobbes, *Leviathan*, 33.
8. For *akrasia*, see Aristotle, *Nicomachean Ethics*, 7.1–10. For the fluttering of vicious passions in the soul, see Long and Sedley, *Hellenistic Philosophers*, 65A, G; and Gill, "Did Chrysippus Understand Medea?"
9. La Mettrie, *L'homme machine*.
10. For an overview of his thought, see Dennett, *From Bacteria to Bach and Back*.
11. In a much-discussed fMRI study on the trolley problem, the choice to not push a person to his or her death in order to save others is framed as emotional, a nonobjective response that must be explained by nonrational factors. The choice to push a person to their death is termed rational because it is quantitatively defensible. Greene et al., "FMRI Investigation."
12. For overview, see Kahneman, *Thinking, Fast and Slow*.
13. Gigerenzer, *Rationality for Mortals*; Gigerenzer, "On the Supposed Evidence."

14. Cited by Porter, *Rise of Statistical Thinking*, 54.
15. Porter, 60–65, 151–92; Hacking, *Taming of Chance*, 123–32; Gigerenzer et al., *Empire of Chance*, 37–79.
16. For these examples, see Porter, *Rise of Statistical Thinking*, 193–230.
17. Schwartz, *Battle for Human Nature*.
18. This is a very large body of literature. Important overviews and sources include Wilson, *On Human Nature*; Pinker, *Blank Slate*; Wade, *Troublesome Inheritance*; and Plomin, *Blueprint*. Important critical analyses include Sahlins, *Use and Abuse of Biology*; Ann Arbor Science for the People Editorial Collective, *Biology as a Social Weapon*; Lewontin, *Biology as Ideology*; Gould, *Mismeasure of Man*; and McKinnon, *Neo-Liberal Genetics*. Key theological discussions include Pope, *Human Evolution*; and Deane-Drummond, *Christ and Evolution*.
19. For a theological analysis, see Nowak and Coakley, *Evolution, Games, and God*.
20. Wilson, *On Human Nature*, 195.
21. Wilson, 208.
22. Lewis, *Abolition of Man*.
23. Other disciplines could serve equally well as an example of this anthropology, such as cybernetics. My focus on behaviorism and its tie to contemporary technologies is inspired by Zuboff, *Age of Surveillance Capitalism*. See also Bernard, *Triumph of Profiling*, 88–91.
24. For theoretical overviews, see Watson, *Behavior*; Skinner, *Beyond Freedom and Dignity*; and Skinner, *About Behaviorism*.
25. Watson, *Behavior*, 1.
26. Skinner, *Beyond Freedom and Dignity*, 24–25.
27. Watson, *Behavior*, 7.
28. Watson, 1.
29. Watson, 14.
30. For review of these experiments, see Schwartz, *Battle for Human Nature*, 120ff.
31. Skinner, *Beyond Freedom and Dignity*, 18.
32. Skinner, 148.
33. Economics takes the ends of action from the individual's schedule of preferences, so it is much more flexible in terms of ends than these other disciplines.
34. Skinner, *Beyond Freedom and Dignity*, 136.
35. Spaemann, "Bourgeois Ethics," 49.
36. For the modern turn to ordinary life, see Taylor, *Sources of the Self*.
37. Rousseau, *Emile*, 66.
38. Skinner, *Walden Two*.
39. Kaye, *Social Meaning of Modern Biology*, 3.
40. See Roediger, "What Happened to Behaviorism?"
41. Agamben, *Homo Sacer*; Arendt, *Human Condition*.
42. Foucault, *History of Sexuality, Volume 1*; Foucault, *Society Must Be Defended*; Foucault, *Security, Territory, Population*. The major problem with Agamben's use of the concept is that he takes what for Foucault and Carl Schmitt are historically specific ideas of biopolitics and sovereignty and expands them to a more totalizing vision of power existing for as long as the state. Moreover, in Foucault, this technology of power, though dangerous, has valuable uses, whereas Agamben describes it as almost completely negative. For a critique of Agamben's use of this concept, see Rabinow and Rose, "Biopower Today."

43. Foucault, *History of Sexuality, Volume 1*; Foucault, *Discipline and Punish*.
44. The best overview is by Kahneman, *Thinking, Fast and Slow*.
45. E.g., Gigerenzer, *Rationality for Mortals*. For Simon's work, see Simon, "Rational Choice."
46. Kahneman, *Thinking, Fast and Slow*, 367.
47. Gigerenzer, "On the Supposed Evidence," 367.
48. Gigerenzer, 368.
49. The most comprehensive popular overview is by Thaler and Sunstein, *Nudge*.
50. Thaler and Sunstein, 105–19.
51. Thaler and Sunstein, 246–49.
52. Thaler and Sunstein, 1–4.
53. E.g., Thaler and Sunstein, 43, citing the food researcher Brian Wansink. Unfortunately, Wansink's research has come under intense scrutiny due to its use of statistics, leading to many retractions and to his resignation; see Servick, "Cornell Nutrition Scientist Resigns." The investigation began when he celebrated how a graduate student was able to discover correlations in a data set that had been missed by a postdoctoral fellow. Observers noted that this seemed like p-hacking, a statistical trick of going over data to find any possible correlation that one can. In any given data set, however, there will be many spurious correlations, so these techniques will lead to false results.
54. Crawford, *World Beyond Your Head*, 31–35. For a theological discussion of this concept, see Vera, "Augmented Reality."
55. Elster, *Ulysses and the Sirens*, 43.
56. Elster, 84.
57. Elster, 82.
58. On Quetelet, see Ewald, *L'etat providence*, 148–68; Gigerenzer et al., *Empire of Chance*, 38–48; and Hacking, *Taming of Chance*, 105–14.
59. Schwartz, *Battle for Human Nature*, 228–39; Braverman, *Labor and Monopoly Capital*.
60. Braverman, *Labor and Monopoly Capital*, 59–106.
61. Davis, "Social Physics Comes to the Workplace," 66. My analysis of social physics draws heavily on this article.
62. Pentland, "Death of Individuality."
63. Pentland, *Social Physics*, 64–65.
64. Pentland, 121–26.
65. Pentland, 32–61.
66. Pentland, 93–96.
67. Pentland, 108–12.
68. Rosenbaum, "IBM Artificial Intelligence."
69. Pentland, *Social Physics*, 40.
70. Davis, "Social Physics Comes to the Workplace," 62.
71. Pentland, *Social Physics*, 20.
72. Hayles, *How We Became Posthuman*, 53.
73. Zuboff, *Age of Surveillance Capitalism*.
74. Zuboff, 63–97.
75. Zuboff, 306–19; Bernard, *Triumph of Profiling*, 27–59.
76. Zuboff, *Age of Surveillance Capitalism*, 212–18; Bernard, *Triumph of Profiling*, 69.
77. Vera, "Augmented Reality."
78. MacIntyre, *After Virtue*.

79. Many commentators have objected to this system on account of privacy, which is certainly a concern. Yet the ethical foundations of privacy as a right have never been entirely clear. It tends to be treated in much the same way as property or bodily integrity, but there are problems with these comparisons. Further, it is unclear how one would justify a right to privacy as a fundamental right on a theological basis. Unfortunately, there is not space to explore this topic here. For one of the few reflections on this topic in theological ethics, see Stoddart, *Theological Perspectives*.

80. Plato, *Laws*, 719e–20.

8

Algorithms and the Demonic

When a man turns away from God he simply gives himself
up to the law of gravity. . . . If we examine human society and
souls closely and with real attention, we see that wherever the
virtue of supernatural light is absent, everything is obedient to
mechanical laws as blind and as exact as the law of gravitation.

—*Simone Weil*

In 2013, Mark Hemmings called the United Kingdom's emergency number because of agonizing stomach pain.[1] The operator asked a series of questions determined by an algorithm about his condition. Despite his frequent cries that he was in agony and his pleas for an ambulance, the operator responded that the algorithm determined that his constellation of symptoms did not require an ambulance. She told him to call a doctor on a nonemergency basis. A few days later, a home health care worker found him unconscious in his apartment. Rushed to the hospital, he died soon after arrival from a heart attack brought on by gallstones blocking his pancreatic duct.

Whereas chapter 7 outlined the anthropology underlying systems of power drawing on probabilistic prediction, this chapter focuses on how they affect human agency. The story of Mark Hemmings illustrates two sides of this effect on agency. The first is the objectification of the targets of this system, which frequently results in forms of systemic injustice. In this vision, people are seen as operating like computers and are manipulated by other machines. Increasingly, much of this manipulation is performed using algorithms tied to forms of artificial intelligence (AI). Theologians, ethicists, and others have frequently approached this issue from science fiction scenarios of general AI, superintelligent conscious machines that could take over the world and kill us all, but most computer scientists do not see such a hyper-development of machine intelligence as likely. As one researcher told me, when we talk about AI, we are just talking about statistics: machine-learning techniques for determining patterns in large amounts of data—that is, assessing statistical regularities in a sample—in order to develop predictive algorithms. Yet we do not need to wait for Skynet for machine intelligence to transform our lives, as whole realms of social decision-making have been handed over to, or are at least assisted by, computer programs: stock trades, piloting, sentencing guidelines, police deployment, employee performance evaluation, the news, and so on. The use of these decision-making systems is set to expand into many more areas, such as autonomous vehicles, autonomous weapons systems, systems of workplace management based on social physics, and websites engaging the regime of surveillance capitalism.

As the example of Hemmings shows, these algorithms have entered medical care. In his case, the algorithm served to enforce certain goals of cost savings to the detriment of treating him as a human being in need of care. Instead of an individual, he was treated as an abstract statistical point in a population. Because of these orientations, Hemmings was denied care that he desperately needed. Many similarly troubling social issues are emerging from this trend: the centralization of power because these algorithms are owned and operated by only a few companies; the way that these algorithms can incorporate and radically expand bias against minorities under the cloak of "objective" data; and the problems of unemployment due to automation.

The second important aspect of this trend is revealed by the actions of the operator, who suffered the subjective effects of management by algorithms. Ethicists discussing AI in areas such as autonomous weapons systems emphasize the importance of having a human in the loop, someone who can step in to make moral decisions. Frequently, however, as the anthropologist Jarrett Zigon points out with regard to Hemmings's case, having a human in the loop is no help for ensuring moral decisions.[2] The tendency of these systems is to remove a sense or even a possibility of human responsibility. The growing trust in the decision-making prowess of machines, what Nicholas Carr calls automation bias, may remove even the little power that the human agent has.[3] The people involved have a semblance of responsibility, putting a human face on automated decision systems, but no true decision-making power. As Zigon says, "The human operator simply acted as the mouthpiece—the voice—of the algorithm."[4] In such a situation, the human in the loop has become inhuman, a mere appendage of the machine. The term "inhuman" may bear too much of a note of moral judgment, suggest too much of a sense of malice.[5] But the operators in these examples bear no malice; they do not act out of cruelty. Instead, they hardly act at all. As Zigon describes, the systems act through them.[6]

When these systems invade areas of human judgment, domains for prudent action are narrowed or erased. For example, many systems of performance evaluation in jobs remove subjective judgment as to the quality of work or special conditions that decrease productivity in favor of evaluation based purely on quantitatively measurable factors. One could even think of the replacement of critical analysis of media like movies by crowd-sourced rankings. The rest of this chapter discusses such systems as forms of algorithmic judgment. By this, I do not merely mean to include systems that make judgments according to simple algorithms (although many do) but also more complex forms of machine learning.

The theological relevance of both aspects of this trend, objective injustice and the evacuation of subjective agency, is highlighted in the early twentieth-century theologian Romano Guardini's *The End of the Modern World*, in which he discusses social organization in terms of the demonic.[7] In this work, which deeply influenced Pope Francis's encyclical on the environment, *Laudato si'*, Guardini traces the changes occurring in society, culture, and human subjectivity between the modern world and what we would call the postmodern world, not only to chart this new age's dangers but also to call people to action to realize its hopeful possibilities.[8] One particularly distinctive aspect of post-modern social systems is that they undermine human agency, constraining action and hiding the true efficacy of those actions that people can still perform. Guardini, of course, was not thinking of algorithms but of bureaucratic organizations. However, those aspects of postmodernity that concerned him are accentuated by algorithmic tools. What he sees as problematic is the way that such systems nullify the human ability to act in good conscience through reason and free will.[9] Because, as discussed in the introduction, reason and free will are distinctive aspects of the *imago Dei*, Guardini sees these systems that evacuate agency as demonic, defacing the image of God.[10]

This chapter explores his concerns over these aspects of the demonic, showing how they apply to new algorithmic tools, in two ways. The first is when individuals are denied the possibility of agency through the use of such decision-making tools by those in power. This denial of agency also undermines the relational aspect of human sociality, as the other becomes an object. Beyond this analysis, however, there is a curious phenomenon brought to light by anthropologists studying human interactions with these systems. People seem to seek out the diminishment of their own agency, first by deploying such systems because they are ostensibly more trustworthy or less biased than any human could possibly be, which is a claim that is simply false, as this chapter discusses. However, other commentators have noted that it also seems to be the case that people desire to remove the burden of agency from themselves. This self-sought denial of agency occurs in a phenomenon explored brilliantly by Natasha Dow Schull, in which interactions with algorithmic systems allow individuals to enter altered states similar to the much-lauded state of flow consciousness, in which they are sucked into games that manipulate them using ideas drawn from behaviorism. Disturbingly, much of the architecture of the digital world is designed to encourage users to enter into sustained interactions in which they are reduced to the most basic behavioristic stimulus/response systems. Here one sees the ultimate outcome of the objectification performed through probabilistic analytics. The person takes on the role of the predictable stimulus/response system governed by probabilistic reasoning, embracing the anthropological vision discussed in chapter 7 and losing contact with higher forms of rationality as well as her role as a source of new action in the world. In this way, the *imago Dei* is disfigured, and the truth of human nature and destiny is denied.

This analysis requires two caveats. First, I am not claiming that algorithms themselves are immoral or demonic. Rather, it is the underlying anthropology that shapes their design and the social systems in which they are used that create problems. A total rejection would deny the obviously beneficial uses of them, from library search engines to simple calculators, or when they are used to consciously place a person's will in the environment, as discussed in chapter 7. My goal is to detect where they can go wrong and seek ways to actually benefit from their tremendous potential for good. This goal requires transforming these underlying structures.

The second caveat is that this treatment is not meant to be exhaustive of the understanding of the demonic. I am not suggesting that when a theologian says demonic, she should think only of the evacuation of agency. There are many other analyses a theologian could deploy, some of which overlap with my discussion: social systems as powers and principalities, the demonic experienced in individual temptation, or the personal aspect of the demonic emphasized by both Guardini and Francis.[11] Each of these interpretations raises a number of questions demanding their own chapters, so here I focus only on the demonic in terms of the reduction of agency, which is the aspect most directly related to the subject of the book.

SYSTEMS OF INJUSTICE

As mentioned above, Guardini was very concerned with emerging social systems, calling such forms of life "non-human."[12] In this, he was contrasting the emerging postmodern era with a modern understanding of the human, which embraced a strong sense of human personality, combined with both a conception of nature and an exaltation of culture. In the contemporary age, according to Guardini, people have become distanced from direct experience with the world. Instead, nature is understood only through the abstract and formalized mechanisms of mathematics and technology.[13] The world loses its "quality of real experience." This has grave implications for an understanding of responsibility: "Responsibility involves growth, growth from an immature process of executing material acts to a mature process of squaring them with ethical standards. But how can ethical standards be applied to areas of work which have become lost in abstract formulae and distant machines?"[14] With this last question, Guardini points to the fact that the development of mature responsibility cannot be understood apart from the structures of daily action, which allow the person to come to know what responsibility is and how her actions affect the world. Attempts to control the consequences of action have moved from the tacit knowledge of prudent actors in human systems to the abstract models of cost/benefit analysis.

Although there are many differences between the Fordist mass society that Guardini confronted in the postwar era and today's society, there remain many similarities in the crucial arena of the "increasing alienation between [human] experience and . . . understanding."[15] People are distanced from the effects of their actions, so they cease to experience any real causality in the world. This is true of many areas of contemporary life: driving leads to carbon emissions that will cause climate change whose effects may not be felt until years in the future, or consumer purchases reinforce capitalist systems of sweatshop labor in distant countries. The central danger of contemporary power structures, according to Guardini, is that they have become "so deranged or falsely arranged that those responsible can no longer be named. . . . When to the question 'Who did this?' neither 'I' nor 'we,' neither a person nor a body of people replies, the exercise of power has apparently become a natural force."[16] This is true of many modern and contemporary systems, but it is expressed with startling clarity in the case of behaviorist models of power, in which it is the environment or device that shapes action. It also becomes apparent in algorithmic decision-making. For example, one of the fundamental unanswered questions for self-driving cars is who would bear responsibility in the event of an accident: the operator, the company, or the programmer? In such cases, it seems that no human would, only a machine that by its nature cannot bear responsibility.[17]

This offloading of responsibility opens the possibility for systems of injustice that are nearly impossible to resist or in which it is difficult to even trace the causal links. As chapter 7 discussed, there are aspects of these tools that arise from motives of increased profit and more centralized power. This argument works on the analogy between algorithmic judgment and Taylorism. Taylor replaced craft judgment with combinations of machines and workers fitted to the machines, who operated as if they were parts of the machine of the factory. This transformation allowed for increased efficiency and decreased labor costs. Workers were replaced by machines, and those still employed did not need to be paid the high wages of the expert artisan.

A similar result occurs for cognitive labor through machine learning and algorithms. The results of millions of expert radiologists' examinations of scans for cancer are fed into a machine that discovers the patterns the radiologists use to discern whether cancer appears in the scan. The machine then develops its own predictive statistical method. This allows for the replacement of the radiologist. Consumers no longer need to pay video store owners or record store merchants to curate a collection and recommend a selection that might meet their tastes but allow algorithms to do that job on Netflix or Spotify. People do not need editors to direct them to the important news; they use aggregators and news feeds. Frontline workers can be paid less if they are just repeating what an algorithm spits out than if they required judgment. All these changes reduce labor costs.

These shifts have a second effect, however: a centralization of power. There are no longer multiple nodes of cognitive expertise in organizations, because cognitive labor is centralized in management and those who program the algorithms. This mirrors the elimination of the practical expertise of craftsmen seen in Taylorism. Other workers become expendable, decreasing their ability to protest decisions. Beyond individual organizations, such algorithmic systems tend to centralize power throughout society and the economy. Because machine learning thrives on more and more information, those companies that gain an early advantage in a sector tend to swiftly attain an almost insurmountable dominance, as with Google in web searches and advertising.[18] This trend centralizes economic power, reinforcing gross wealth inequalities and undermining the operation of free market competition. Finally, the way that these modes of surveillance and machine learning can be networked conjures totalitarian scenarios of political and social control. Though many might be tempted to dismiss such Orwellian nightmares, the emerging Chinese system of social credit (let alone the darker picture of its security apparatus in Xinjiang) should give such scoffers pause. This interlocked system analyzing personal responsibility, economic productivity, and political reliability and tying the results to benefits like decreased hotel costs as well as to basic liberties like freedom of movement suggests the baneful uses to which the growing number of new authoritarian regimes may put these technologies.

OBJECTIONS

Despite such reasons to be skeptical of these technologies, there are some genuinely good motivations for these algorithmic tools; and these, I would guess, are the intentions that consciously motivate most of those who develop them. Here, I briefly discuss four. To take one already mentioned, such algorithmic tools should improve efficiency. This is not a bad thing. Algorithms speed up operations because they can handle more data than humans. Although they do obviate the need for some jobs, this is also not always a problem. Few would say that it was a negative outcome when human computers, as they were called—who performed the detailed mathematical calculations for industry, science, and the military—were replaced by digital computers or calculators, which would allow anyone to swiftly perform such calculations at their desk. Insofar as such efficiency provides a net benefit to society, it may be something to be welcomed.

On a similar note, these algorithms may provide more accurate predictions. They can handle the tremendous amount of data produced every day and transform these data into useful insights. Humans are much slower and less able to integrate all these reams of Big Data. Thus, such programs can help to predict new health issues, determine signs of a disease, find patterns in social media that suggest a danger of political violence, or detect terrorists. Such predictive accuracy could be a tremendous gain.

Third, as objective machines, they could reduce bias. Many decisions in society pertaining to hiring or sentencing may be biased due to characteristics like race or sex, perhaps due to unconscious bias on the part of managers and judges. As the anthropologist Hugh Gusterson notes, "There is an idealistic impulse underlying much bureaucracy: the ideal that everyone will be treated equally, fairly, and in accordance with rationally configured administrative procedures."[19] Perhaps machines could avoid such subjective bias by inserting objectivity into the process.

Finally, these machines promise safety. Perhaps the most popular example of this claim regards self-driving cars.[20] Tens of thousands of people die every year on the road. By removing the distracted, fallible, sometimes drunk human drivers from the road and entrusting traffic flow to interlocked, coordinated self-driving cars, proponents argue that those numbers could be reduced to near zero. Or take predictive policing algorithms that use past crimes and other kinds of data to predict where future crimes might occur. They allow police departments to concentrate resources in those areas and prevent it. Thus, AI may lead to greater security, one of the chief aims of our society.

These would be strong reasons in favor of these technologies. The problem is that they are all questionable, especially given the current system of power that uses these programs and its underlying anthropology. The easiest to refute is the claim that algorithms eliminate bias. There have been many examples showing that algorithms are often no less biased than humans. Often, seemingly objective systems of predictive risk can be used to hide social bias. For example, Amazon developed a machine-learning system to sort through résumés.[21] The developers fed in the résumés of candidates who were hired or not hired in the past so that the program could learn the characteristics of the population of hirable employees. Yet, when tested, the program systematically excluded women. Prior bias in Amazon's hiring practices became embedded and intensified in the program. Amazon never could determine how to correct the problem. Past data include past discrimination, even in predictive policing algorithms.[22] Seemingly objective statistics can hide structural racism. Non-machine learning algorithms constructed by individuals can incorporate bias as well. An algorithm meant to predict the probability of recidivism to inform parole decisions was systematically biased against African Americans, under-predicting white recidivism. It is unclear why this happened, because the algorithm was proprietary.[23] This points to another problem: the opacity of these systems. Machine-learning systems cannot tell the operator why they made a decision, so one must take the result on faith. They learn on their own and come up with their own forms of prediction. This leads to questions of how the user can ever be certain of their accuracy and efficiency.

Further, there are reasons to question claims of safety. Although these systems might improve some forms of routine safety, their systematic, centralized nature creates risks of catastrophic failure.[24] As chapter 10 discusses, if something unpredictable happens, the system is put at great risk. Centralization itself creates new vulnerabilities. Take the interconnectedness necessary for the machine learning and the consequent software updating necessary for self-driving cars. This system means that if the program develops an error or vulnerability, it will be repeated in every car. These cars are also vulnerable to malign actors, as they can be easily hacked. Further, these programs are vulnerable when faced with scenarios that they have not encountered.[25] Generally, society previously has handled such problems by distributing decision-making authority to individual human actors, reducing systematic vulnerabilities and allowing flexibility in the face of novelty. Such distribution is nonideal, if not impossible, for AI. Moreover, though frequently systems allow humans to take over in case of unforeseen situations, these human–machine combinations do not work very well in practice. The human operators fall out of practice, eventually finding themselves unable to make the necessary judgment.[26] They also tend to trust the systems over their own sense of the world, so disempowered have they become. These systems therefore will not ensure safety.

The deeper problem with these seemingly beneficent reasons, however, is the picture they paint of human practical reason. These justifications for AI all rely on a deep antipathy to the human mind. Human reason is biased, inefficient, lacks the ability to keep up with the world around us, and is ultimately untrustworthy. People need machines to organize their lives for them. Behind these reasons lies, even more than the "nonhuman" that Guardini discusses, an antihumanism found also in transhumanism and some forms of deep ecology.[27] Pope Francis and the Congregation for the Doctrine of the Faith rightly reject this antihumanism.[28] Made in the image of God, humans have the responsibility to care for themselves and the world around them.

HUMAN ABDICATION OF WILL

Given these problems, it would be easy to describe the broader concern with algorithms as purely a concern over power. A hermeneutic of suspicion suggests that these phenomena are merely the latest step in capitalist expropriation or government centralization, perhaps justified by an antihumanist ideology. There is some truth to these characterizations, but they are not complete. As these systems remove personal responsibility, they also have implications for our self-understanding. Guardini argues, "Once action ... is no longer morally answerable, a peculiar vacancy appears in the actor.... He no longer seems master of the act; instead, the act seems to pass through him, and he is left feeling like one element in a chain of events."[29] The person becomes a natural cause rather than a free, personal cause. As Weil says in the epigraph to this chapter, "he gives himself up to the law of gravity." This is exactly what Zigon describes happening in the case of the operator in the example that opened the chapter. The operator became a node for transmitting the decisions of the algorithm. This is, of course, not to claim that this did not happen under older bureaucratic forms. Instead, algorithms mark an acceleration of older trends.

If explanations were to merely foist blame on others (capitalists, managers, bureaucrats), they would miss what is perhaps the most disturbing aspect of this trend, which is that people in some cases desire this abdication of responsibility. Thinking of German capitulation to Nazism, Guardini reflects, "In the long run, domination requires not only the passive consent, but also the will to be dominated, a will eager to drop personal responsibility and personal effort."[30] Already, people are choosing the loss of agency.

This choice occurs in one of two ways. The first is merely the shirking of the weight of responsibility and prudence in favor of a purely technical morality, a morality that would give a clear answer through a moral calculus. Guardini notes a fallen human tendency: "In us there is the inclination to make things easier for ourselves, to do away with our burdens."[31] He describes the two sources from which people draw for such a technical morality. The first is a deontological system of total rules. This formalism is damaging: "Our moral life is becoming impoverished because it is becoming a mere matter of routine: because for long, under the influence of a rationalistic ethical code, of Kantian formalism, and of an empty moral schematism, it was regarded as a fulfillment of prescriptions."[32] The other is a detailed utilitarian cost/benefit analysis, which hides the use of power "behind aspects of 'utility,' 'welfare,' 'progress,' and so forth."[33] When people seek security in a system of total prediction that will give them control over the future, the managerial responsibility that they assume must be made secure by a moral system. However, falling back on a calculus of either a deontological or utilitarian type fails to display the properly free Christian and human virtue of prudence.

Algorithms are a grave temptation to such a moral failure. Already in the early 1980s, Joseph Ratzinger had determined that the abdication of moral responsibility would be one of the chief dangers of technology. People would seek safety through clear rules, thus embracing a freedom-denying form of rigorism condemned by the Magisterium.[34] These fears have been confirmed by the onset of new technologies. Many of the decisions in which algorithms are now being employed are properly ethical judgments: parole, medical treatment, insurance coverage, loan eligibility, and so on. People long to be divested of the burden of choice for such decisions and thus welcome a seemingly more objective decision-maker. Marie David argues that such desires to abdicate responsibility lie behind the push for self-driving cars.[35] One might argue that this is merely the result of the explosion of choice in contemporary life, if it were not for the fact that it predates it.

Natasha Dow Schull shows that this is the case even for less weighty decisions tied to temperance and health. Her case study of the Quantified Self movement shows the rapid shift from the embrace of increased responsibility that technology enables to design decisions that offload responsibility onto the device. The Quantified Self is a movement that seeks to track and quantify ever greater aspects of our lives, using self-logging sensors like Fitbit: it records heart rate, blood pressure, number of steps taken, sleep patterns, and so on.[36] The person can then use this information to transform her life in targeted ways and hopefully improve her health. It has also been expanded to other areas of life, such as productivity or mood. Though there are many problems with the attempt to know oneself by knowing one's numbers, what is interesting for this chapter is the shift that has occurred with regard to these technologies. Initially, these tracking devices sought to give the person greater self-knowledge.[37] The individual tried to analyze and interpret her data herself. Such self-analysis would give her insights to change her routines. Paradoxically, as Andreas Bernard suggests, quantified self technologies promised to promote "the autonomy of its customers by means of behavioristic control mechanisms."[38] All this was carried out through her own agency, and the individual's reason and will were necessary components.

Swiftly, however, the instability of this model made itself known, and the technology design changed. Instead of being merely informative, the devices became directive. They are now disciplining, in the Foucaultian sense of both surveilling and constraining behavior through data-based nudges. Take the HAPIfork, for example.[39] An early tracking device might have just told the user how long she was sitting at meals, how many times she used her fork, and the interval between uses. All this information would have allowed her perhaps to understand that she was eating too quickly, a behavior that can exacerbate weight gain. Thus, she could have attempted to eat more slowly. In contrast, HAPIfork records the interval between each time the user raises a fork to her mouth and vibrates if the time interval is too short, indicating that she is eating too quickly. This nudge provides a Pavlovian external signal to train one to eat more slowly. This kind of external direction is also included in many other devices, such as the Fitbit that will buzz if the user has been sitting "too long" to encourage her to stand or take a walk.

In such cases, agency has been transferred from the person to the device, with the person becoming the obedient follower of the device's directives. It is not the same as the externalization of will discussed in chapter 7, because the user is no longer consciously engaged in setting the routine. She is relying on the device to direct her. Although one could take this as her delegating agency to the device's programmers, albeit a delegation taking the singularly unpleasant form of a fork vibrating in her mouth, it is not an intersubjective reliance on another, because the programmers are anonymous. In any event, the important aspect of this example for my argument is the trend toward increased reliance on the machine and what it indicates. This is not a grasp for power over the lives of users on the part of the technology company, because designers made this shift in response to consumer desire: "Consumers of wearable technology are—quite desperately—looking for a way to relieve themselves of the work of anticipation, or at least to share the burden."[40] Directive devices sell better because consumers tire of the need to track such things. Consumers are "desiring *not* to be in charge; the technology presents itself as a solution to this desire" (emphasis in the original).[41] Although one might be sympathetic to the desire to avoid this kind of self-analysis, it still is fascinating that people want to have their behavior directed in this way.

If that first set of examples points to a delegation of agency, which may or may not be troubling depending upon the exact situation, a second set of examples points to a troubling desire to lose agency altogether, to engage in a form of ersatz agency managed by algorithms. Many programs manipulate aspects of human psychology tied to reward and expectation in order to help individuals attain a state of altered consciousness similar to that of the flow state described by the psychologist Mihaly Csikszentmihalyi.[42] The foundational work in this area is Schull's *Addiction by Design*, which describes the evolution of machine gambling.[43] Designers of gambling systems realized that if they could use features of their interface to set the win rate to a certain point, crafted in relation to the specific player, then they could entice players to play for longer periods.[44] In these designs, they are drawing on Skinner's work on variable reinforcement.[45] Cognitively, humans get pleasure from the moment of expectation that occurs after they hit the button. Uncertainty adds to this pleasure, as long as the winnings occur just frequently and unpredictably enough.

As this shows, these systems do not seek to eliminate choice, because people also enjoy the feeling of making simple choices. But the focus is on simplicity, having only a feeling of agency in the world rather than a true ethical engagement with reality. One gambler explained, "I was addicted to making decisions in an unmessy way, . . . to engaging in something where *I knew what the outcome would be*. . . . Either I'm going to *win* or I'm going to *lose*. . . . So it isn't really a gamble at all—in fact, it's one of the few places I'm certain about anything."[46] In these simple decisions, gamblers escape the world of complex prudential or risk analysis. This form of simple, certain action is so desirable that players will stay at the machines for hours, enduring great physical discomfort, with one woman even wearing two pairs of wool pants so that others would not notice that she was wetting herself in her many consecutive hours of play.[47]

Even more than the experience of simplified choice, however, the gambler desires to enter into a certain state of consciousness, described as the "machine zone." Players are not playing to win; they want to enter "a steady, trancelike state that 'distracts from internal and external issues.'"[48] This state is tied to an interruption of their everyday temporality, separating them from the stream of time and its endlessly ramifying choices.[49] By escaping time, they also escape their often-tragic pasts and their failed relationships. Even more troublingly, this experience eliminates all intersubjective relationality as they become attuned to the machine alone.[50] In the end, the players even seek to escape themselves, to disappear, to be nothing.[51] For one player, the video poker machine is "a vacuum cleaner that sucks the life out of me, and sucks me out of life."[52] In another article, Schull describes how an online poker player desires to become a robot so that she can respond to games optimally with neither thought nor emotion.[53] As willed action disappears into automaticity, these players get closer and closer to what Schull refers to as self-erasure or self-liquidation.

This paradigm of tailoring algorithms to drive people into altered consciousness and ersatz action has become a more generalized design principle, so it is important not to tie it only to clear pathologies such as addiction.[54] It is used in computer games, of course, but also in Netflix binge watching, in Facebook likes, swiping right on Tinder, and many other domains. I think of all the times that I have logged onto my computer just to check my email and have lost myself in searching the web, coming back to conscious life only to notice that a half hour of wasted time has passed. Companies use these techniques and algorithms to suck people into zones of altered experience that lead them to spend more time on each site, time that translates into advertising dollars.

The desire to escape from oneself is an even a broader phenomenon that sometimes occurs in the real world in a way that does not depend on algorithms, as many anthropologists have found. Joshua Burraway describes the blackout state intentionally sought by homeless addicts as a way to escape their troubled pasts and bleak futures by exiting from time and memory.[55] Caitlin Zaloom describes how commodity traders try to disconnect themselves from their total rational understanding of the world so that they can enter into "the zone," in which they are completely responsive to market movements: "Traders speak of their best trading moments in ways that make them sound like mystical engagements. They need to abandon self-consciousness to gain full access to the market's interior and use discipline . . . to enhance their abilities to read, interpret, and ultimately merge with the market."[56] These all become ways to make behavior automatic rather than freely responsible. Though more widespread than just computer programs, AI provides a finely honed tool to give these experiences to broader segments of the population.

THE EMERGENCE OF THE DEMONIC

In these dual aspects of algorithmic judgment, theological concerns emerge. As Guardini notes, "There is a growing sense of there being no one at all who acts, only a dumb, intangible, invisible, indefinable something which derides questioning. . . . Seemingly incomprehensible, it is simply accepted as a 'mystery,' . . . and as such draws to itself those sentiments, in distorted form, which a man is meant to reserve for his fate, not to say, God."[57] Zaloom's traders submit to the market, speaking of it in religious ways.[58] Schull's gamblers ask, "What is this thing controlling me?"[59] Others see AI as the solution to our social problems. Many in contemporary society put their faith in the power of expert quantitative risk analysis and new technologies (nudges, social physics, AI) to solve the problems of medicine, science, workplace management, urban design, warfare, and so on. Faith in God disappears into this alternative faith, which is ultimately an idol.

This external form of idolatry has an internal counterpart. As Schull describes them, these systems make use of personal desires to escape oneself. People face existential meaninglessness and are struggling with the demands of contemporary life: work stress, unemployment, failed relationships. More deeply, they face the anxiety of increased choice and responsibility. They want to escape this anxiety but can do so only through manufactured choice. Fundamentally, they are despairing, one variety of which is the desire to escape oneself. They are like the people described by Kierkegaard: "For what he . . . despairs over is precisely this: that he cannot consume himself, cannot be rid of himself, cannot become nothing."[60] Through algorithms, as well as by other means, a person can achieve a similitude of this desired nothingness.

Yet this internal and external vacancy the person experiences with the loss of agency does not remain void. It "is succeeded by a faithlessness which hardens to an attitude, and into this no man's land stalks another initiative, the demonic." As Guardini argues, "There is no being without a master."[61] Through growing power over the world, humanity has become responsible for it, a duty of stewardship emphasized by Pope Francis.[62] However, "When man fails in his responsibility toward the being which he has taken from nature, that being becomes the possession of something anonymous," something demonic.[63] We have given over much of the management of society and the environment to impersonal markets or bureaucratic and technological systems, systems that structurally undermine individual abilities to act as agents responsible for others. Humans are no longer acting responsibly toward that for which they are stewards. Systems seem to run on their own, leaving the question as to what is directing them. This description of the problem points back to a fundamentally Augustinian analysis of such social systems deprived of human responsibility that ensnare humans in another logic. Nature abhors a vacuum, so the emptiness caused by the contemporary evacuation of agency longs to be filled. Guardini offers a threefold framework of the demonic: a certain form of alienating social or cultural arrangement that becomes idolized; a vacancy within the self, longing to be filled; and a personal presence that ultimately lies behind both.

Guardini would distinguish such frameworks as demonic because they undermine the ability of the person to understand himself as a free actor in the world. In this way, they undermine, or rather parody, the image of God— insofar as this is characterized by reason and free will. The person divests himself of agency, entrusting it to the algorithm. Though the person engages in action (pushing buttons, swiping right, clicking likes), these are pointless actions with no efficacy in the world. As the individual becomes more embedded in such practices, an emptiness appears that will be filled by something. Sometimes the emptiness is already in service to something, such as the market idolized by commodity traders, which is seen by them as having providential power to punish the disobedient. This service leads to a parody of mystical experience. Losing oneself in God becomes merely losing oneself in the machine.

CONCLUSION

These problems represent the culmination of the first two parts of this book. Faced with the responsibility for all possible futures placed on him by managerial responsibility and knowing that he will bear the brunt of the consequences of his choices under neoliberal responsibility, the person blinks. Dizzied with anxiety over the future, he falls, plunging into immanent goods and false choices. He forgoes the freedom with which he was endowed in order that he might use it to seek the true, eternal good. Instead, he gradually becomes enmeshed in false goods, and his exercise of freedom becomes more and more ensnared by automatic responses. He is *delivered over* to something outside him, which is the original meaning of addiction in Latin and law.[64]

This is not only the situation with electronic devices and behavioristic systems. Many today—facing the meaninglessness of a purely immanent world, crushed by the weight of responsibility, undermined by unjust systems, and lacking a viable future or a viable self—seek solace in various releases: drugs, food, or the ultimate ersatz freedom, the freedom of self-destruction in suicide.[65] Diseases of despair surround us, devouring our contemporaries. Much of this is an attempt to erase the meaningful connection of past, present, and future that makes up the self.

These problems are not new. People have always sought to avoid freedom for excellence by the false freedom of choice of lesser goods. This is the life of the flesh, which entraps our will, the law of sin that wars against the spirit.[66] What is unique about today's situation is that there are much more powerful systems of governance that aid this drive for self-erasure. They seek to control us by embracing the semblance of freedom found in stimulus/response behaviors, and thus move beyond freedom and dignity. They will grant the immanent goods we desire, in a paternalistic fashion, just as long as we undertake our role as an appendage of the machine. It seems inevitable, and even those in power seem to have no control. Arendt said that only scientists acted in the modern world, but, in the contemporary world, only the environment or technology acts.[67] The future is foreclosed in a predictable network by erasing the capacity for novel human action, one of the primary sources of uncertainty in the Aristotelian vision, and thus better ensuring control by those with political or corporate responsibility.

As we drift further and further into this future, the task for part III of the book is to recover a picture of human action under uncertainty that can escape this iron cage. The answer is found by realizing that freedom and action can exist only when responsibility is limited. One can find these limits only by entrusting oneself to another. Chapter 9 first explores Christian responsibility envisioned as a response to God, entrusting oneself to God, a response that enables new action by drawing on past narratives and faith in God's providence. With this framework, we can envision uses for quantitative risk assessment and these other technologies in the process of prudential reasoning that do not cause problems. Such action, however, can occur only within forms of community that enable dependence, an entrusting of ourselves to others. Only such a mode of action and community will enable people to form a relationship with time that is not exclusively characterized by anxiety and regret.

NOTES

Weil, "Love of God," 49.

1. Cheney-Lippold, *We Are Data*, 201–5.
2. Zigon, "Can Machines Be Ethical?," 1011–14.
3. Carr, *Glass Cage*; David, "AI."
4. Zigon, "Can Machines Be Ethical?," 1013.
5. Guardini, *End of the Modern World*, 109–10n2.

6. This is an intensification of what Kathryn Tanner has described as the self evacuation of call center employees in *Christianity and the New Spirit of Capitalism*, 68–70.

7. Guardini, *End of the Modern World*.

8. By postmodern, I do not mean to highlight those thinkers who generally are described by that adjective—Derrida, Deleuze, et al. Instead, I mean to refer to a time period and its social structures.

9. Guardini, *End of the Modern World*, 70, 123–34.

10. Guardini, 133–36.

11. Guardini, 126; Francis, *Gaudete et exsultate*, 160–61.

12. Guardini, *End of the Modern World*, 70. In German, he used the word "*nicht-humanen*"; Guardini, *Das Ende Der Neuzeit*, 85.

13. Guardini, *End of the Modern World*, 69. For a similar critique of the technological buffers surrounding contemporary experience, see Crawford, *World beyond Your Head*.

14. Guardini, *End of the Modern World*, 70.

15. Guardini, 70.

16. Guardini, 123.

17. The literature on the problem of machine responsibility is vast, but for overview see Bostrom and Yudkowsky, "Ethics of Artificial Intelligence."

18. Zuboff, *Age of Surveillance Capitalism*.

19. Gusterson, "Introduction: Robohumans," 5.

20. For discussion, see David, "AI and the Illusion"; Crawford, *Why We Drive*.

21. Dastin, "Amazon Scraps Secret AI Recruiting Tool That Showed Bias against Women."

22. Richardson, Schultz, and Crawford, "Dirty Data, Bad Predictions."

23. Angwin et al., "Machine Bias." For a more general discussion of racial and other kinds of bias in these systems, see Benjamin, *Race after Technology*; Eubanks, *Automating Inequality*.

24. Taleb, *Black Swan*; Goldin and Mariathasan, *Butterfly Defect*.

25. Larson, *Myth of Artificial Intelligence*.

26. Carr, *Glass Cage*.

27. For discussions of the antihumanism of these movements, see Dupuy, *Mechanization of the Mind*; McKenny, "Transcendence, Technological Enhancement, and Christian Theology."

28. Congregation for the Doctrine of the Faith, *Instructions Dignitas Personae on Certain Bioethical Questions*, 27; Francis, *Laudato si'*, 78, 90.

29. Guardini, *End of the Modern World*, 125.

30. Guardini, 165. For his more explicit reflections on German responsibility for the Holocaust, which also develops some of the themes of the loss of responsibility in the face of seemingly inevitable bureaucratic power, see Guardini, "Jewish Problem."

31. Guardini, *Conscience*, 49.

32. Guardini, 32.

33. Guardini, *End of the Modern World*, 133. For this desire for a ready ethical algorithm, see Hasselberger, "Ethics beyond Computation."

34. Ratzinger, "Technological Security."

35. David, "AI and the Illusion."

36. For background on the Quantified Self, see Droge, "What Is Quantified Self?"; Lupton, *Quantified Self*; Schull, "Sensor Technology and the Time Series Self"; Schull, "Data for Life."

37. For a nuanced discussion of the positive benefits of this way of using these devices, see Schull, "Data-Based Self."

38. Bernard, *Triumph of Profiling*, 90.
39. Schull, "Data for Life," 323. For more details on this product, see "HAPIfork."
40. Schull, "Data for Life," 329.
41. Schull, 330.
42. Csikszentmihalyi, *Flow*.
43. Schull, *Addiction by Design*. For later work on these problems, see Alter, *Irresistible*; Zuboff, *Age of Surveillance Capitalism*.
44. Schull, *Addiction by Design*, 118.
45. Schull, 108.
46. Schull, 208.
47. Schull, 179.
48. Schull, 18.
49. Schull, 203.
50. Schull, 193.
51. Schull, 12.
52. Schull, 187.
53. Schull, "Abiding Chance," 564.
54. Alter, *Irresistible*.
55. Burraway, "Remembering to Forget."
56. Zaloom, *Out of the Pits*, 135.
57. Guardini, *End of the Modern World*, 125.
58. Zaloom, *Out of the Pits*, 139.
59. Schull, *Addiction by Design*, 233.
60. Kierkegaard, *Sickness unto Death*, 49.
61. Guardini, *End of the Modern World*, 83.
62. Guardini, 83; Francis, *Laudato si'*.
63. Guardini, *End of the Modern World*, 84.
64. "Addiction, n."
65. For the notion of the lack of a viable self, see Davis, *Chemically Imbalanced*.
66. Rm. 7:14–15, 22–23.
67. Arendt, *Human Condition*, 323–24.

PART III

A Christian Approach to Risk and Decision Theory

9

Christian Responsibility

The new man we have in mind is also profoundly aware of
the dangers inherent in present-day conditions. . . . Current . . .
contempt for bourgeois dependence on carefully precalculated
security . . . seem[s] to point that way. The man in question can
live danger. . . . Yet he does not treat danger as a mere adventure;
his typical reaction to it is a sense of responsibility for the world.

—*Romano Guardini*

Whoever wishes to guide others toward the pure development
of their individuality must guide them towards a trust in
God's providence and towards the readiness to regard
the signs of this providence and to follow them.

—*Edith Stein*

Part I of this book explored the problems and temptations that can arise
when the techniques of quantitative decision theory dominate practical
reason. Part II showed the dangers in these techniques' treatment of others
as objects or instances of a population. Taking these dangers into account,
this chapter and the other chapters in part III ask how a Christian should go
about engaging these techniques, which have very powerful uses for good
and can prevent great harm. To explore this question, this chapter examines
alternatives to the secular visions of responsibility discussed in chapter 6.
These Christian understandings of responsibility see it as always engaged
with another person, either another human or God. In so doing, it eschews
the totalizing responsibility of the managerial paradigm, the "precalculated
security" Guardini criticizes, because the individual actor cannot be held
to account for the whole world. The impersonal providence of the market
also is inadequate, with its treatment of danger as "mere adventure." Instead,

the third model looks to the personal, providential care of the living God that Edith Stein embraces and aims to manifest this providence to others. The intellectual roots of this model of responsibility are found not in utilitarianism or liberalism but in early Christian thought as it was influenced by Stoicism. Before engaging these discussions, it is first necessary to situate this idea of responsibility in relation to practical reasoning and prudence. This framing will show how this chapter's investigation will contribute to a broader framework for the problem of risk and practical reason that is the aim of part III and the book as a whole.

TWO EMPHASES IN PRUDENCE

There are many steps in a prudential decision, but here I highlight two essential aspects: the initial perception of a situation that inspires the intention toward an end, and the determination of a plan to pursue that end. These two aspects are in fact inseparable for proper action, but they are conceptually distinct.[1] Indeed, two of the major schools of ethical thought in Antiquity tended to primarily focus on only one or the other of these aspects. Stoics focused on the initial source of action in a person's response to a situation, asking the question, Does this inspiration to action arise from a proper judgment of the situation and the world? In contrast, Aristotelian discussions of action tended to focus on planning the means to achieve the end and determining the morality of these means. In modern action theory, especially of the Catholic variety, this second aspect emerges as a detailed examination of the different parts of action. These two schools highlight different but interrelated parts of the moral life.

For the philosopher Josef Pieper, prudence is at heart about correctly perceiving a situation: "The pre-eminence of prudence means that realization of the good presupposes knowledge of reality. He alone can do good who knows what things are like and what their situation is. . . . Realization of the good presupposes that our actions are appropriate to the real situation, that is to the concrete realities which form the 'environment' of a concrete human action; and that we therefore take this concrete reality seriously, with clear-eyed objectivity."[2] The actor finds herself in a certain situation, confronted by a certain state of the world. Her response to this situation begins with an interpretation: What is required of me here? What ends must be pursued? It is this interpretive step of moral judgment that the Stoics made central, arguing that vice and error always arise from a misperception of reality. If the agent judges that money is a good, for example, then she will be moved to pursue money. The Stoics thus encouraged the agent to consider money, and all material and bodily goods, as indifferent, things that could be either good or bad for the person. In this way, she would consider the better question of whether pursuing money at this time would be proper. Is this object that presents itself to desire good absolutely, and if not, how does it relate to the true good?

For the Stoics, passion and action flow from (and passions, in some sense, just are) judgments about the situation facing the actor. That is why judging perceptions rightly is the key to Stoic ethics. As Epictetus says again and again, our judgments are the only things that are up to us.[3] The actor cannot ensure that action will succeed or that all the consequences of action will be good, but she can ensure that she first judges the situation well. To have that right judgment, her whole perception of the world must be correct. She must properly ascertain her relations and obligations, recognizing the true value of the goods and the possible ends that the world places before her. Key to this model of ethics is a proper response to the world embodied in right judgment of the moment driven by true perception. In many ways, decision theory distracts the agent from this moment of action by diverting attention to future possibilities.

The second essential step of action, the one to which Stoics paid much less attention, is the turn from that basic judgment of the world to the pursuit of the means to the end that the agent intends. It is this step that Aristotelian theories highlight, as discussed in chapter 2, though of course the initial interpretation of perception is important for Aristotle. The actor develops the facts recognized about the world into a practical syllogism and then takes counsel about the possible means to achieve his end. For Aristotelians, prudence is primarily about choosing the means to an end—that is, the selection and command of one of these action plans. Such a vision of action is much more focused on the future and planning than the Stoic one but still differs from decision theory in its focus on the end.

These two aspects of action, though conceptually distinguishable, belong together, and they were joined by the Fathers of the Church in late Antiquity, a synthesis found in the writings of John Damascene.[4] In him, one finds both the response to the initial perception followed by the selection of an end. Later, Thomas Aquinas enriched this schema with the full wealth of Aristotelian philosophy. Thus, both aspects are joined in the Thomistic understandings of action. Still, there is strength in noting the difference between these aspects of prudence so that neither is lost. Catholic or analytic action theories have a tendency to analyze the second aspect of planning but frequently lose sight of the importance of a global orientation to the world, endangering ethics with a dry proceduralism.[5] Virtue theory has helped to remedy this neglect. Conversely, a situationism or phenomenological approach focused only on perception can lose track of moral constraints on action. Ethics benefits from a detailed analysis of each of these aspects of action.

Around the middle of the twentieth century, many Christian ethicists centered their thought on the first aspect of action, leading to a Christian ethics of responsibility.[6] This ethics of responsibility, as we will see, differed strongly from the managerial and neoliberal models of responsibility discussed earlier in this book. For the most part, it has fallen out of favor, partly due to its inability to provide action guidance in the way that a rule- or rights-based ethic can, but for other reasons as well. As the theologian Gerald McKenny discusses, this focus on responsibility sought to recover human freedom in the face of two threats: the preponderance of law in early modern Christian ethics and the growth of bureaucratic forms of power.[7] With regard to the legal aspects of ethics, the recovery of virtue and prudence gave much of what a responsibility ethics sought to provide. Yet the call for responsibility can still play an important role in the face of the increasingly manipulative models of power deployed by bureaucratic systems that were discussed in part II of this book. Here I seek to understand Christian responsibility not as an independent ethic but as a modality for understanding this first aspect of prudence. This chapter seeks to grapple with a proper way of perceiving the world that can serve as the spring of moral action. Christian responsibility is the interpretation of this world of action as a calling from God, an interpretation different from managerial or neoliberal responsibility. If one perceives the world rightly, then technical cost/benefit analyses of immanent goods will not dominate action.

However, there is still a need to choose the proper means to attain one's end. In such choices, probabilistic analysis can play an important role. Exploring this second aspect of prudence, the Aristotelian aspect, will be the role of the next chapter. Yet both perception and planning take place in complex social structures that shape both perception and possible paths of action. This third aspect of prudence was considered by the ancients in their political works. These aspects require a deeper analysis of justice and charity. Chapter 11 examines what kinds of social structures shape thinking about risk well and what kinds can properly mitigate risk. If the reader finds that this chapter and chapter 10 do not adequately address the effects of structures of sin, that is because these considerations have been delayed until chapter 11.

CONSCIENCE AND RESPONSIBILITY

This chapter, then, explores how the actor perceives the world in a way that leads to the right intention of a particular end. As noted, many twentieth-century Christian ethicists focused on this problem.[8] Inspired in part by the dangers of totalitarian conformism, and in part by Kantian concerns over heteronomy, these authors staked out a space for the creative action of the individual in response to moral situations. This space stood in contrast to subservience to social or legal norms. As chapter 5 showed, this legal framing of moral action has received the most historiographical attention. For much of the late medieval and early modern periods, moral action was interpreted under the dialectic of law and freedom, with casuistry seeking to determine where law applied and how much space there was for freedom. The goal of these responsibility ethicists was to reframe ethics as the use of one's free action in the service of God.

Protestant and Catholic authors—Karl Barth, Dietrich Bonhoeffer, H. Richard Niebuhr, Bernhard Haring, Romano Guardini, and many others—discussed this modality under the framework of responsibility. Catholic authors also sometimes used the term "conscience" in these discussions, as will become apparent below, making it necessary to distinguish these terms.[9] Conscience, though central to Catholic moral thought, has many different meanings. The earliest meaning emerged in Greek and Latin Antiquity from Stoic thought.[10] For the Stoics, conscience is synonymous with self-consciousness, as illustrated by the many languages that use the same word for both concepts, such as French (*conscience*) and Latin (*conscientia*). It was a particular consciousness of one's moral character, of how one has responded to ethical demands. Such consciousness could spur reform or, as in Pauline thought, accuse one in an ex post facto judicial role.[11] This juridical role of accusation was also found in Epicurean practices.[12]

Hannah Arendt captured the tie between moral conscience and self-consciousness. She observed that there is a doubling of the self in any form of thought, but especially moral thought, because thought is a conversation with oneself.[13] To have a proper conversation, the person must want to spend time with her interlocutor; she must be her own friend.[14] As Aristotle argued, however, only a virtuous person can be a true friend. The person thus must not be in basic contradiction with herself, or she becomes her own adversary.[15] Thus, self-knowledge of fault, if not corrected, torments the person, forcing her to flee herself, not being able to stand the conversation with the vicious person that she herself is.[16] From this insight springs the Stoic analysis of travel: "Though you may cross vast spaces of sea, . . . your faults will follow you whithersoever you travel. Socrates . . . said: 'Why do you wonder that globe-trotting does not help you, seeing that you always take yourself with you.'"[17] Ethics is necessary merely to live with oneself.

For Aquinas, conscience is no longer a retrospective analysis of one's action but is rather the judgment of practical reason in response to a particular situation, "the application of knowledge to some action."[18] Conscience is thus much more closely tied to immediate action in this strand of the tradition. The later casuistical tradition developed the legal undertones of these two forms of conscience, to make it a courtroom in which the demands of law and individual freedom contest in particular cases according to "the practical principles of canon and human law."[19]

In response to the sentimentalists, a fourth strand emerged in which conscience was no longer merely a judgment on the self or situation but also became the voice of morality itself. Rousseau exemplifies this vision: "I have only to consult myself about what I want to do. Everything I sense to be good is good; everything I sense to be bad is bad. . . . Conscience is the voice of the soul."[20] In this vision, "The acts of conscience are not judgments but sentiments."[21] This voice could speak to the individual from beyond the constraints of law and tradition, which are corrupting or inauthentic in the Romantic imagination. In twentieth-century and contemporary Catholicism, all these aspects merged into conscience as a creative individual action of moral imagination in response to the particular situation. For the moral theologian Charles Curran, "The holistic understanding of conscience . . . recognizes the complexity and manifold aspects of decision making," using the four aspects of "reason, grace, emotions, and intuition."[22] Yet this seems a hypertrophy of conscience leading it to consume all the functions of practical reason in a somewhat conceptually undifferentiated mass of elements.[23]

Conscience is therefore an equivocal concept. In this work, I only use the term in a more constrained sense, corresponding to the Stoic/Arendtian or Thomistic formulation, wherein it identifies, respectively, a judgment on the moral quality of one's character or of particular action. The sentimentalist confuses conscience with the passions, with discernment, or with the grounds for moral judgment. The other understandings of conscience as legal space or as creative freedom are related variations on a modality of practical reasoning, a way of seeing the world and moral action in the world. The best insights from these more recent explorations of conscience can be captured through the lens of responsibility with less confusion. In the rest of this chapter then, I use the term "responsibility" in many places where an author such as Haring or Guardini might speak of conscience, and I may use their quotations about conscience to refer to responsibility.

ASPECTS OF CHRISTIAN RESPONSIBILITY

Christian responsibility can perhaps best be illustrated by contrasting it with behaviorist modes of understanding moral action. In these, as shown in the managerial forms of behaviorist technique analyzed in chapter 7, the situation facing the actor appears in the light of physical or biological science: the situation arises from the chance concatenation of circumstances emerging from the blind effects of physical laws. In each situation, the salient goal is future stability and survival through the attainment of certain immanent goods. To attain those goods, the actor engages in calculative reason, working through an estimation of the probable outcomes of possible action. In this calculation, the world, others, and the self are treated objectively, in two senses. First, there is the universal objectivity of this form of calculative rationality. The answer as to what to do in a situation would be the same for everyone, and the same techniques can be used to compute the proper course of action in each situation. Second, it treats others (and the self) as objects to be manipulated. Generally, this manipulation takes place through the use of the environment to shape behavior in a stimulus–response manner. It is thus objective, calculative, universal, and future-oriented. Christian responsibility distinguishes itself from each of these aspects.

Dialogue

First, Christian responsibility is fundamentally intersubjective.[24] Its primary paradigm is dialogue. In his 1963 work *The Responsible Self*, the Protestant theologian H. Richard Niebuhr distinguished three forms of moral thought founded in three visions of the human: utilitarianism, based on the idea of man the maker, who is in control;[25] deontology, based on the vision of a person as citizen or legislator under communal law;[26] and responsibility. This last is founded in "the image of man-the-answerer, man engaged in dialogue, man acting in response to action upon him."[27] It is a social vision of each person existing in a dialogue with others and most especially with God. The world is not determined or a chance concatenation of events. Instead, each situation is consciously brought about by others. This modality of perception also looks at things as part of a patterned whole: "We interpret the things that force themselves upon us as parts of wholes. . . . And these large patterns of interpretation we employ seem to determine . . . our responses to action upon us."[28] By understanding these larger patterns, the agent seeks responses that are fitting for the current situation. Because people exist in an ongoing dialogue, each person is accountable for his or her responses; they can be called by others to account for themselves. This vision is not an atomistic understanding that looks at what may flow from each individual action.

Although this model has been most prominently developed in Protestant ethics, it also has Catholic exemplars. For Bernhard Haring, "The pure type of religious ethic is of the nature of response, in which moral conduct is understood as response to the summons of a person who is holy, who is absolute."[29] The individual acts to realize a fuller relationship with God in response to His call. In some places, however, one sees Haring coming to a closer engagement with managerial responsibility than one finds in Niebuhr, and thus to the risk-based vision of the future. There is occasionally a focus on choice between multiple future possibilities: "The moral decision requires humble and docile attention to the will of God our Creator and Father from the very beginning, but often it is completed by faltering or bold hazard of choice among a multitude of possibilities that lie open before us."[30] For Haring, the actor also becomes responsible for possibly foreseen, even though unintended, effects of action.[31]

Another Catholic exemplar for this responsible mode of engagement in action is Romano Guardini, although he also uses the language of conscience. It is through conscience that one discerns God's will for one's life and for a specific situation and thus acts appropriately. He notes, "The sentence 'I am responsible' . . . signifies that I am asked and must answer. . . . The question to which a personal answer must be given can be asked only by another Person, . . . God."[32] Guardini speaks of conscience as something in me "which responds to the Good, as the eye responds to light."[33] Note the framing in terms of response and dialogue. John Paul II also remarks upon this centrality of dialogue to conscience. As he argues in *Veritatis splendor*, "The importance of this interior *dialogue of man with himself* can never be adequately appreciated. But it is also a *dialogue of man with God*, the author of the law, the primordial image and final end of man" (emphasis in the original).[34] This Good to which one responds is "something living and spiritual" that "touches my conscience in this way."[35] It asks to be realized and is shown in the occasion, the situation in which one finds oneself.[36] Responsibility requires obedience—not to abstract law, as in many caricatures of moral theology, but to a person, God, in a singular conjuncture of circumstances, although, as we will see, virtue and law give material and direction to aid in obedience and discernment.

This attention to dialogical features of action attenuates some of the dangers of too great attention to reason and free will as essential to the image of God. This focus, as developed in chapter 8, may strike many as too closely related to the isolated Enlightenment individual acting on his or her own, focused on rationality and choice. Such a vision of the person has been widely criticized by communitarian, feminist, and many other thinkers. It seems to ignore the social and structural influence on human education and action. Further, a focus on reason and free will may ignore the fundamentally relational understanding of the human that the Trinitarian understanding of the image of God provides.[37]

Although Guardini was concerned that the person develop a sense of interiority that would allow action independent of the mass, he was in no way embracing Enlightenment individualism. Indeed, his focus on "person" instead of "personality" was essentially a move away from such an Enlightenment view of the self-constructing individual.[38] The person could develop to the highest degree of free human action only by deepening in relationship. Most important, this meant one's relationship with God: "Man becomes genuinely a 'Person' when he is faced toward God, is left inviolate in his dignity, is robed with duties no other can assume."[39] However, he also believed that the emerging society that focused less on the individual personality allowed greater room for comradeship and shared devotion to the common good.[40]

More to the point, however, Guardini highlights the fact that one cannot have true relational personhood without developing one's reason and free will more fully. There cannot be an I–Thou relation if there is neither an "I" nor a "Thou." There has to be a "living polarity of person to person," or else "both the genuine 'Thou' and the genuine 'I' are lost."[41] The Trinity is a communion of persons after all. Drawing on a Levinasian understanding of ethics, Zigon shows how such personal responsibility is necessary for a relational ethics.[42] The operator in the story of Mark Hemmings told in chapter 8 failed ethically precisely because she had not developed the independence and mature responsibility to respond to the other on the phone, instead abdicating her reason and will to the algorithm. Sociobiological and neurobiological accounts of the person go even further, theoretically dissolving the individual into networks of genes, neurons, or memes. Intersubjective consciousness would be a folk illusion. As the critical theorist Jürgen Habermas feared, a communicative ethics based on dialogue is impossible in such an account of the person.[43] Intersubjectivity requires subjects, and care requires persons who have the ability to take responsibility.

Interpretation of the Particular and Definite

Second, note the importance of the situation in this vision. One's central interlocutor in this dialogue is God, the ground of the world's existence, who makes gestures and statements and asks questions of the person through the situations in which she finds herself. The world is not a mere outcome of chance and necessity.[44] Everything can be interpreted as an address to the person by God, as the result of His providence for us. As Niebuhr argues, the Christian must see "the presence only of One action in all actions upon it."[45] All things emerge from the one Word of God in Creation from eternity. This shifts the vision of action. Proper prudence must seek above all to interpret every situation as an action by God and then seek to determine what God is saying. Right action, then, consists of responding appropriately to God in faith and trust through word, deed, and thanksgiving: "And my response in every particular action takes the form of response also to the One that is active in it."[46] As Oliver O'Donovan frames it, Christians must "come to know ourselves as agents summoned by God to answer him in action."[47] Life becomes an ongoing dialogue with God and our neighbors, one in which we seek the correct grammar in which to express our love and gratitude.

This interpretation takes account of the individual's unique calling. It is God's demand for her since the situation in which the Good is revealed is nothing less than an expression of God's providence, of God's call to her in the particular moment.[48] Guardini argues that a belief in providence does not lead to a quietism, "but that we should participate in God's care for His kingdom, and share the responsibility for this absolutely decisive concern."[49] Guardini explains that conscience is "the organ of living reality and of the nearness of God, of God's demands."[50] It reveals "the task lying before me, and makes it irrevocably mine."[51] Because of this, action need not lead to anxiety. The Christian knows that God is guiding her through love and holds Creation in His hands.[52] Guardini's work contains similar insights as those found in Niebuhr's work, but developed in such a way as to address many of the concerns raised by risk-based decision theory. There are not a near-infinite set of pregiven possibilities of choice in every situation that call for the minimization of risk. Rather, there is the specific call from God to realize the eternal in the moment. This call is highly particular to the individual, the outcome of her personal history. As Mordecai tells Esther, "Who knows? Perhaps you have come to royal dignity for just such a time as this."[53] In this

"Who knows?" Mordecai demonstrates the difficulty of a certain interpreta
tion of a situation, the provisional nature of all human attempts to discern
God's will. O'Donovan similarly sees the possibility for individual obligation:
"When Paul obeyed the dream summoning him to Macedonia, his course of
action was not only not dictated by a rule, but was one that Jesus at one point
had forbidden his disciples (Matt. 10:5). So we may have obligations which
do not replicate those of any other person."[54] Similarly, Ignatius of Loyola
foresees that God may call different people to take opposing stances on the
same questions, such as when the pope attempted to make a Jesuit a cardi-
nal.[55] Ignatius discerned a need to oppose this move but recognized that God
may call the pope to follow through. Therefore, Ignatius should not be angry
that his own will is thwarted, and no Christian should be too concerned
about outcomes. God may call him to a failed action. This is an important
caveat. God does not call the Christian to will the ultimate providential outcome, but what He wills for us to will, which is revealed through Scripture
and our networks of obligations.[56] In Aquinas's example, the wife of a thief
need not will the thief's execution, even if that is the judge's just sentence
and God's will. The demand of her relationship makes it appropriate for her
to will his release. Responsibility looks to the call of the particular person.

This emphasis is even more apparent in the works of Barth and Bonhoeffer. God can call people to follow his commands in a paradoxical way.
Here I will not embrace Barth's problematic idea of the *Grenzfall*, or Bonhoeffer's call for "a complete renunciation of every law" in the *ultima ratio*.[57]
These seem to allow too much, such as the possibility of committing intrinsically evil actions, opening the door for utilitarianism. Who cannot think
themselves entitled and called to commit evil, destructive actions in a time
of emergency? The valuable intuition behind these ideas, however, is that it
is not always obvious what God calls a person to do. God can call individuals
to respond to a situation in surprising, difficult, and self-sacrificial ways. Nor
are these ideas just blank checks for free action. For Barth and Bonhoeffer,
actions are always under judgment. A person acts, seeking to follow God's
commands, but it is not until all is revealed at the eschaton that he will know
whether he has discerned correctly. Because it is not a strict utilitarian or
deontological calculus, there is always the risk of falling into sin through not
properly attending to God's will.

This is in contrast to managerial responsibility. This mode of rationality is
not calculative. It is interpretive. Nor is it universal. It is intensely particular.
Nor is it a probabilistic decision-making. It is definite and singular. There is
a good to which God calls us in each situation. Yet it also does not embrace
risk, instead seeking the call of God to a singular action.

The Temporality of Now

Christian responsibility also contains a distinct vision of time. As chapter 3 discussed, the Christian vision of time is not the flat chronicity of physics-based secular time. For Niebuhr, time is not envisioned as a line filled with future events that can be completely planned. Instead, it is affected by others in each instance. It is time-full, with each moment of "existence in encounter, in challenge and in response. To be in the present is to be in *compresence* with what is not myself."[58] Because time is an affair of encounter, the course of events is not predictable. One can seek to plan based on past encounters, "but the future which makes a difference to my present action is the future of impending questions to be addressed to me to which I do not know the answer, of actions upon me by new compresences, or of unfamiliar actions upon me by those who have been present to me in my past."[59] The social nature of existence removes the predictability of time.

It is also not an obsessive grasping for control over the future. It is characterized by a concern with the present, with the situation as it presents itself in its urgency: "O that today you would listen to his voice!"[60] The fact that it is *today* is essential. Commenting on this verse, O'Donovan says, "To exercise agency effectively we must consider the time we occupy, formed by what we have learned to love, following what has been achieved for us, yet hearing and making answer now, in this new and instant moment."[61] The future can beckon with its endless possibilities, but the kairos, the opportune moment, is key. This makes it a very different temporal framework from that of managerial responsibility.

Moreover, unlike in probabilistic decision theory, the future is not a mere choice between possibilities. Because the future is living, Guardini says that it requires "real creation; not a mere carrying out of a rule, but the creative realization of something which does not as yet exist."[62] It is the creation of something new, similar to Arendt's understanding of the function of human action. Yet, for Guardini, it is something new that already exists: good action consists of "giving an earthly form to the Eternal and Infinite" to that which exists already through God's creative action but has not yet been given form in time.[63] Time is not dead, pregiven possibilities; rather, it is always alive to the potentiality of the eternal because "conscience . . . is the point where the Eternal enters time."[64]

Edith Stein reflects on this importance of the moment, of now, in order to reject Heidegger's anxiety-ridden understanding of human temporality discussed in chapter 2. The person cannot just hasten into future possibilities because "all moments present a fullness that should be brought out," because

every now is a contact between the temporal and eternal.[65] The resolute com
mitment to chosen possibilities advocated by Heidegger will not relieve the
guilt engendered by the focus on lost possibilities. Instead, it is only when a
person understands time in terms "of an *order* or a *plan*, which the human
being has not herself projected, but in which she nevertheless is included,"
that she can distinguish the limitations of finitude from the denial of obligation.[66] "Even the holy one" will lack time "to fulfill all that is required of him"
and will fail in discernment, but "he will find rest in the confidence that God
preserves the one who is of good will from a tragic mistake, and makes his
involuntary errors serve a good end." As Stein's analysis shows, this framework removes anticipatory regret; there is no need to look at that from which
one is missing out. One is called to the task at hand. Guilt arises only through
the rejection of God's call.

Providence and Limits to Responsibility

Christians can confidently take these risks and engage novelty because they
are aware that there is a providence guiding history. Stein's discussion and
her epigraph for this chapter already note the importance of providence. It is
not the ersatz providence of the invisible hand but the loving providence of
a personal God. Faith in providence and attention to God's call to determine
how one might participate in providence also constrain responsibility, which,
paradoxically, actually enables true responsibility. As Robert Spaemann discusses, "Being responsible for absolutely everything undermines the very
idea of responsibility. . . . A comparison of possible alternative worlds would
be an impossibility, and once we had compared them we would have no criteria for evaluating them."[67] Decision theory is an impossible theory to live.
It is only once he can rely on another who bears ultimate responsibility that a
person can act in the world in which he is placed. Such limitations eliminate
the anxiety over consequences. As Bonhoeffer says, "It is precisely because
it is not its own master, because it is not unlimited and arrogant but crea-
turely and humble, that it can be sustained by an ultimate joy and confidence
and that it can know that it is secure in its origin, its essence and its goal, in
Christ."[68] The limitation of responsibility and the attention to God's command thus, far from removing freedom, enable agency. As Spaemann notes,
"That is why Fichte spoke of 'faith in divine providence' as a condition for
moral action."[69]

John Cassian, the father of Western monasticism, describes how obedience eliminates anxiety over the future.[70] In his *Conferences*, he describes the
"interminable worry" that could attack hermits in the wilderness. Despite

escaping to the desert for the solitude in which to seek perfection, the holiest solitaries were beset by numerous visitors: younger monks seeking spiritual guidance, laypeople seeking intercession, other solitaries showing comradeship. The uncertainty as to whether someone would arrive that day, how many would come, how to meet the demands of hospitality, and how patterns of ascetic prayer would be disrupted could be crippling to the attempt to seek spiritual peace and contemplative perfection. That is why one of the Desert Fathers recommended the communal cenobitic life: through obedience, one did not have to concern oneself with the evils of tomorrow. The cenobite could trust that the needs for hospitality would be met as long as everyone did what was demanded of them. In this way, obedience can dispose of anxiety as the person trusts in God's guidance. Yet Cassian's monk consciously chooses a vocation and a social institution that requires obedience as a means to the attainment of the ultimate end of eternal life.

Moreover, the guilt for past responsibility, which can never be undone in the managerial or entrepreneurial framework, can be removed through the grace of forgiveness. For Spaemann, "It is what has gone wrong in a life, its guilt, that locks us into situations that deprive us of personal freedom to engage, as it were, freely and immediately."[71] As Arendt intuited, God liberates us from the past through the power of forgiveness. This reliance on God limits one's responsibility, allowing agency. It gives a release from past failures and the courage to face the future.

A caveat is important here. Relying on divine providence does not entail an expectation of worldly success or avoidance of suffering, as in versions of the prosperity gospel. God may be calling one to a personal cross, to share in Jesus's suffering. Sometimes the situation will reveal itself as a test, something to be endured. The great spiritual writers speak of difficulties discerning God's will in times of spiritual desolation, apparent abandonment, and suffering. Trust in providence is not meant to be a mistaken conviction that all will turn out well in a temporal sense or a Pollyannaish glad game. Instead, it is a path that leads to peace, but only through the difficult struggles with the self and the world that make up a Christian life.

CARE AND THE LIMITS OF RESPONSIBILITY

Although this vision may seem to be veering toward a neoliberal vision of risk as something to engage, it does not, because of its focus on obedience and care for others. In Bonhoeffer's words, humans have been given deputyship by God to care for others.[72] There are spheres of life that guide and constrain our actions. In each sphere, a person is given certain tasks and people for which he is responsible. His aim is to care for those others in line with God's command. However, responsible "conduct is not established in advance, once and for all, that is to say, as a matter of principle, but it arises with the given situation."[73] One must determine what form of care God calls for in the concrete situation.

As Bonhoeffer suggests, insight into the scope of responsibility comes from social roles. In every social position, others are put in one's care in particular ways. The importance of social relations is also seen in Aquinas's order of charity, in which the person owes more to those more closely united to her.[74] Cicero is perhaps the clearest ancient source for the way that individual characteristics and social roles shape moral action. Drawing on the Stoic philosopher Posidonius, he describes four roles, four *personae*, that shape the moral duties of each person.[75] First is the general one of a rational creature, which is the role that dictates the more universal ethical commands.[76] The second role is the one provided by each person's natural aptitudes and temperaments, which shapes what sort of life he is equipped for and what kinds of tasks he should assume. Although these first two are from nature, the last two roles arise from chance and choice. Contingencies place the individual in particular positions, such as having wealth, or confronts him with particular demands. Other roles he chooses for himself, such as taking up a career in law or philosophy.

Hans Jonas analyzed how these roles make an impact on modes of responsibility. Most obviously, this comes through naturally assumed roles like parenthood, Jonas's primary example of responsibility.[77] Parenthood illustrates many of the marks of responsibility: it involves a power disparity and thus is nonreciprocal.[78] The infant is not responsible for the parent. It is also total and continuous through the early life of the child.[79] The parent is totally responsible for children: their bodily needs, their education, their spiritual development, and so on. In contrast, some responsibilities are self-chosen, such as that of the politician.[80] Political responsibility is total and continuous, providing care for all aspects of communal life.[81] Unlike parenthood, however, one seizes this responsibility for oneself because of a calling. As Jonas argues, "He who feels the calling for it in himself seeks the call and demands it as his right. Public peril in particular, meeting with the conviction to *know* the way to salvation and to be fit to *lead* it, becomes a powerful incentive for the courageous to offer himself and force his way to responsibility," as Churchill did in 1940.[82] Yet this sense of calling could be wrong.

Foucault argues that the most clearly delineated role responsibility in Christian ethics is that of pastors.[83] Scripture is clear about the greater responsibility of those given spiritual care of others, like prophets and pastors. God prophesies through Ezekiel: "If I say to the wicked, 'You shall surely die,' and you give them no warning, or speak to warn the wicked from their wicked way, in order to save their life, those wicked persons shall die for their iniquity, but their blood I will require at your hand."[84] This heavy weight appears in all its difficulty in the sermons of those Church Fathers who were bishops, such as Augustine.

Other responsibilities are self-chosen but more limited. The teacher is responsible for students' education. The business owner is responsible for employees and customers. These role responsibilities provide a limitation, delimiting who falls under the person's care. Yet the responsibility for others also contains limitations on one's duties. It is not the responsibility of managerial responsibility, because it is sharply limited, recognizing that the individual cannot have complete control over the future. It is limited by creatureliness, one's own limitations, so there is no need to attempt to make the world "into the kingdom of God."[85] It is also limited by ignorance of the ultimate good or evil of the action and its consequences—limited insight and foresight. Unlike in the universalized managerial system of utilitarian ethics, each person is not responsible for maximizing all goods for everyone in society. There are people responsible for the community—politicians, for example—but generally all can look to certain others for whose care they are accountable.

Moreover, the aims of these forms of responsibility limit one's power and one's liability. Both parenthood and political life, though forms of total responsibility, aim at socializing the persons in their care into the free way of life of the citizen.[86] They aim to foster the "autonomous causality of the life under his care," preparing the child or citizen for freedom.[87] Raising a child requires giving him freedom. The politician seeks to preserve the preconditions for political existence, so she must not seek to determine all aspects of peoples' lives, as in a behaviorist model, but enable freedom.[88] The other must be recognized as a responsible agent in his own right.[89] Moreover, the parent must also accept God's plan for the other. She cannot try to exercise optimal control over the other's characteristics and future, as in the case of the procreative beneficence discussed in chapter 2. The actor exercises concern for another but does not suffer from the dangers of pride and anxiety because she recognizes limits and trusts in God. The fulfillment of parenthood is in the abdication of responsibility at the child's adulthood and ultimately when the grown child can assume responsibility for the parent once the parent sinks into the vulnerability of old age.[90] These are forms of responsibility limited and bounded by the child's maturation and the freedom of action of one's fellow citizens. Even prophets cannot control action as much as they may warn. Ezekiel is told, "But if you warn the wicked, and they do not turn from their wickedness, or from their wicked way, they shall die for their iniquity; but you will have saved your life."[91] A person must respond as best she can to God's promptings, but ultimately the consequences are not in her hands.

This understanding inevitably changed when pastoral power moved into the hands of the state. Taking responsibility for the whole population and for each citizen individually in all areas of life, the modern secular state cannot rest content in responsible action regardless of the consequences. It only judges the actions of its functionaries based upon statistical outcomes, for example, visible, quantifiable consequences. This fact shifts political reasoning in the direction of consequentialism, which also affects individual responsibility.

But a Christian might ask, does not the Gospel call us to love our neighbors as ourselves, calling us to deep responsibility for each of them? Does not the parable of the Good Samaritan show that everyone is our neighbor? Does this not mean a universal responsibility for the greatest good, as in utilitarianism? Such questions would seem to stand against the limitation of responsibility in this schema and in favor of a more consequentialist stance.

Indeed, these considerations do indicate that our care is not limited to those for whom we are responsible through our social roles, for "Do not even the Gentiles do the same?"[92] However, parables such as that of the good Samaritan show that the expansion of one's responsibilities will come through a careful situational attentiveness to God, as revealed in encounters with others.[93] The Good Samaritan encounters the man beset by robbers in the road; he did not seek him out. Lazarus starved to death in the doorway of the rich man. Dives is not called to account for all the poor of Jerusalem but for ignoring the poor man near him. The enemy whom one is to love is already entangled in a relationship of hostility. Opportunities and duties to show forth God's love beyond the scope of immediate social roles will appear if the agent is attentive to God's voice in his life and the vulnerability that lies before him. These opportunities will appear vocationally: the call to take on a pastoral role, a call to work in the sphere of international aid, a calling to medicine, each of which involves assuming a role of increased responsibility. But God's call to love the neighbor also appears in daily encounters: the homeless person passed on the street, the community action group in the parish, increased involvement with a particular community after a mission trip, the family in crisis at a child's school.[94] If the Christian is constantly attentive to God's voice in everyday situations, she will find many times that she is called to extend her responsibilities beyond those of specific social roles. These extensions come from following God's call and are particularly directed rather than being a generalized responsibility for universal welfare.[95]

This particular-versus-universal calling of responsibility is well illustrated in Evelyn Waugh's Sword of Honor Trilogy. The main character, Guy Crouchback, though old, joins the army at the outbreak of World War II. He wants to bravely take his role in the events of history, assume his part of the responsibility for the fate of the world. But over the course of the war, he becomes disillusioned through involvement with a foolish incursion in Africa, the British disaster in Crete, and repeated experiences of bureaucratic folly and personal humiliation. Finally, it becomes apparent to him that the way he is called to serve God is not to take responsibility for the great events of history. Instead, he is called to adopt an illegitimate child. This involves the humiliating step of taking back the wife who ruined his life by abandoning him years before, who is now penniless and pregnant by another man. Responding to a friend's claim that it is none of his business, he says,

> "It was made my business by being offered."
> "My dear Guy, the world is full of unwanted children. . . . What is one child more or less in all that misery?"
> "I can't do anything about all those others. This is just one case where I can help. And only I, really. . . . So I couldn't do anything else."[96]

This reflects Jonas's claim that the vulnerable newborn elicits the most archetypical claim for responsibility: "Here the plain being of a de facto existent immanently and evidently contains an ought for others, and would do so even if nature would not succor this ought with powerful instincts or assume its job alone."[97] Yet beyond Jonas's metaphysical and moral insight, Guy can regard it as a call to him from God. He draws on his father's insights into the humiliating treaties the Vatican entered into before World War II: "Quantitative judgements don't apply. If only one soul was saved that is full compensation for any amount of loss of face."[98] It is important to note this rejection of quantitative comparison when the concern is with the call to aid souls. Theresa of Avila warns that the desire to do quantitatively more can be a temptation: "The devil sometimes puts ambitious desires into our hearts, so that, instead of setting our hand to the work which lies nearest to us, and thus serving Our Lord in ways within our power, we may rest content with having desired the impossible."[99] Doing the simple task within our power is better than fruitlessly aiming at maximization.

MEMORY

Responsibility thus consists in responding to God's will. Yet it is not the blind assertion of creativity. Nor is it a foolish overconfidence that one can easily interpret a situation. Spiritual writers are clear on the dangers of discernment, as Satan can appear as an angel of light.[100] Conscientious decision requires carefully seeking the right course of action. In order that the Christian might do this well, God has not abandoned him merely to his own reason in this process of discernment but has given him many tools. As Haring notes, he must bear "the responsibility for his free decision in his own particular situation," even while using "the assistance which God offers through authority, through community, through prudent counselors in seeking to discover the divine will."[101] These resources come from one's own and one's community's past experiences.

Aquinas explains the importance of memory for prudence.[102] One needs experience to acquire prudence because experience teaches "what is true in the majority of cases," which is the kind of norm that should direct us in practical matters.[103] Aquinas explains, "It behooves us to argue . . . about the future from the past."[104] This experience can be gained on one's own, for which one needs a good memory, or through others, which is why a prudent person needs docility, the willingness to learn from others.[105] These insights from the past are then applied to the future. One uses the general understanding of what happens in the majority of cases to foresee the future and properly order future contingents to the appropriate end.[106]

This memory, though looking toward past events, is not the simple use of the past as a matrix for probabilistic prediction of the future. Instead, it is the engagement of the past to create a certain kind of narrative imagination, a form of perception. Through docility to the past, one learns the broad Christian narrative of salvation history. Actions must be consistent with that narrative.[107] They must cohere with how God has commanded His people to act in the past. Actions must be assimilable to the models of the Christian life that one finds in that narrative; most centrally in the life of Christ but also the imitations of Christ found in the lives of the saints. The diversity of saints in the Catholic tradition allows for people in every form of life and vocation to find a model to enlighten their path. Through these examples, one sees how others have responded well to God and thus learn the grammar and patterns of a proper responsibility.

Though the moral life is not a series of rule-following exercises, the tradition of Christian moral discourse is also helpful in shaping the moral imagination. The casuistry described in chapter 5 does not provide a deductive method for assuring the actor that she has chosen the correct action, but it does provide a guide as to what sorts of actions are appropriate responses to God's will in certain kinds of situations. Importantly, it indicates what sets of actions are never appropriate, the intrinsically evil actions that can never be ordered toward God, thus preventing a slide into utilitarianism through rationalization.[108] In most cases, however, it merely provides a heuristic that can help guide reflection, leaving much room for discernment. Ultimately, it is through prayer and discernment that one discovers God's will.

CONCLUSION

Saint Joseph perhaps serves as the best exemplar of this model of responsibility. As Pope Francis notes, Joseph, as well as Mary and Jesus, also had to declare his own fiat in response to God's difficult calls, which were in his case revealed in dreams: accepting a pregnant wife, fleeing to Egypt, returning to Nazareth.[109] In so doing, "Joseph set aside his own ideas in order to accept the course of events and, mysterious as they seemed, to embrace them, take responsibility for them and make them part of his own history."[110] He embraced and responded to the mysterious, providential unfolding of God's will. This acceptance did not mean that Joseph was just a passive observer of events. Instead, he showed "creative courage" in fulfilling the ends to which God called him, difficult ends of caring for Mary and Jesus in the foreign land of Egypt.[111] God called him to take responsibility for his family. Through his actions, Joseph becomes a model of Christian practical reasoning.

From this analysis, a number of differences emerge between relational, Christian responsibility and both managerial, especially behaviorist, forms of responsibility and neoliberal responsibility. First, the liability for others is real, against an individualist form of neoliberal responsibility, but it is limited, as opposed to the unlimited anxiety of managerial responsibility. It is limited because it is intersubjective, taking the will and freedom of the other, the other's calling and personal destiny, seriously. The other must be allowed to herself be an actor. These responsibilities are thus limited in scope by social role responsibilities (parent, teacher, employer, et al.) but also in extent. The actor is only placed in relationship with certain others and thus does not have total responsibility.[112] Of course, one must be cognizant and open to being called forth into new relationships of care. Responsibility is also limited by finitude, the fact that humans are not God. God cares for the fate of the world. The actor can trust that God is placing her in the situation

where her action is necessary and will reveal the proper response, given care
ful discernment.

This relationship with God reveals the second difference. The aim is
not success in the market through risk-taking and foresight, as in neoliberal responsibility. It is not self-preservation; nor is it the immanent goods
through which concern is incited under managerial responsibility. Instead, the
Christian aims at the transcendent good, at beatitude. This beatitude is realized through knowledge and love of God, a love expressed through uniting
one's will with God's. It is through loving the image of God in others, even
enemies, and through actions of care, that the Christian wills as God wills,
who "makes his sun rise on the evil and on the good" alike.[113]

This last point illustrates the third difference. The environment is not a
market indicating a price, as in neoliberal responsibility. Nor is it a tool for
the manipulation of behavior, as in behaviorist power. Instead, it is truly a
world, a creation, a space of meaning. It is, in each situation one finds oneself,
a communication from God. As such, it demands interpretation. Thus, indicating a fourth difference, interpretive rather than calculative reason should
rule action. Moreover, it is a specific communication to each individual at
every moment. The situation is not a featureless object, a book open to everyone's universal reason. Neither is it probabilistic in its orientation. It asks for
a definite response arising from a particular person's disposition and history.

As such, it is an urgent call. It does not leave room for tinkering and
gradual experimentation, as the behaviorist model would require. Each historical moment demands a response that is irreversible. The Christian must
act in the today in which she finds herself. There is a demand for a creative
response.

This relational view of responsibility has many advantages, combining
the best aspects of managerial and entrepreneurial responsibility. Like the
entrepreneurial framework, it calls the Christian to risk. As seen in the parable of the talents, God calls us to risky endeavors that are far from sure bets.[114]
Security is a danger for the Christian. God does not call us to embrace a
rationally calculable future, but a new heaven and a new Earth that are right
now available in some way through the inbreaking of the kingdom of God.

Yet this relational responsibility does not entirely reject managerial
responsibility. In some areas of life, one's role appropriately calls for quantitative risk assessment.[115] Those who run businesses must seek to predict possible financial futures. Those developing government policy should develop
cost/benefit analyses and engage the precautionary principle. As chapter 10
discusses, in specific roles, such decision theory can be a valuable adjunct to
prudence.

In these ways, Christian relational responsibility eliminates many of the problems of managerial and entrepreneurial responsibility while maintaining their valuable insights. It constrains the use of quantitative risk assessment and its temporality to certain roles. The person can do this because he trusts in providence and thus has no desire for total control over the future. The Christian responds in faith to the situation where he finds himself. However, this stance is difficult. Quantitative risk assessment arose from the early modern desire to conquer Fortuna in all areas of life, giving stability and control to society. The problems facing us emerged from an understandable desire for security. The next chapter more closely investigates how one might properly use these forms of risk assessment.

NOTES

Guardini, *End of the Modern World*, 200–201.

Stein, *Essays on Woman*, 193.

1. My analysis of Thomistic practical reason is indebted to Westberg, *Right Practical Reason*.
2. Pieper, *Prudence*, 25. One finds this insight in other ethics, such as Barbara Herman's discussion of the perception of morally salient aspects of a situation in Kantian ethics. See Herman, *Practice of Moral Judgment*.
3. E.g., Epictetus, *Discourses*, I.1.
4. Westberg, *Right Practical Reason*, 126–28; John of Damascus, "Exposition of the Orthodox Faith," 2.22.
5. E.g., proportionate reasoning about noncombatant casualties can go badly astray if one does not keep in mind the fundamental Christian opposition to war. Similarly, decisions about ordinary and extraordinary means of care can become restrictive if one does not keep in mind that death is not the end of human existence.
6. Although the authors I discuss in this section were, as a rule, critical of Stoicism, their dependence on Stoic forms of thought appear at key points in their discussions. Crouter, "H. Richard Niebuhr"; Haring, *Law of Christ*, 1:136.
7. McKenny, "Responsibility."
8. For review, see Jonsen, *Responsibility*; McKenny, "Responsibility"; Keenan, *History of Catholic Moral Theology*.
9. For overview, see Curran, "Conscience"; Keenan, *History of Catholic Moral Theology*.
10. Sorabji, *Moral Conscience*, 11–36.
11. Rm. 2:15–16.
12. Sorabji, *Moral Conscience*, 24–25.
13. Arendt, *Life of the Mind: Thinking*, 185.
14. Arendt, 188.
15. Arendt, 186.
16. Arendt, 190.
17. Seneca, *Epistles*, 28.1–2.
18. Aquinas, *Summa theologica*, I-II.19.5.
19. Tutino, *Uncertainty in Post-Reformation Catholicism*, 63.

20. Rousseau, *Emile*, 286. One finds elements of this vision of conscience as the voice of God in the soul in many modern forms of ethics. E.g., see Newman, *Letter to the Duke of Norfolk*, chap. 5. In the Thomistic tradition, this aspect of conscience would be equivalent to *synderesis*, the knowledge of the first principles of natural law that cannot be effaced from the mind, although it can be darkened by vicious habit. For these different senses of conscience, see Pinckaers, "Conscience and Christian Tradition"; Pinckaers, "Conscience and Virtue of Prudence."

21. Rousseau, *Emile*, 290.

22. Curran, "Conscience," 17.

23. For critique of this position, see Pinckaers, "Conscience and Christian Tradition"; Pinckaers, "Conscience and Virtue of Prudence."

24. There are also philosophers who used this approach, perhaps most notably Emmanuel Levinas. See Levinas, *Totality and Infinity*; Levinas, *Otherwise than Being or Beyond Essence*; Waldenfels, *Phenomenology of the Alien*. My analysis bears solely on Christian theological developments.

25. Niebuhr, *Responsible Self*, 48.

26. Niebuhr, 51.

27. Niebuhr, 56. In this work, I do not adopt Niebuhr's system as a whole, but neither do I provide a detailed critique of those aspects with which I disagree. I merely focus on his general approach to responsibility as it relates to God.

28. Niebuhr, 60–61.

29. Haring, *Law of Christ*, 1:35.

30. Haring, 47.

31. Haring, 106–8.

32. Guardini, *Freedom, Grace, and Destiny*, 21.

33. Guardini, *Conscience*, 24. He also addresses responsibility in this work, but he uses it primarily in terms of being answerable, of accountability. See Guardini, 47.

34. John Paul II, *Veritatis splendor*, 58.

35. Guardini, *Conscience*, 28.

36. Guardini, 29.

37. LaCugna, *God for Us*.

38. Guardini, *End of the Modern World*, 62–66.

39. Guardini, 65.

40. Guardini, 66.

41. Guardini, *Freedom, Grace, and Destiny*, 41.

42. Zigon, "Can Machines Be Ethical?"

43. Habermas, *Future of Human Nature*, 105–8.

44. Monod, *Chance and Necessity*.

45. Niebuhr, *Responsible Self*, 126.

46. Niebuhr, 123.

47. O'Donovan, *Finding and Seeking*, ix.

48. Guardini, *Conscience*, 57.

49. Guardini, *Freedom, Grace, and Destiny*, 230.

50. Guardini, *Conscience*, 55.

51. Guardini, 68.

52. Guardini, 58–61.

53. Es. 4:14.

54. O'Donovan, *Finding and Seeking*, 227.
55. Toner, *Discerning God's Will*, 47–50.
56. Aquinas, *Summa theologica*, I-II.19a10.
57. Bonhoeffer, *Ethics*, 236; Barth, *Church Dogmatics*, II/2, III/4. For a discussion of these positions, especially Barth's, see McKenny, *Analogy of Grace*, 225–87; Yoder, *Karl Barth*, 57–102; Biggar, *Hastening That Waits*, 7–45; Clough, *Ethics in Crisis*, 89–103; Werpehowski, "Karl Barth"; Bowlin, "Barth and Werpehowski"; and Puffer, "Taking Exception."
58. Niebuhr, *Responsible Self*, 94.
59. Niebuhr, 95.
60. Ps. 95:7.
61. O'Donovan, *Finding and Seeking*, 145.
62. Guardini, *Conscience*, 32.
63. Guardini, 33.
64. Guardini, 39.
65. Stein, "Martin Heidegger's Existential Philosophy," 79.
66. Stein, 78–79.
67. Spaemann, *Persons*, 99.
68. Bonhoeffer, *Ethics*, 231–32.
69. Spaemann, *Persons*, 100.
70. Cassian, *Conferences*, 19.5–9.
71. Spaemann, *Persons*, 100.
72. Bonhoeffer, *Ethics*, 221ff.
73. Bonhoeffer, 224.
74. Aquinas, *Summa theologica*, II-II 31.3.
75. Cicero, *On Obligations*, bk. I.107-119. For the importance of these roles in Stoic ethics and the Stoic conception of the self, see Reydams-Schils, *Roman Stoics*.
76. This *persona* is where the duties belonging to the natural law, such as human rights, emerge. As noted in the introduction, my analysis here does not question the necessity of such clear ethical constraints, but I do not address them in much depth because my focus is on the actions that do not fall in the domain of the intrinsically evil.
77. Jonas, *Imperative of Responsibility*, 95.
78. Jonas, 93–94.
79. Jonas, 101, 105.
80. Jonas, 96.
81. Jonas, 101.
82. Jonas, 96–97.
83. Foucault, *Security, Territory, Population*, 115–90.
84. Ez. 3:18; see also the discussion of false shepherds in Ez. 34.
85. Bonhoeffer, *Ethics*, 229.
86. Jonas, *Imperative of Responsibility*, 102.
87. Jonas, 107.
88. Jonas, 118.
89. Bonhoeffer, *Ethics*, 231.
90. Jonas, *Imperative of Responsibility*, 108.
91. Ez. 3:19.
92. Mt. 5:47.
93. For a longer discussion of this parable, see Francis, *Fratelli tutti*, 63–83.

94. This distinction between response to the person and bureaucratic forms of universal ized responsibility is at the heart of the discussion of Ivan Illich's view of charity and the Church by Taylor, *Secular Age*, 737–42. For a further defense of the initial primacy of role responsibilities, see Pope, *Evolution of Altruism*.

95. There remain questions of more structural issues of injustice that chapter 11 addresses. Some of these are dealt with through personal choices (e.g., buying products that are ethically made) and through general political involvement as part of the duties of citizens. Others, such as international development, seem more difficult to solve from the perspective offered here. On these issues, see China Scherz's work discussing the ways in which modes of charity characterized by personal interaction, such as school sponsorship or developing a long-term engagement with a particular community, are much more efficacious than the managerial modes of development that currently predominate. See Scherz, *Having People, Having Heart*.

96. Waugh, *Unconditional Surrender*, 623–24.

97. Jonas, *Imperative of Responsibility*, 131.

98. Waugh, *Unconditional Surrender*, 491.

99. Theresa of Avila, *Interior Castle*, 232.

100. 2 Cor. 11:14.

101. Haring, *Law of Christ*, 1:47–48.

102. For the importance of memory to medieval ethics, see Yates, *Art of Memory*; and Carruthers, *Book of Memory*. This section draws on Scherz, "Prudence, Precaution, and Uncertainty."

103. Aquinas, *Summa theologica*, II-II.49a1.

104. Aquinas, II-II.49a1 ad3.

105. Aquinas, II-II.49a3.

106. Aquinas, II-II.49a6.

107. For the importance of narrative, see MacIntyre, *After Virtue*; and Hauerwas, *Community of Character*.

108. John Paul II, *Veritatis splendor*, 80.

109. Francis, *Patris corde*, 3.

110. Francis, 4.

111. Francis, 5.

112. One Christian author who does seem to claim total responsibility for evil is Fyodor Dostoyevsky, who has Elder Zosima make such an argument in *The Brothers Karamazov*. As Robert Spaemann argues, this is not really a consequentialist moral claim but a mystical claim for the need for spiritual perfection. See Spaemann, "Individual Actions," 151–52.

113. Mt. 5:45.

114. Mt. 25:14–30.

115. The development of our technological world has made this framework of relational responsibility seem especially lacking in certain instances, as noted by Schweiker, *Responsibility and Christian Ethics*, 45.

10

The Role of Risk Assessment in Prudential Judgment

As the past has ceased to throw its light upon the future,
the mind of man wanders in obscurity.

—*Alexis de Tocqueville*

As the analysis thus far shows, the quantitative risk analysis used in decision theory and the policy arena presents many problems. On the personal level, it creates anxiety, encourages improper understandings of responsibility, and reinforces an insidious focus on financial security. On the societal level, it creates powerful incentives to undermine autonomy, reshapes temporality, and centralizes power. On the theological level, it undermines trust in providence, a grasp of the eternal, and a proper response to God. Given this list of consequences, a reader would be excused for expecting an argument that the Christian should entirely reject quantitative risk analysis.

Such a rejection would be a mistake. Quantitative analysis of the probability of future scenarios is an extraordinarily powerful tool when used correctly. One might say of it what Foucault said of any form of power: it is not bad, just dangerous.[1] The danger is that such a form of knowledge tied to power will attempt to colonize our entire lifeworld by reshaping the approach to any practical situation. Quantitative risk analysis can present an underlying theoretical model of the world as consisting of predictable and controllable objects. This model, if it becomes hegemonic, tends to deform the first step of practical reasoning: the perception of the world that shapes the actor's response. If one judges the world correctly, however, as created by God and filled with free actors, then it is possible to use these techniques in limited ways. The task of ethics, then, should be to determine the proper use of this technology and to ensure that the requisite limits are maintained. To do so, it is necessary to determine what this technique is good for and where it productively adds to prior models of action.

The proper role for quantitative risk analysis is in the second step of practical reasoning, that of action planning and selection. O'Donovan, drawing on a discussion by Maximus the Confessor, suggests that "the essential element in deliberation . . . is not a comparison but a *search*" (emphasis in the original).[2] Deliberation explores possibilities for the best way forward. In this search, the actor should use all the tools that she can to identify a solution. Quantitative risk analysis is just such a tool. As O'Donovan notes, the emphasis should not be on the comparative aspect of this decision procedure, its promise of placing all possibilities before the actor so that she can find a definitive calculation of the best way forward. Instead, the responsibility to judge right action always lies with the agent. It is always a choice. Nor should the actor dwell on comparisons with other possibilities. Yet the procedure of risk assessment can help to open these considerations up for the step of counsel.

The best-developed model of this second step of practical reason is the Thomistic understanding of prudential judgment, which describes a number of ancillary virtues and aids for proper judgment. As chapter 9 discussed, judgment in the Thomistic tradition is dependent on memory, on the individual using her past experiences, the experience of trusted advisers, her culture, and her tradition of discourse to inform judgment. But it is in the strength of this model, its reliance on history, that a weakness appears. With the rapid development of technology, new forms of social organization, and ongoing attempts to regulate the social world, policymakers are frequently confronted with devices and situations for which memory does not prepare them, for which it is no longer the case that *historia magister vitae*, that history serves as a teacher, as the Ciceronian saying goes.[3] Such novel developments can lead to disastrous effects if not taken into account. It is this break that Tocqueville highlights in the epigraph to this chapter. With these changes and the resulting inadequacy of past experience, the individual is left rudderless in dealing with new situations.

Moreover, as chapter 6 discussed, actors can also become overly focused on certain kinds of dread risks, such as recently experienced or overwhelming dangers. Certain kinds of death or economic outcomes can dominate an analysis. In the process, such analyses can obscure other less common but still significant dangers. Threats to the marginalized are especially easy to ignore because historical experience has frequently included prejudice. Further, the desire to mitigate dread risks can lead actors to ignore the unwanted side effects of mitigation strategies. It is necessary in many cases to force one-self to broaden one's considerations during deliberation.

It is here that quantitative risk analysis can help to make up for defects in older forms of deliberation. As Mary Hirschfeld has discussed in relation to economic analysis, it can help to uncover unusual and nonintuitive effects of policies. It drives the actor to be attentive to a broad array of problems. This is why theologians and policymakers need to embrace it in certain situations. Risk analyses based in decision theory serve as an aid to deliberation by redirecting attention from conspicuous dangers and benefits to the less obvious problems in a policy. This use allows the redescription of Hans Jonas's emphasis on precaution as not so much a deontological norm but a virtue, a disposition to be attentive to the unseen. Because its role here is merely to broaden the deliberative search rather than select the one best option, neither precaution nor a risk analysis threaten to replace human agency and judgment but rather enrich it. In this way, they do not have the same bad effects as when they are used under the form of managerial responsibility. Even then, however, its use should be restricted to certain domains so that it does not overwhelm actors with choices. Decision theory based in risk analysis should cease to be a complete model of decision-making and become what its most sophisticated practitioners already view it as: an aid to prudence in a restricted domain of decisions.

THE STRUCTURE OF PRUDENCE

As a first step, it is important to lay out the Thomistic framework of practical judgment. According to Aquinas, in line with much of the virtue tradition, prudence is "right reason about things to be done" and regulates the means to attain an end.[4] It governs the process of deciding on action. First, as chapter 9 discussed, through rightly formed prudence, a person recognizes the salient practical aspects of a situation, the goods to be pursued and evils avoided. Then the person develops an intention to attain an end.[5] If a proper course of action is not immediately apparent because of the uncertainty of contingent singulars, the prudent person takes counsel on the possible means available to attain the end in the situation along with the benefits and types of harm of each.[6] Then the person judges between these options and chooses one before finally executing the action plan.[7] It is this last step of command that is the proper act of prudence,[8] while the other steps are governed by the three potential parts of prudence: counsel, synesis (judgment of the ordinary), and gnome (judgment of exceptions).[9]

To function properly, prudence needs other ancillary virtues, "things which need to concur for the perfect act of prudence," which are called the quasi-integral parts of prudence.[10] There are eight of these: memory, understanding, docility, shrewdness, reason, foresight, circumspection, and caution. These parts of prudence relate to the temporality of prudence, as described in the section of Cicero's *De inventione* that served as a source of the parts of prudence for the medieval tradition.[11] As Cicero defines these parts of prudence, "Memory is the faculty by which the mind recalls what has happened. Intelligence is the faculty by which it ascertains what is. Foresight is the faculty by which it is seen that something is going to occur before it occurs."[12] This shows how practical wisdom involves an intelligent relation to all three dimensions of time: past, present, and future. The actor recognizes the important lessons from the past in memory, which allows him to understand and interpret the present, which in turn enables him to foresee the future.

Aquinas uses this same temporally inflected model. As chapter 9 discussed, experience teaches "what is true in the majority of cases," which is the kind of norm that should direct us in practical matters.[13] Experience can come from a person's own life, her memory, or from others' experience, which requires docility, a willingness to learn from others.[14] Insights from the past allow foresight with regard to the future so that she can properly order future contingents to the appropriate end.[15] Circumspection (literally, the act of looking around oneself) illuminates particular aspects of the present circumstances that may make the means unconducive to the end.[16] Similarly, caution helps to identify possible obstacles to success or types of evil that may come from good actions.[17] Thus, the actor foresees the future and takes steps to prevent dangers arising from action.

MEMORY IN THE CONTEXT OF NEW DANGERS

The importance of memory reveals a problem. Traditionally, history was taken as a model for current action. The virtuous person learned how to act in a present crisis from important past exempla. Underlying this vision was a conception of the world whereby the basic shape of political and personal life remained relatively stable between the past and the present. Because the past actor faced the same basic conditions as the present actor, the present actor could analyze the future outcome of a policy based on how it had played out in the past. Many ancient historians justified their work based on this principle.

As the historical theorist Reinhard Koselleck has shown, this way of using history came under attack beginning in the Enlightenment, but with a certain finality during the Age of Revolution.[18] New ideas of progress and historical change convinced people that the present is radically different from the past, so past exempla may mislead.[19] New situations demand new responses. Even in daily life, the speed of changes made past custom and practice an unreliable guide.[20] Moreover, Enlightenment and Revolutionary thinkers saw the future as something to be constructed, as an open site for utopian ideals.[21] Relying on the past would thus be a reactionary closure of possibilities.

One need not accept Enlightenment narratives of progress to see the kernel of truth in these arguments. First, relying on the past can blind the actor to important failures in past practice. One can see clear examples of such failures in the field of machine learning. Machine-learning systems are forms of artificial intelligence that learn to make predictions based on past data with little guidance from programmers. Huge amounts of past data (e.g., mammograms) are fed into the program, which then develops an algorithm to predict an outcome (the presence of breast cancer) based on features it identifies. But problems arise if there are defects in the data set used to train the algorithm. Such defects can become a problem when applied to groups, such as Amazon's résumé-sorting algorithm discussed in chapter 8 that was biased against women. The overwhelming proportion of men in the industry led to past sexist biases becoming ingrained in the system, creating an even more powerful system of discrimination. Similar examples of bias with regard to race have been found in other algorithms based on machine learning for health care, facial identification, parole, and many other areas.[22] Past inequities can make poor grounds for future judgments.

Furthermore, problems can arise when a calculative vision of the future is taken as conclusive in situations of uncertainty. With regard to this problem, the economist Frank Knight distinguishes between situations of risk and uncertainty, as discussed in chapter 6.[23] A decision under risk concerns decisions in which one knows the probabilities of different negative outcomes with an approximate certainty because the decision is made with regard to a situation that is a member of a large group. In contrast, uncertain dangers are those of which one does not know the probability, or of which one may not even be aware, and which therefore cannot be mitigated or insured. The COVID-19 pandemic; the September 11, 2001, terrorist attacks on the United States; World War I; or inventions like the iPhone are examples of uncertainty, the novelty emphasized in chapter 3.

Uncertainty is a central problem for contemporary action. It is difficult to predict the outcomes of actions and even more difficult to foresee the possibility and effects of rare events. Though considerations of uncertainty and contingency have always had an important place in human action, two aspects of modernity have accentuated their importance. First, society depends on complex, interconnected systems in areas such as communications, transportation, finance, and medicine, systems that have vastly increased the efficiency of contemporary society but at the cost of increasing fragility through amplification of the effects of small events.[24] A glitch in the trading algorithm of a single firm can send markets plunging, floods in Thailand can bring the global computing industry to a halt, and a disease outbreak in China can shut down the world. Moreover, increasingly complex causal chains make the future effects of actions more opaque to the decision-maker because it is difficult to predict what will result from any intervention, as Guardini argued. For example, it is unlikely that US regulators would have let Lehman Brothers fail in 2008 if they had known that this policy would precipitate the global financial crisis.

A related problem rests on the novelty of technological developments, which bring many advantages in their train but also greater and to some extent unknown risks, because no one has ever had experience with them. These new technologies increase dangers of random shocks to the system as they amplify the power of individual actors, meaning that a malign hacker, a do-it-yourself bioweapons designer, or even a foolish trader can have outsize effects. The unknown and the unpredictable play an ever-larger role due to otherwise beneficial developments in technology and social organization. Ironically, many of these technological innovations and increasingly complex social organizations explicitly aim at the reduction or control of risk. The attempt to tame risk therefore leads to a fragility that makes society vulnerable to uncertainty.

As briefly discussed in chapter 6, Nassim Taleb has criticized the risk assessment methodologies of decision theory, especially their use in finance, because of their dependence on past and present data, which blinds them to such novel events.[25] In complex systems, like markets or nature, rare events—what Taleb calls Black Swan events, because of their tendency to overturn previous generalizations based on inductive reasoning—can have an outsize effect. Such events will not be captured by risk assessments, so these will be blind to absolutely crucial considerations. Too much confidence in extrapolative calculations from past data can lead to future disaster. Despite the claims of subjectivists, probability theory does not apply well to singular events, especially novel ones. Truly important events are not calculable, thus showing the failure of predictive risk analysis when one confronts risks of catastrophes. Yet older frameworks of prudence dependent on past experience are in some ways just as vulnerable to the novel situation. One must always consider the novel.

THE VIRTUES OF PRECAUTION

In response to this uncertainty with regard to the past, Hans Jonas has proposed the principle of precaution, as discussed in chapter 6. His imperative of responsibility is to "act so that the effects of your action are compatible with the permanence of genuine human life."[26] This principle attempts to address the imbalance between our increased power to cause harm and our decreased predictive knowledge of the future. Understood in this way, the principle of precaution has a clear relationship with the quasi-integral parts of prudence delineated by Aquinas. As expressed throughout *Laudato si'*, this principle encourages decision-makers to be docile to a greater range of experiences and expertise than might be present among a standard group of policymakers—to engage in interdisciplinary explorations,[27] solicit the opinions of affected segments of society, and pay close attention to the experiences of the marginalized whenever a project is planned.[28] Based on this broader set of experiences, policymakers can circumspectly identify a range of possible risks. Out of caution, projects should be delayed until there is more knowledge of the dangers they entail or until they are altered so as to mitigate possible risks. In this way, the prudent person can respond to dangers that she suspects but does not know will happen.

Yet framed in this way, the precautionary principle does not quite meet the problem of uncertainty. First, it assumes that people already have some knowledge, even if not certain or reliable knowledge, of possible dangers. Thus, it does not address the unknowns with which novelty and uncertainty confront us. Second, as chapter 6 discussed, it may itself create new risks. All mitigation strategies create risks, and sometimes a risky strategy is necessary to prevent a greater disaster. At its most extreme, precaution can lead to inaction.

It is the framing as an imperative that gives the precautionary principle such strength to inhibit action in problematic ways. However, though Jonas formulated the imperative of precaution in Kantian language, his argument as a whole suggests a concern for the development of a certain habit of thinking and feeling about the dangers of action. He speaks, for instance, of cultivating the emotion of fear, or of developing heuristics.[29] Precaution is a disposition toward thinking about the future, one that presupposes the act of imagining possible dangers. Initially, there will be little knowledge, or even inkling, of possible dangers of a new technology; there will be situations "where that which is to be feared has not yet happened and has perhaps no analogies in past or present experiences."[30] It is thus incumbent upon decision-makers to employ the faculty of imagination to conceive possible scenarios: "The anticipatory conjuring up of this imagination becomes itself the first, as it were introductory, duty of the ethics we are speaking about."[31] The role of fiction, especially science fiction, in arguments over new technologies suggests the importance of imagination. Much of bioethics draws on the novel *Brave New World* as a touchstone over which to argue. Visions of AI have been shaped by the fictional Skynet and HAL-9000. Although such imaginative works obviously should not be determinative for ethical arguments, they are useful in broadening possible ethical considerations and thus have a valid role to play. Jonas calls for a casuistry based in such imagination. Moreover, artistic works possess the second relevant aspect of imagination: imagination can evoke a proper emotional response to possible dangers; "it can instill in us the fear whose guidance we need," impelling policymakers to investigate or mitigate potential dangers.[32] Of course, after further investigation and reflection, one may decide that an imagined scenario is actually not possible or can be prevented easily. Still, the imagination is an essential aid in areas for which one lacks the knowledge otherwise needed to generate possible scenarios.

It therefore makes sense to think of precaution less as a principle than as a virtue, a habitual disposition. If it is a virtue, then one could retrieve Jonas's intuitions in this area by integrating them into the Thomistic tradition. One could envision two new quasi-integral parts of prudence: imagination and precaution. These are quasi-integral because, though they are ancillary to prudence as not tied immediately to the action of command, they are virtues necessary for the proper action of prudence in the contemporary world. As virtues annexed to counsel, precaution lacks the self-defeating aspect of a principle, the effect of stymieing action due to the ever-present possibilities of bad effects. Instead, it broadens the set of considerations.

RISK MANAGEMENT AND UNCERTAINTY

In any situation—but especially ones where there is a possible new technology, new regulation, or new form of social organization—the past can mislead. Black Swan fallacies can cause a blindness to unseen risks. Bias can sway our judgments. Individuals can become too focused on conspicuous dangers rather than the agglomeration of smaller everyday risks. Similarly, an excess of precaution can block action, preventing good. People may misestimate the impact of individual risks. For all these reasons, memory and precaution need additional aids.

It is in such decision settings that quantitative risk analysis can help. Here, Andrew Yuengert or Mary Hirschfeld's research on economic analysis in relation to prudence may provide a paradigm for deploying decision theory.[33] Both are clear that economic analysis alone cannot govern human action. The discipline lacks the necessary substantive understanding of the good provided by a rich anthropology, leading to an oversimplified model of how economic actors seek the good in terms of preferences. True prudence needs to grasp ends.

Yet both these authors emphasize that economic analysis is far from useless. It reveals nonintuitive effects of action. To take an example from Hirschfeld, rent control eventually shrinks the housing stock, ultimately harming the poor that it aims to help.[34] Such insights are essential for proper foresight, and theologians have ignored them for too long. Formal analysis, though limited, can be very powerful in giving a sense of possible outcomes resulting from major alterations to complex systems, outcomes that are invisible to intuitive judgments because of systemic complexity. Economic analysis introduces new considerations into the process of deliberation.

Similarly, quantitative risk assessment allows policymakers to broaden their field of vision. Ideally, risk analysts are trained to introduce all the effects that they can think of, even minor and unlikely ones into their analysis. But for this to work properly, these decisions cannot be merely the reserve of bureaucratic experts. Policymakers must also consult the communities that will be affected by a policy and include lay expertise.[35] Adding these voices makes judgment more robust and just.

This is not to say that it will make the policy decision foolproof. Data analytics and lay expertise can be just as constrained by past experience as other forms of human judgment, as the example of risk models driven by machine-learning algorithms show. If the situation changes or some other event makes the new data set different from the training data, then these predictions will be wrong and just as much constrained by an inapplicable past. That is why these tools should not be thought of as a calculative decision tool but as an aid to deliberation. Similarly, precaution taken too firmly can go awry, overblowing fears of future danger. None of these methods will lead to a sure solution.

THE IMPORTANT BUT LIMITED ROLE
OF QUANTITATIVE RISK ANALYSIS

Quantitative risk analysis and precaution can play an important role, but it is a limited one. Good risk analysts recognize these limits. To quote Ernest Braun again, risk analysis frequently errs, but "nonetheless, it is an essential aspect of the human condition that we attempt to foresee the future in an effort to shape it."[36] Jonas himself recognized that the statesman could undertake nearly impossible risks based on his sense of calling. These probabilistic tools can expand our horizons of considerations, but they cannot make the ultimate judgment of human goods and the situation that is the role of prudence.

The problem is that all too often, people put too much faith in these tools. They become a replacement for prudence rather than its aid. Democratic societies seek a transparent and sure method for arriving at decisions, one that mathematical analysis and quantified risk/benefit equations seem to offer.[37] These replace prudential judgments dependent on tacit knowledge and the discernment of the situation and the individuals involved. Such a mode of judgment seems too elitist, too closed to examination to be appropriate for a democratic people. Yet the hope in certainty and transparency must fail. Instead, politicians must train themselves in prudent judgment: judgment informed by quantitative analysis, of course, but not determined by it.

The other limit to the sphere of this analysis is that it best serves in policy contexts. If restricted to the political, this form of analysis becomes an aspect of what Aquinas calls regnative prudence rather than general prudence. Regnative prudence directed toward the common good is tied to the government and command of a city or kingdom. As Aquinas argues, "A government is the more perfect as it is more universal, extends to more matters, and attains a higher end. Hence prudence in its special and most perfect sense, belongs to a king who is charged with the government of a city or kingdom."[38] It is this kind of prudence that protects nations and the entire human community from undergoing disasters caused by unpredicted effects of actions. It is especially important because it pertains to broad environmental effects, which affect the common good of the whole human community and the natural order.

However, this restriction does not mean that the broader public should not be exposed to the principles of statistical analysis. All who live in a democracy contribute to governance. It is thus essential that the public have a basic sense of how this analysis is done, its strength, and its weaknesses. Otherwise, public discourse is likely to be hijacked by demagogues arguing in equally dangerous directions. On one hand, some will seek to downplay risks that are actually there, like climate change. On the other hand, a politics of fear may focus on the most conspicuous risks while ignoring dangerous side effects of policy responses, such as the growth of the surveillance state in response to domestic or international terrorism or the effects of climate mitigation efforts on the poor. Only a well-educated populace can avoid these dangers.

However, such a technical analysis is not well suited for personal life. There, it frequently causes anxiety because the larger context is out of the individual's control. Even in policy contexts, this should not be thought of as a universal tool but as something to apply in a restricted set of decisions: new technologies and regulations, for example. Policymaking with regard to risk should preferentially aim at creating and sustaining structures within which risks will already be limited. Chapter 11 investigates what such structures might look like.

NOTES

Quoted by Koselleck, *Futures Past*, 31.

1. Foucault, "On the Genealogy of Ethics," 256.
2. O'Donovan, *Finding and Seeking*, 181.
3. Koselleck, *Futures Past*, 28.
4. Aquinas, *Summa theologica*, I-II, q. 57, a. 4. This discussion largely follows Westberg, *Right Practical Reason*. Much of this chapter draws on Scherz, "Prudence, Precaution, and Uncertainty." See also Scherz, "Risk, Prudence, and Moral Formation in the Laboratory."
5. Aquinas, *Summa theologica*, I-IIa12.
6. Aquinas, I-II.14a1, a2.
7. Aquinas, I-II.13a3, 15a3, 16a4.
8. Aquinas, II-II.47a8.
9. Aquinas, II-II.51.
10. Aquinas, II.II.48a1.
11. The others come from Macrobius, *Commentary on the Dream of Scipio*, 1.8.7.
12. Cicero, *On Invention*, 2.53.160.
13. Aquinas, *Summa theologica*, II-II.49a1.
14. Aquinas, II-II.49a3.
15. Aquinas, II-II.49a6.
16. Aquinas, II-II.49a7.
17. Aquinas, II-II.49a8.
18. Koselleck, *Futures Past*, 26–42.
19. Koselleck, 37.
20. Rosa, *Social Acceleration*.
21. Koselleck, *Futures Past*, 39.
22. Obermeyer et al., "Dissecting Racial Bias"; Guynn, "Google Photos Labeled Black People 'Gorillas'"; Angwin et al., "Machine Bias." More generally, see Benjamin, *Race after Technology*.
23. Knight, *Risk, Uncertainty, and Profit*, 20.
24. Goldin and Mariathasan, *Butterfly Defect*; Taleb, *Antifragile*; Perrow, *Normal Accidents*. This section and my later discussion of Taleb are from Scherz, "Prudence, Precaution, and Uncertainty."
25. Taleb, *Antifragile*, 8–9.
26. Jonas, *Imperative of Responsibility*, 11.
27. Francis, *Laudato si'*, 110.
28. Francis, 183.
29. Jonas, *Imperative of Responsibility*, 25–31.

30. Jonas, 27.
31. Jonas, 27.
32. Jonas, 27.
33. Yuengert, *Approximating Prudence*; Hirschfeld, *Aquinas and the Market*.
34. Hirschfeld, *Aquinas and the Market*, 43.
35. For discussions of the complicated terrain of expertise, see Collins and Evans, "Third Wave"; Wynne, "Seasick"; Jasanoff, "Breaking the Waves."
36. Braun, *Technology in Context*, 32–33.
37. Porter, *Trust in Numbers*.
38. Aquinas, *Summa theologica*, II-II.50a1.

11

The Epimethean Society

Hope . . . means trusting faith in the goodness of nature,
while expectation . . . means reliance on results which are
planned and controlled by man. Hope centers desire on a person
from whom we await a gift. Expectation looks forward to satisfaction
from a predictable process which will produce what we have the
right to claim. The Promethean ethos has now eclipsed hope.

—*Ivan Illich*

The US government . . . is best thought of as
a giant insurance company with an army.

—*Paul Krugman*

The myth of Prometheus has served as an inspiration for countless writers on technology. In the earliest form of the myth that we have in Hesiod, Prometheus both steals Zeus's fire to aid humans and also defrauds the gods of the best portion of the sacrificial animal.[1] Zeus has his revenge, chaining Prometheus to a mountain to have his liver eaten by an eagle. The other aspect of Zeus's revenge has received less attention in technology ethics. In a story that many scholars think Hesiod mistold to accentuate his misogynistic point, Zeus orders Hephaestus to forge a beautiful woman and asks the gods to crown her with all gifts, including the craftiness of Hermes, naming her Pandora, the all-gifted. He sends her to Prometheus's brother, Epimetheus, along with a sealed jar (mislabeled as a box by Erasmus).[2] Either Pandora or Epimetheus, depending on the source, is overcome with curiosity and opens the jar. Out spring all the evils of human life. The only thing left in the jar is hope, which still remains to give light to human existence.

In later interpretations, both Prometheus and Pandora have symbolized technology. Prometheus, meaning foresight, clearly relates to technologies of prediction, with Aeschylus also giving him the gift of prophecy. Aeschylus further notes that he has hidden human death from mortals, perhaps suggesting the way that technology drives us to attempt to escape finitude.[3] Many have taken this story to represent the evils of technology. In the epigraph to this chapter, Illich is perhaps drawing on Goethe's retelling of the story.[4] Goethe presents Prometheus as a straightforward utilitarian attempting to conquer nature. Epimetheus, in contrast, serves as an embodiment of the contemplative life. He waits upon a return of Pandora promised by Elpore (Hope) and Eos (Dawn), "a gift unthought of."[5] Prometheus rejects this gift because he does not enjoy novelty, preferring to depend upon human means. Eos counters him, saying that "timeless good and beauty" can only come from the gods.

In this story, we see themes of this book: the problems of the foresight of decision theory, technological control, concerns over novelty, trust in God and others, and hope. Illich develops this mythical contrast into a picture of contrasting social orders: a Promethean one based on predictive control, and an Epimethean one based on intersubjective trust and engagement. The earlier chapters in this book have chronicled how society has adopted this Promethean ethos, one relying on planning based in the predictive management of risks. It has gone so far that Paul Krugman can see the function of government as largely that of an insurance company, managing future risks. Security has become a right emerging from a system of control. The common good is now centered on risk reduction. Yet I have suggested ways that this form of social organization can cause dramatic unintended consequences, as Illich and the myth of Pandora suggest, increasing personal anxiety, intensifying social control, and undermining trust in providence. The first section of this chapter recapitulates the strategies and problems of this risk society.

Needless to say, the Promethean society is not the Christian social vision, with the Sermon on the Mount, like Goethe, calling Christians to trust in God for the future rather than anxiously planning for the next day. Yet this trust does not mean that Scripture is heedless of risk. Indeed, the Old Testament frequently refers to ways to confront future contingency, both in institutional forms, seen in the Law, and in personal action, described in the Wisdom Literature. However, these institutional and individual ways of dealing with risk are all tied to other ideals of justice and virtue. None focus solely on security. By examining these structures, I hope to gain insight into non-Promethean forms of social life that can care for individuals in the face of the uncertainty of life, while avoiding the trap of seeking total control. It is essential that a way be found to create a social structure open to hope and interpersonal trust, what Illich calls an Epimethean form of life, one founded in trust in others, especially God.

MODES OF CONTROLLING RISK

To summarize much of what has already been discussed, contemporary society has developed four major strategies for controlling risk. The first is to train individuals to be responsible for their future welfare.[6] This goal in part requires training them in the decision theoretical model of practical reason. At each decision point, they must consider the multiple futures that lie before them, the risks of harm that each bears, the possible benefits that emerge from each, and the likelihood of these risks' and benefits' realization. By becoming provident for themselves, individuals relieve society of much of the burden of caring for them.

This strategy was primarily deployed in classical liberal societies of the nineteenth century.[7] Those who were not able to conquer the contingencies of life through planning and hard work were left to suffering, individual charity, or sporadic forms of state relief. Though this model fell out of favor with the growth of the welfare state, it has seen a revival in the last forty years, one tied to the neoliberal model of responsibility discussed in chapter 6.[8] Social means of confronting risks have been transformed in order to require greater individual responsibility. Pension plans became 401(k)s, mandating that individuals rather than institutions manage retirement funds. Single-payer health insurance was forgone in the Affordable Care Act in favor of subsidized health insurance exchanges. Markets now manage the information requirements of dealing with future risks. For people to operate well in these systems, however, they must be trained in this economic rationality of planning and personal providence. Toward this end, programs to train people in responsibility are now included in the prerequisites for participation in welfare programs. Addiction treatment includes training in responsibility, even in the setting of the Russian Orthodox Church.[9] The unemployed and single mothers must work to receive benefits, thus demonstrating responsibility. The goal of these programs is to train people to be skilled risk managers so that society does not need to address their risks.

Yet individual providence will not always be sufficient. Some risks are too great, almost inevitable, overwhelming responsible risk management. Some people will fail to become responsible. Moreover, behavioral economics reveals human reason to be faulty, unable to properly use decision theory. Many times, people are accused of being too lazy to act in their interests. In such cases, social authorities can use predictive analysis of behaviors to nudge people in the appropriate direction to reduce risks, a second strategy for managing risks. Through regulation and, increasingly, through manipulation by electronic devices, planners can shape the environment in ways that drive people to the proper choice. In this way, risk is reduced both by making people more predictable and by shaping their behavior to minimize risk.

Policymakers must also control the effects of their own actions. Thus, the third strategy of cost/benefit analysis at the policy level predicts the effects or minimizes the risks of major social decisions. Finally, policymakers and business leaders have deployed structural systems of control in order to predict and minimize natural risk as well as maximize efficiency. Pesticide usage minimizes the risk of crop failure. Just-in-time manufacturing reduces the financial risks of too large inventories. Instruments like derivatives and other forms of debt repackaging into new financial products minimize financial risks to the individual investor, distributing risks throughout society. When risks cannot be controlled, they can be insured against or redistributed, allowing financial reparations for realized risks. Thus, policymakers and business leaders deploy targeted instruments to directly control particular risks.

Society has thus developed powerful systems of predictive control to dam and dike Fortuna. These systems have greatly reduced many risks. Yet they also introduce their own problems. To take the last two strategies first, intricate control of particular risks can leave systems vulnerable to rare events, as was discussed in chapter 10. Mistakes are swiftly amplified by the complex systems used to govern risks, especially with regard to unexpected events or new technologies for which decision-makers have little experience.[10]

The strategies for managing individual responsibility for risk fare little better in this analysis. Systems of behavioral control rely on the manipulation of individuals. Unseen forces in the environment push people toward choices, possibly subverting their activity as free agents and shaping their ends toward lesser goods. These strategies centralize power in the hands of those controlling the system, creating the danger of abuse. Who guards the guardians? Or rather, who will manage the risk created by the risk managers? Even worse, no one could be in charge, with action directed toward the maintenance of an impersonal, inevitable system.

Finally, the encouragement of individual responsibility creates its own problems. People become anxious when faced with too many possibilities. They regret the past choices that have led them to forgo other goods. They feel responsible for their entire fate, becoming obsessed with security and success, yet unsure of how to obtain it in the face of increasing precarity. This is an unsustainable social framework and one that presses against a number of Christian ideals. Without systems to support those who suffer from risks, who fall on hard times, or who cannot support themselves, it is difficult to not become swept up in solicitude for worldly things.

Ultimately, Promethean hubris and Promethean planning turn into what Gunther Anders calls Promethean shame.[11] Technologies of control promise much, but these promises are never fulfilled. Financial and technical management of risk fail spectacularly, as seen in the 2008 financial crisis or the 2011 Fukushima nuclear disaster. On a personal level, few people save enough for retirement. It can seem that people are unable to live up to their machines: their reason is too faulty; they lack foresight; they are too unpredictable. Thus, we trust more and more in automated systems, hoping that they will find the wisdom to guide us through uncertainty. But these idols will ultimately fail.

BIBLICAL VISIONS OF RISK AND SOCIETY

Scripture expresses skepticism about such centralized, quantitative systems of control. For example, God sent a plague upon Israel as punishment for David's census.[12] The census that coincided with Christ's birth marks the distinction between earthly imperial power and the kingdom of heaven. Even when centralized systems of risk management providentially save lives, they can still be put to malign ends. Joseph's centralized system of grain storage and distribution may have saved Egypt and the surrounding peoples from the worst effects of seven years of famine, but, ultimately, this power was used to enslave everyone to the pharaoh.[13] These are thus dangerous tools of human power.

However, Scripture does not seem opposed to all systems that address contingency. This is seen most clearly in the Law of Israel.[14] A number of its provisions served to limit exposure to and the consequences of natural and social dangers. One of the greatest risks for the Near Eastern peasantry was that of crop failure due to bad weather, pests, or just bad luck. Such failures could drive a farmer into debt as he borrowed money or seed in order to survive and plant for the next year. Eventually, a cycle of indebtedness and crop failure could force the farmer into debt slavery, drive him to sell a family member into slavery, or lead him to sell his ancestral fields. Ideally, however, this would not be an unbounded free fall. Through the seven-year sabbath, debts were remitted and slaves were freed periodically.[15] Debt was limited. At the Jubilee, lands reverted back to their ancestral owners, so that even the loss of land was limited.[16] Even beyond these general forms of debt relief, limits were set on loans. Usury was banned among Israelites so that debt could not endlessly grow.[17] Essential items taken as collateral, like cloaks, had to be returned.[18] Risks were allowed to play their course, but only for so long. Eventually, their effects were limited. It was not a targeted management of individual risk, as is found in crop insurance, but social structures that broadly alleviated the greatest consequences of risks gone bad. As the denunciations of the prophets suggest, these buffers against risk were ideals that were rarely implemented, but they still provide a valuable framework.

Another danger was the loss of family caregivers through death or abandonment. Widows and orphans could be left in grave want, or parents could be ignored by children. Structures were in place to care for these vulnerable people. Levirate marriage provided care for widows without children.[19] The commandment to honor father and mother set social demands to care for parents. Caring for widows and orphans was a social duty of the powerful and a mark of virtue.[20] The institution of gleaning limited the maximally efficient usage of cropland, which allowed the poor to eat.[21] Again, social structures and norms were in place to limit these dangers, in theory. These protections were not to occur through actuarial methods like life insurance, but through communal commitment and interpersonal trust in others. Even in the last century, some Mennonite communities rejected life insurance as contradicting this biblical witness of communal caring for the bereaved.[22]

However, Scripture also reveals a need for individual action and dispositions that address future contingency. The Wisdom Literature, for example—especially in what are called the more lucid variants, like Proverbs and Sirach—offers advice on how to live.[23] Wisdom assumes that such advice would generally lead to both a just life before God and reasonable worldly security. As in Aquinas's model of contingency and practical reasoning, these books presume a fairly predictable set of natural regularities. The world is created as an orderly system, and action turns out for the most part in a certain way, even if contingent events can make action plans fail. The sage can take advantage of these natural regularities to avoid and manage risks so that life turns out well. For example, dealing with kings is a risky business: the sage should know that he will have to repay the favors he receives and that he should keep quiet unless absolutely necessary.[24] He should never pledge himself as surety on another's loan, for he will likely be betrayed.[25] Work hard, like the ant.[26] Do not stray from the marriage bed, as it creates dangers from jealous spouses and manipulation by courtesans.[27] The best route is to rejoice in the wife of one's youth.[28] All these admonitions serve to guide individual action in the face of common risks, not through quantitative decision theory but by encouraging particular dispositions and norms of action.

What distinguishes these forms of risk management through social institutions and individual dispositions is that they were not solely or even primarily aimed at controlling risks or ensuring immanent security. Each of them also served higher ends. The Jubilee restoration of property and the institution of gleaning demonstrated God's ultimate dominion over the Land that He gave to Israel. Debt relief and slave manumission evinced God's call to human freedom and reenacted His salvific actions in the Exodus. Usury and other restrictions on loans aimed at justice and a demonstration of solidarity among God's people. Levirate marriage ensured the continuity of the name. Care of widows and orphans imitated God's beneficent care of all, especially the poor. Honoring one's parents enacted piety and acknowledged one's origins. Such structures had ends beyond security and the mere management of risk.

Moreover, the individual dispositions recommended in the Wisdom Literature aimed beyond worldly success to a flourishing that included worldly security, but only as it involved virtue and right relationship. Silence in the face of the powerful demonstrates prudence and control. Fidelity in marriage is good in itself beyond whatever risks it might help one avoid. All these texts argued that fear of the Lord was the foundation of Wisdom. They did not aim at Promethean control but a hearkening to the Law of God that directed the sage toward fulfillment. All these dispositions aimed at higher, true goods, while at the same time limiting risk.

By aiming at these higher goods, these controls sought to benefit individuals. The sages of course sought to influence the disciple. Wisdom calls out to the novice on the street, attracting people to her way of life.[29] Yet this influence is not a form of manipulation. Immanent desires are not induced in order to shift behavior in a socially useful manner. Choice architecture and the environment are not altered. There are sanctions in the Law for clear violations; but for many of the positive prescriptions of the Law and Wisdom, what is provided is rather an invitation to a form of life. The sages sought to shape the novice through rational discourse, proverbs, and examples, appealing to reason and will. It is Dame Folly that incites base desires that lead to ruin.[30] Wisdom is gained through an apprenticeship in a way of life and form of reasoning about the world. Bare manipulation is ruled out.

The Wisdom Literature also recognizes the limits of prudential management. This is especially clear in so-called skeptical Wisdom books like Job. Despite his virtue, living according to temperance, justice, and prudence does not save Job from material and physical ruin. Ecclesiastes suggests the vanity of the whole game of earthly risk management, as all ends in death in any case. Thus, the genre was clear on its limits. Even the more lucid books of Wisdom recognize the limits of control. No matter how one plans, God's will will be realized.[31] Ben Sira recognizes that even the virtuous would be tested by the Lord.[32] Yet there is still a deep trust in God, that in the end He will bring justice out of a trial. Those chastised and tested will emerge purified, just as Job was restored to more than he had before his trial. Even Ecclesiastes ends with a basic directive toward the fear of the Lord.[33] Wisdom relies on the orderliness of Creation to generally bring security but ultimately accepts that there will be suffering. But even then, sages trusted that God would ultimately bring good out of the experience. Trust in providence, and in God's justice, undergirds this whole system.

It was ultimately this trust that would be reaffirmed in the New Testament in the Sermon on the Mount. Do good, seek the kingdom, and trust that needs will be taken care of, even if there would be suffering on the path. Of course, new and sometimes continuous forms of individual behavior and social structure would arise to serve these needs in the Church. Without an independent nation and social order, different forms would be devised to enforce norms surrounding risk, ones more dependent on personal dispositions and communal engagement. People were to work to support themselves and their dependent relatives.[34] Suffering and persecution were inevitable, so like Paul, Christians should be self-sufficient, ready to live under any circumstances through God's help and the virtues of courage, temperance, and prudence.[35] Yet the poor were not left to themselves. The Church cared for them and for widows, a ministry that would blossom into an intensive structure of care for the vulnerable by late Antiquity.[36] Thus, needs were provided for through social structures and individual virtue, but in a way that aimed at higher goods and forms of flourishing, such as temperance, charity, and solidarity in Christ.

These modes of addressing contingent dangers avoid many of the problems that appear in contemporary society. First, they do not create fragile systems because they do not seek total control of risk. They accept that some misfortune will happen and rely on communal structures rather than impersonal systems to address the aftermath. Second, they are not manipulative. They call to the individual to seek her own flourishing by aiming for higher goods like virtue, solidarity, and piety. They appeal to reason and will rather than desires. Finally, they do not induce anxiety. They ask the person to follow a basic template of action and disposition that corresponds well with natural and social regularities. Although temporal security is not ensured, there is an expectation that such a mode of action is more likely to lead to it. Even if it does not, the fundamental call is to trust in God, who will bring good out of whatever occurs.

LATER CHRISTIAN MODELS

These ideals were maintained in later instantiations of Christian social arrangements. For example, consider the guild system.[37] Guilds sought to control risk through mutual agreements among producers. The size of the craft was constrained by the need for an extensive apprenticeship, thereby limiting competition. Similarly, prices were controlled by the group. Through these measures, running a business became more predictable, limiting future risk due to market fluctuations or increased competition.[38] Frequently, these groups also had benefits that buffered against major crises for members as well as the broader community: paying for burials, help for widows, care of the sick.[39] They increased business predictability while also providing support in the face of larger risks.

After the destruction of the guild system, mutual aid societies, labor unions, and other kinds of voluntary organizations provided similar services to offer care in the face of risk.[40] These could not regulate business under the liberal form of society, but they could buffer risk. They were formed among people with some kind of shared background: an occupational group, immigrants from the same country of origin, or a religious faith. They provided social outlets but also material support in the face of hardship. These also sometimes paid for burials; they might provide support to widows or those suffering illness. Some contracted with doctors in order to provide medical benefits, with early forms of medical and life insurance arising out of these groups. In many countries, these organizations provided structures upon which later social insurance programs were built.

These were the kinds of groupings that shaped the imagination of early Catholic Social Teaching. *Quadragesimo anno*, for example, envisioned a multitude of such organizations.[41] The guild system would be expanded in industrial society to include owners and workers in broader corporatist organizations. These groups would share the efforts of planning and regulating the growth of their industries, thus buffering future uncertainty and conflict. They would ensure the wage levels necessary to fully support a family as well as save enough in order to acquire property that would lead to a secure old age.[42] Other, smaller Christian groups would provide different kinds of mutual social and material support. This was a vision of a form of social organization that buffered individuals against the risks of market society but not through impersonal methods.

Instead of objective modes of managing a population of risk, they are forms of interpersonal engagement. In this way, they are sustained by a very different social imaginary than that of risk management. Probabilistic techniques depend on viewing a group as a population with regularly realized risks. These can be predictably addressed through actuarial techniques. It does not matter who the members of a population are, nor really their willed action. One can treat them in the same way as a population of animals for modeling purposes. They are objects for management.

In these other models, however, the members of the organization exist in community. They are formed for a purpose beyond merely the management of risk in many cases. Guilds and the corporatist organizations envisioned by early Catholic Social Teaching are aimed at the flourishing of a certain kind of craft. Even mutual aid societies and unions generally aimed at forms of social support and engagement that extended beyond merely the material: festivals, celebrations, meetings, and the like. They were grounded in a sense of community that was greater than mere population risk, such as occupation or nationality. In this, they see others as subjects who are due care beyond the contractual obligations of the insurance contract, forming deeper social bonds. Care is thus intersubjective. Risk is ultimately not addressed through impersonal mechanisms but through a personal commitment to others.

These groups are not neutral toward individual action. The older forms of guilds and mutual aid societies enforced social norms using classic modes of community enforcement and ostracization. Some of these prohibitions were aimed at reducing risks, and thus costs, by ensuring better health, reducing the risk of scandal for the guild, and so on. Yet these restrictions also served a higher good. These groups ideally sought to form individuals in virtuous behavior aimed at a certain kind of good life that it was assumed that the members shared. There was an ideal of a craftsman that the guild purportedly supported. This is not a modulation of behavior aimed at reducing population risk and thus cost. Instead, it is a shaping of character toward a certain ethical ideal that is believed to be good in itself but that also reduces risk. Such a mode of organization is thus aimed at true goods before security and pursues these goals through modes of interpersonal trust.

BROADER LESSONS FOR SOCIAL GOVERNANCE

These last few examples were all private, or what one might now call nongovernmental organizations, but that does not mean that the government played no role. States created the framework in which guilds flourished, and it required liberal state action in order to dismantle their prerogatives. *Quadragesimo anno* envisioned state support for its corporatist organizations. Moreover, state programs stepped in during crises and problems too grave for private groups. Ultimately, in many countries, states cooperated with these organizations to provide the first forms of social insurance. There is a need for contributions from actors at all levels of social complexity, from the family up to international organizations. Although it would be absurd in the space available to me in this book to try to map out a whole system of institutions that would embody a Christian vision of the social management of risk, here I highlight three primary lessons that the examples discussed in this chapter suggest for designing institutions and policy frameworks.

First, social structures should aim at limiting the types of harm from realized risks rather than attempting to control, manage, and eliminate all risk. Social actors have created highly fragile systems in order to maximize efficiency and ensure returns: systems of just-in-time production that require complex, easily disrupted, global supply chains; financial systems that opaquely distribute risks in a way that allows the decrease of the price of one asset class, such as home prices, to collapse global credit systems; too-big-to-fail business; internet servers vulnerable to hacking. Instead, we should aim at what Taleb calls robust or antifragile systems. Taleb encourages looking at the properties of systems to see how to limit the possible harm from unforeseen events. He describes three possible properties of systems, states, or plans of action in relation to volatile, unforeseen events: fragility, robustness, and antifragility.[43] Some systems or courses of action are fragile, meaning that usually they turn out well, but a shock event can lead to rapid collapse and loss. A famous example is the collapse of the power grid of the Eastern United States in 2003 as a result of a tree falling on a powerline, leading to a blackout affecting 50 million people.[44] Or one could consider the example of investing in the stock market, which generally gives a good return on investment but occasionally loses much of its value, as in 2008. Most modern systems are fragile because they have been designed primarily with efficiency in mind. A robust system or course of action is one that is resistant to shocks because it has multiple, redundant safeguards. Thus, DARPA designed the internet to use multiple nodes so that it would still function after a nuclear attack. The analogue for investing would be a diversified portfolio of extremely safe investments. In contrast to fragile courses of action, and going beyond robust systems, Taleb encourages what he calls antifragile courses of action: those that flourish in volatility and uncertainty, taking advantage of them. He argues that entrepreneurial markets as a whole are antifragile (although not for the individual entrepreneurs who go bankrupt); the same holds for an investment portfolio composed mostly of extremely safe investments but with some long-shot bets like venture capital or an option to short a market.[45] Prudent actions and prudently designed systems should aim at robustness or antifragility in the face of uncertainty. Although a prudent person will frequently be able to take advantage of uncertainty, she should at least aim for robustness, which is all that can be achieved in some circumstances.

The way to ensure a system's robustness is to pay attention to its maximal exposure to harm rather than to the expected average benefit and risks. The folly of the utilitarian weighing of the probability-adjusted benefits versus the probability-adjusted types of harm is that it cannot take into account the unknown and thus always tends toward fragility. One cannot know for certain the probability of future events, so such calculations are mere guesses. Instead, one must look at how much harm could occur if everything went even worse than could possibly be expected from past experience. With Jonas, the person concerned with systemic robustness knows how to view the future with a proper heuristics influenced by fear as well as hope.

There are many ways to get a sense of maximal exposure to harm. One could look to see if the action is nonlinear, which means that bad effects would accelerate exponentially in relation to possible bad events rather than merely increasing at a linear rate.[46] For example, the system of derivatives and credit default swaps that was in place before the 2008 financial crisis was predictable as long as housing prices remained stable. Because of its complexity, however, once housing prices started falling, the economic losses swiftly accelerated out of anyone's control. If one sees that bad effects accelerate, then it suggests that the results of an unforeseen event could be catastrophic. Alternatively, one could look for safeguards capable of containing increasing harms. In finance, one can have a stop-loss order, whereby an investment is sold once it decreases to a certain price in order to limit loss. In other areas, processes should be reversible once bad effects appear. If harms can be limited, then it suggests that an action meets the test of precaution. It makes little sense to act in such a way that one exposes oneself or others to great harm in the event of an unforeseen disaster in exchange for limited or even great gains. Such benefits can be erased very swiftly.

At first glance, it may seem that what Taleb gives us is merely a way of calculating effects of actions, one that may be more akin to utilitarian cost/benefit analysis than prudential judgment, even if it is a significant advance over most versions of the former. Yet what Taleb is really trying to suggest is a different way of perceiving courses of action and ways of organizing society. Antifragile systems thrive on volatility and uncertainty, much like a competitive marketplace. Robust systems are resistant to instability. They tend to be local, distributed, and reliant on subsidiary forms of organization.[47] The failure of one piece of the system will not bring about the collapse of the whole. Such systems are not as efficient, and they allow for some harm to occur. Yet they prevent wholesale collapse.

At the personal level, there is also the need to limit the effects of failed risk-taking. For example, bankruptcy allows people to start over after becoming overly indebted due to business failure or personal emergency. Yet, just as society has forced more people to assume responsibility for their own risks, the government tightened the bankruptcy laws in 2005.[48] There has also been an assault on the social support system. Frequently, people are on forms of relief only for a few months, but they serve as crucial services in order to help one get back on one's feet. These programs need support, especially if carried out through other forms of mutual aid and charity.

Second, instead of focusing on managing specific risks, social planning should aim at true goods. For example, much money has been poured into preventive health services: screening for risks, treatment of risks like high blood pressure, and management of these risks.[49] Pharmaceutical companies, insurance companies, and health data analytic companies are all investing heavily in this management of specific individual risks. Yet the greatest benefit to health comes from the provision of goods that are not directly aimed at specific disease risks. Over the last two centuries, better food supplies, clean water, clean air, and sanitation have done far more than medicine to raise life expectancy.[50] Designing cities that are safe for walking, public transportation, and neighborliness would do more for health by increasing exercise and decreasing stress than many medications. Reducing poverty through better jobs would eliminate damaging social determinants of health.[51] More should be done to aim at such goods.

Third, society should aim at shaping dispositions, but not through the manipulation of specific risk behavior, especially if that is mediated through forms of consumerism. Instead, it should encourage virtues that more broadly reduce risks. For example, Pope Francis cites Patriarch Bartholomew's call for the need for a broader asceticism among Western consumer societies.[52] Rather than using the climate change crisis merely to shape which variety of good one buys (a new electric car vs. a gas-guzzling sport utility vehicle), people should strive to reduce the overconsumption at the heart of the problem. Instead of anxious management of future risk, the individual should prudently seek higher goods.

CONCLUSION

In these ways, society could reduce the anxious striving for risk reduction. Instead, it could encourage people to seek true goods within supportive social structures, safe in the knowledge that risk will be limited for both the individual and society. Of course, wise leadership would sometimes require a risk/benefit analysis, but such exercises would only fall on some shoulders at certain times. More of the burden would depend on individual and communal prudence and charity. Such a social form would not depend on manipulation. Instead, it would be focused on relations of intersubjective trust.

In these ways, we might move beyond the Promethean society of control that Illich criticizes to a more Epimethean society, one based on trust in others and on hope. Hope, as Joseph Ratzinger stated, "appears when we have something to expect beyond our own production."[53] If one only trusts in the future because one thinks one can control it, then one is presumptuous rather than hopeful. Ultimately, hope can only be founded in God by trusting in His providence. This does not mean that risks will not be realized, that suffering will not occur. Sometimes, God permits or calls us to participate in the sufferings of Christ; but Christians can trust that they will be sustained in perseverance. This sustenance comes in part through God's providence working through individuals and the Christian community. Our trust in God allows us to trust in others. As Arendt argued, a social future can only be sustained through the institution of promising, through personal, willed engagement.[54] Thus, what this chapter offers is not a prediction of a sure future sustained through ironclad planning. Instead, it is a suggestion for a society founded on hope and trust, seemingly the most fragile of things, but in reality the only foundations robust enough to see us through the challenges we face.

NOTES

Illich, *Deschooling Society*, 105.

Krugman, "Insurance Company with an Army." Krugman is commonly cited as the source for this description, although he admits that the phrase did not originate with him. He credits an official of the George W. Bush administration, but I was unable to verify that attribution.

1. Hesiod, "Theogony," ll. 507–616; Hesiod, "Works and Days," 47–105. My discussion of this myth draws on the magisterial account of its life in art and literature given by Panofsky, *Pandora's Box*.

2. Panofsky, *Pandora's Box*, 14–26.

3. Aeschylus, "Prometheus Bound," l. 248; Gadamer, *Enigma of Health*, 156.

4. Panofsky, *Pandora's Box*, 125–36.

5. Panofsky, 128.

6. Foucault et al., *Foucault Effect*; Dean, *Governmentality*; O'Malley, "Governmentality and Risk."

7. Ewald, *L'etat providence*, 85–108.

8. For critique of these shifts, see Hacker, *Great Risk Shift*; and Mounk, *Age of Responsibility*.

9. Zigon, *HIV Is God's Blessing.*
10. Goldin and Mariathasan, *Butterfly Defect*; Taleb, *Antifragile.*
11. Anders, "On Promethean Shame."
12. 2 Sm. 24.
13. Gn. 47:13–26.
14. This interpretation draws on Baker, *Tight Fists or Open Hands?*; Bergsma, *Jubilee from Leviticus to Qumran*; Guillaume, *Land, Credit, and Crisis*; Yoder, *Politics of Jesus*; and Fager, "Land Tenure in the Biblical Jubilee."
15. Dt. 15:1–18.
16. Lv. 25:8–17.
17. Ex. 22:25–27; Lv. 25:36–37; Dt. 23:20–21.
18. Ex. 22:28.
19. Dt. 25:5–10.
20. Jb. 29:11–12.
21. Lv. 19:9–10. For a reflection on gleaning in modernity, see Varda, *Gleaners and I.*
22. Tracy, "Insurance and Theology"; Nolt, "Problems of Collectivity and Modernity."
23. For lucid wisdom, see Legaspi, *Wisdom in Classical and Biblical Tradition.* See also Murphy, *Tree of Life.*
24. Prv. 23:1–4.
25. Prv. 6:1, 17:18, 22:26.
26. Prv. 6:6–11.
27. Prv. 5, 6:22–35.
28. Prv. 5:18.
29. E.g., Prv. 1:20–21.
30. Prv. 9:13–18.
31. Prv. 16:9, 19:21.
32. Sir. 2:1–6.
33. Jb. 12:13.
34. 2 Thess. 3:6–15, 1 Tm. 5:4.
35. Phil. 4:11–13.
36. For widows, see 1 Tm. 5. For the Church's broader relation to the poor as it developed through late antiquity, see Brown, *Poverty and Leadership.*
37. For an overview of guilds, see Black, *Guild and State.* For the influence of the ideals of guilds on Catholic corporatist movements and Catholic Social Teaching, see von Ketteler, *Social Teachings*, 325–32; Nell-Breuning, *Reorganization of Social Economy*, 259–60; Bowen, *German Theories of the Corporative State*, 75–118; and Elbow, *French Corporative Theory*, 13–22. For a broader discussion of the social embeddedness of economic life under the ancien regime, see Polanyi, *Great Transformation.*
38. As liberals and Marxists emphasize though, these restrictions limited the function of the competitive market, potentially slowing economic development and disadvantaging consumers.
39. E.g., see Rosser, *Art of Solidarity in the Middle Ages.*
40. For discussions of these organizations as they relate to various forms of insurance, see Witt, *Accidental Republic*, 71–103; Ewald, *L'etat providence*, 204–14; and Starr, *Social Transformation*, 206–9.
41. Pius XI, *Quadragesimo anno.* For background on the encyclical and corporatist doctrine, see Nell-Breuning, *Reorganization of Social Economy.* For a more recent discussion

placing these theories in the overall history of Catholic Social Teaching, see Shadle, *Interrupting Capitalism.*

42. Leo XIII, *Rerum novarum,* 46.

43. Taleb, *Antifragile,* 21–27.

44. Goldin and Mariathasan, *Butterfly Defect,* 106–7.

45. Taleb, *Antifragile,* 74–80.

46. Taleb calls this "convexity vs. concavity"; see Taleb, 267–89.

47. For recent arguments encouraging a more subsidiary form of social organization, see Bruni and Zamagni, *Civil Economy*; and Milbank and Pabst, *Politics of Virtue.*

48. Coco, "Cultural Logics"; Hacker, *Great Risk Shift.*

49. For critical discussions of preventive medicine, see Greene, *Prescribing by Numbers*; Welch, Schwartz, and Woloshin, *Overdiagnosed*; Dumit, *Drugs for Life*; Aronowitz, *Risky Medicine*; Ehrenreich, *Natural Causes*; and Scherz, "Risk, Health, and Physical Enhancement."

50. McKeown, *Modern Rise of Population.*

51. Marmot, "Social Determinants of Health Inequalities."

52. Francis, *Laudato si',* 9.

53. Ratzinger, *Fundamental Speeches,* 91.

54. Arendt, *Human Condition,* 243–47.

Conclusion

Nearly all vices are rooted in the future.

—C. S. *Lewis*

The widespread use of the technologies and ideologies of probabilistic prediction has transformed society. Institutions focus on individuals as members of populations, using behaviorist techniques implemented through algorithms to remold behavior. Individuals in both private and public life take upon themselves the burden of possibility, scanning the future for dangerous consequences and regretting forgone goods. People desperately reach for security, even while social arrangements push them toward ever more precarity. But we are not condemned to this fate. There are different ways of relating to risk, technology, the future, and responsibility. Trust in God can still provide a clear path toward ultimate certainty amid the confusion of life. Social institutions can provide a bedrock of protection without the need to manage behavior and without reducing people to quanta of populations. We can retain the benefits of quantitative risk analysis while limiting its dangers by integrating it within a prudence directed toward true goods. Information technologies can serve practical reasoning, allowing the deposition of will into the environment rather than its replacement. Problems arise only when decision theory metastasizes from a useful model into the normative form of all practical reason, shaping a mistaken anthropology.

To consider the practical difference that an altered vision might make, let us return to the observations with which the book opened. During the COVID-19 pandemic, individuals were flooded with constantly changing predictions emerging from multiple models, which in part helped fuel the polarization and conspiracy theories driven by social media. To confront shortages of medical supplies, rationing programs emerged based on algorithms predicting the probability of patient survival. Although the first two issues deepened anxiety and made an adequate response to the pandemic more difficult, the last proved unacceptably controlling. As should now be clear, these scenarios arose from the vision of probabilistic prediction and population management that depends upon and shapes emerging information technologies.

How would the vision offered in this book have altered these approaches? In the first place, a turn from the primacy of prediction and populations would encourage a focus on the individual and concrete. Some of the most successful early responses to the pandemic—like those of Vietnam, Germany, South Korea, and Taiwan—depended upon a strategy of testing individuals for the disease, tracing the contacts of infected people, and requiring them to quarantine.[1] This is the classic public health strategy for dealing with infections. To do this well, authorities need to deploy real people as contact tracers, who can explore who the infected person's contacts are, determine modes of transmission, and convince contacts to go into quarantine. Most Western countries have grievously underinvested in public health infrastructure, especially personnel who could staff this approach. Later successful responses relied on the provision of concrete vaccines, once available.

Flooded with conflicting predictions and information, the public in many countries became anxious and distrustful. Policy decisions changed rapidly, often for unclear reasons. Fatigue set in, the vigilance necessary for lockdown measures faded, and many groups (parents, small business owners, and minorities) felt their concerns were not addressed. Although the approach suggested here would not solve these problems, because it was a tragic crisis requiring great prudence, it would alleviate some issues with this approach. First, analysis of the uncertainties of the different models could take place within policymaking circles rather than in the public glare of the media. The focus could be on the variety of ends sought in the response rather than merely stopping the disease. Trade-offs would need to be recognized and justified. This would leave many of the population-level measures in place but with a clearer sense of public justification. It might also reduce anxiety on the personal level.

Conspiracy theories and news siloes are harder to address. Ideally, people would seek news and analysis in multiple venues offering a variety of perspectives. At least, one or two trusted sources could describe diverse viewpoints on important issues. Yet even before the introduction of news feed algorithms, market segmentation among traditional media outlets created difficulties for this ideal. Too many interests find untruths and slander conducive to their purposes. This is an old problem, as the skill of older forms of media at encouraging the spread of such conspiracy theories as those surrounding *The Protocols of the Elders of Zion* showed even in the nineteenth century.[2] But shifting the way algorithms function could limit the rapid expansion of these conspiracy theories. At least, they might not be presented to the unsuspecting web browser as a way to increase the traffic on a site. Limiting various behavioristic techniques such as automatically loading the next video also might prevent users from being sucked deeper into an unreal universe.[3]

In the health care sector itself, there could be much greater circumspection about predictive algorithms like the sequential organ failure assessment score used to determine who receives intensive care. Although this algorithm is relatively simple, medical centers are deploying more powerful and opaque machine learning systems that share just as much possibility for racial bias based in past injustice.[4] Such systems should only be used with precaution and the knowledge that they can easily systematize and expand injustice against the poor and marginalized. Moreover, these algorithms should not serve as the final arbiter of who receives care. These life-and-death decisions should ultimately depend on clinical judgment, especially when comparing very similar cases.[5] Algorithms can serve as tools for assisting that judgment or even as checks on the possibility of subjective bias, but such decisions cannot entirely be taken out of human hands. In these ways, the framework presented here can provide models for addressing practical issues. More important, it provides a theoretical reorientation that would apply to many contemporary issues.

FROM VIRTUE TO THE VIRTUES

The most straightforward application of my analysis regards the role of risk in virtue theory. The Stoic approach to virtue illuminates the themes of the relationship between perception and judgment, the role of providence in the moral life, various understandings of responsibility, and differing conceptions of temporality. But this approach might cause concerns among virtue theorists. Frequently, scholars contrast Stoic and Aristotelian ethics, especially on the issue of security and the value of immanent goods.[6] Further, Stoics had a much stronger idea of the unity of the virtues than did Aristotle.[7] The different virtues in Stoicism reflect situational application of a single practical wisdom rather than the perfection of different affective and rational faculties as in Aristotle. This explains why this work has had so little discussion of individual virtues like temperance or courage. However, though these distinctions show important differences in these two forms of virtue ethics, they do not mean that the analysis offered here cannot be applied to an Aristotelian model of virtue. After all, Aquinas combined Stoic and Aristotelian models of prudence, and both systems affirm the unity of the virtues. Much of the book's argument can be formulated in terms of the seven traditional Christian virtues, although doing so does not provide the clearest illumination of what differentiates practical reason under probabilistic prediction from older forms.[8]

From a negative perspective, the model of probabilistic prediction that I critique undermines virtue by forming people in vice. In this decision-theoretical paradigm, faith becomes confidence in oneself and one's ability to use the tools of technical control to ensure security rather than trust in God. Hope is turned from eternal good to temporal goods, both by the internal dynamic of decision theory and by the algorithmic tools that manipulate desires. The lust for temporal security causes the person to shift attention away from others' needs, undermining charity. God is ignored, and others are treated as objects for manipulation rather than subjects for communion. One uses others to ensure one's own security rather than seeking after their true good. This quest for security also leads to injustice: greed, usury, and manipulation. Not only are others denied the goods they deserve, but social structures also fail to allow them a proper forum for free participation. Goods are hoarded, and action becomes the domain of experts who control data. Prudence is deformed by the focus on the multiple options that confront the individual at any moment rather than on proper ends. The constant enticement of worldly goods corrupts temperance. Courage is sapped by anxiety over the future and fear for security. This mode of engaging the world thus undermines virtue and increases vice.

Reciprocally, recovering virtue and a better mode of practical reason can confront these vices. Enriching one's faith leads to an ever-deepening trust in God and hearkening to His call in one's life. Hope deepens through a developing focus on His promise of eternal reward and continuing temporal strength, despite the struggles and crosses that one bears in the world and the mysterious nature of God's providence. Along with a drive toward union with God's will through concurrence with providence in action, charity encourages an intersubjective engagement with others oriented toward their true good rather than their manipulation for one's own security. This leads to a commitment to just social arrangements in terms of the distribution of temporal goods, protection from the worst results of common risks, and the ability to freely participate in achieving the common good. A proper prudence focuses on true ends, while also taking into account the considerations raised during deliberation by well-performed, but limited, cost/benefit analyses. This focus on true goods gives a proper shape to temperance. The trust in God and desire for true goods inspires courage in the face of risk. Virtue and a proper approach to risk are thus intertwined in the contemporary world.

All this, however, requires a right attitude toward contingency. Given that probabilistic prediction has become so embedded in personal, social, and material worlds, such a change will not come easily. It will require regulation of technology and reshaping policymaking. These changes can occur, however, only if individuals themselves stop thinking and perceiving in these ways. More important, they can occur only if decision theory ceases to be the normative form of practical rationality and is replaced by a richer model of prudence. Risk-based modes of practical reasoning are deeply embedded in contemporary subjectivity because of two hundred years of efforts, so the desired shift will be difficult. It will require a great deal of work on ourselves and on our communities. But only in these ways can we emerge from many of our most pressing problems to a proper faith in God and care for others.

NOTES

Lewis, *Screwtape Letters*, 76.

1. Lewis, "Where Covid Contact-Tracing Went Wrong." These strategies can cease to be effective once the disease becomes too widespread.

2. For discussion of this and the broader context of anti-Semitic conspiracy theories, see Arendt, *Origins of Totalitarianism*.

3. Alter, *Irresistible*.

4. Obermeyer et al., "Dissecting Racial Bias."

5. Sulmasy and Hibner, "Catholic Ethics."

6. Annas, *Morality of Happiness*; Bowlin, *Contingency and Fortune*.

7. On this aspect of Stoicism, especially as it affects ideas surrounding the passions, see Sorabji, *Emotion and Peace of Mind*; Graver, *Stoicism & Emotion*; and Scherz, "Grief, Death, and Longing."

8. In neither the body of the book nor this conclusion do I address some issues that are important to the Christian virtue theorist, such as the relation between acquired and infused virtues, the ontological seat of the virtues, and whether virtues can be held singly. How the framework presented here would address such questions would require an investigation of a different kind.

Bibliography

"Addiction, n." In *OED Online*. Oxford University Press. www-oed-com.proxy01.its.virginia
.edu/view/Entry/2179?redirectedFrom=addiction&.

Aeschylus. "Prometheus Bound." In *Persians: Seven against Thebes—Suppliants—Prometheus Bound*, translated by Alan Sommerstein, 442–563. Loeb Classical Library 145. Cambridge, MA: Harvard University Press, 2009.

Agamben, Giorgio. *Homo Sacer*, translated by Daniel Heller-Roazen. Stanford, CA: Stanford University Press, 1998.

Albree, George. *The Evils of Life Insurance*. Pittsburgh: Bakewell and Mathers, 1870.

Alter, Adam. *Irresistible*. New York: Penguin, 2017.

Anders, Gunther. "On Promethean Shame." In *Prometheanism*, edited by Christopher Muller, 29–96. Lanham, MD: Rowman & Littlefield, 2016.

Angwin, Julia, Jeff Larson, Surya Mattu, and Lauren Kirchner. "Machine Bias." ProPublica, May 23, 2016. www.propublica.org/article/machine-bias-risk-assessments-in-criminal
-sentencing.

Ann Arbor Science for the People Editorial Collective. *Biology as a Social Weapon*. Minneapolis: Burgess, 1977.

Annas, Julia. *The Morality of Happiness*. New York: Oxford University Press, 1993.

Anscombe, G. E. M. *Intention*. 2nd ed. Oxford: Blackwell, 1963.

Arendt, Hannah. *Eichmann in Jerusalem*. New York: Penguin, 1994.

———. *The Human Condition*. Chicago: University of Chicago Press, 1998.

———. *The Life of the Mind*. Vol. 1, *Thinking*. New York: Harcourt Brace Jovanovich, 1978.

———. *The Life of the Mind*. Vol. 2, *Willing*. New York: Harcourt Brace Jovanovich, 1978.

———. *Love and Saint Augustine*. Chicago: University of Chicago Press, 1998.

———. *Origins of Totalitarianism*. New York: Harcourt Brace Jovanovich, 1973.

Aristotle. *Metaphysics*, translated by Hugh Lawson-Tancred. New York: Penguin, 1998.

———. *Nicomachean Ethics*, translated by Terence Irwin. 2nd ed. Indianapolis: Hackett, 1999.

———. *Physics*, translated by Robin Waterfield. Oxford: Oxford University Press, 1999.

———. *Politics*, translated by Carnes Lord. Chicago: University of Chicago Press, 2013.

———. "Topics." In *A New Aristotle Reader*, edited by J. L. Ackrill, 60–80. Princeton, NJ: Princeton University Press, 1987.

Aronowitz, Robert. *Risky Medicine*. Chicago: University of Chicago Press, 2015.

Augustine. *The City of God against the Pagans*, translated by R.W. Dyson. Cambridge: Cambridge University Press, 1998.

———. *Confessions*, translated by F. J. Sheed. 2nd ed. Indianapolis: Hackett, 2006.

Baker, David. *Tight Fists or Open Hands? Wealth and Poverty in Old Testament Law*. Grand Rapids: Wm. B. Eerdmans, 2009.

Balthasar, Hans Urs von. *The Christian and Anxiety*, translated by Dennis Martin and Michael Miller. San Francisco: Ignatius Press, 2000.

Barlow, John Perry. "Crime and Puzzlement," 1990. www.eff.org/pages/crime-and-puzzlement.

Barth, Karl. *Church Dogmatics*. New York: T. & T. Clark, 2010.

Beabout, Gregory. *Freedom and Its Misuses: Kierkegaard on Anxiety and Despair*. Milwaukee: Marquette University Press, 1996.

Beck, Ulrich. *Risk Society*. London: Sage, 1992.

Benjamin, Ruha. *Race after Technology*. Medford, MA: Polity, 2019.

Bennett, Jana. *Aquinas on the Web?* London: T. & T. Clark, 2012.

Bergsma, John. *The Jubilee from Leviticus to Qumran*. Boston: Leiden, 2007.

Bergson, Henri. *Matter and Memory*, translated by Nancy Margaret Paul and W. Scott Palmer. New York: Macmillan, 1913.

———. *Time and Free Will*, translated by Frank Pogson. New York: Macmillan, 1910.

Bernard, Andreas. *The Triumph of Profiling*, translated by Valentine Pakis. Medford, MA: Polity, 2019.

Bernstein, Peter. *Against the Gods: The Remarkable Story of Risk*. New York: Wiley, 1998.

Biggar, Nigel. *The Hastening That Waits*. New York: Oxford University Press, 1996.

Binkley, Sam. *Happiness as Enterprise*. Albany: State University of New York Press, 2014.

Black, Anthony. *Guild and State*. Piscataway, NJ: Transaction, 2003.

Blumenberg, Hans. *The Legitimacy of the Modern Age*. Cambridge, MA: MIT Press, 1985.

Bobzien, Susanne. *Determinism and Freedom in Stoic Philosophy*. New York: Oxford University Press, 2002.

Boethius. "The Consolation of Philosophy." In *Theological Tractates: The Consolation of Philosophy*, translated by H. F. Stewart, E. K. Rand, and S. J. Tester, 130–436. Loeb Classical Library 74. Cambridge, MA: Harvard University Press, 1973.

Boltanski, Luc, and Eve Chiapello. *The New Spirit of Capitalism*, translated by Gregory Elliott. New York: Verso, 2005.

Bonhoeffer, Dietrich. *Ethics*, translated by Neville Smith. New York: Touchstone, 1955.

Borges, Jorge Luis. "The Garden of Forking Paths." In *Collected Fictions*, translated by Andrew Hurley, 119–28. New York: Penguin, 1998.

Borgmann, Albert. *Technology and the Character of Contemporary Life*. Chicago: University of Chicago Press, 1987.

Bostrom, Nick, and Eliezer Yudkowsky. "The Ethics of Artificial Intelligence." In *The Cambridge Handbook of Artificial Intelligence*, edited by William Ramsey and Keith Frankish, 316–34. Cambridge: Cambridge University Press, 2014.

Bouk, Dan. *How Our Days Became Numbered: Risk and the Rise of the Statistical Individual*. Chicago: University of Chicago Press, 2015.

Bourne, Hannah, Thomas Douglas, and Julian Savulescu. "Procreative Beneficence and In Vitro Gametogenesis." *Monash Bioethics Review* 30, no. 2 (2012): 29–48.

Bowen, Ralph. *German Theories of the Corporative State*. New York: Russell and Russell, 1947.

Bowlin, John. "Barth and Werpehowski on War, Presumption, and Exception." In *Commanding Grace*, edited by Daniel Migliore, 83–95. Grand Rapids: Wm. B. Eerdmans, 2010.

———. *Contingency and Fortune in Aquinas's Ethics*. New York: Cambridge University Press, 1999.

Braun, Ernest. *Technology in Context*. New York: Routledge, 1998.

Braverman, Harry. *Labor and Monopoly Capital*. New York: Monthly Review Press, 1998.

Brock, Brian. *Christian Ethics in a Technological Age*. Grand Rapids: Wm. B. Eerdmans, 2010.

Brown, Peter. *Poverty and Leadership in the Later Roman Empire*. Waltham, MA: Brandeis University Press, 2001.

Brown, Wendy. *Undoing the Demos*. New York: Zone Books, 2015.

Bruni, Luigino, and Stefano Zamagni. *Civil Economy: Another Idea of the Market*, translated by N. Michael Brennen. Newcastle: Agenda, 2016.

Burraway, Joshua. "Remembering to Forget: Blacking Out in Itchy Park." *Current Anthropology* 59, no. 5 (2018): 469–87.

Burrell, David. *Aquinas: God and Action*. Notre Dame, IN: University of Notre Dame Press, 1979.

———. *Freedom and Creation in Three Traditions*. Notre Dame, IN: University of Notre Dame Press, 1993.

Byers, Sarah Catherine. *Perception, Sensibility, and Moral Motivation in Augustine: A Stoic-Platonic Synthesis*. New York: Cambridge University Press, 2013.

Caduff, Carlo. "What Went Wrong: Corona and the World after the Full Stop." *Medical Anthropology Quarterly* 34, no. 4 (2020): 467–87.

Carlson, Elof. *The Unfit*. Cold Spring Harbor, NY: Cold Spring Harbor Laboratory Press, 2001.

Carr, Nicholas. *The Glass Cage*. New York: W. W. Norton, 2015.

Carroll, Sean. *Something Deeply Hidden: Quantum Worlds and the Emergence of Spacetime*. New York: E. P. Dutton, 2019.

Carruthers, Mary. *The Book of Memory*. New York: Cambridge University Press, 1990.

Cassian, John. *The Conferences*, translated by Boniface Ramsey. Ancient Christian Writers 57. New York: Paulist Press, 1997.

Ceccarelli, Giovanni. "Risky Business: Theological and Canonical Thought on Insurance from the Thirteenth to the Seventeenth Century." *Journal of Medieval and Early Modern Studies* 31, no. 3 (2001): 607–58.

Cheney-Lippold, John. *We Are Data*. New York: New York University Press, 2017.

Childers, Timothy. *Philosophy and Probability*. New York: Oxford University Press, 2013.

Cicero, Marcus Tullius. *On Invention. The Best Kind of Orator: Topics*, translated by H. M. Hubbell. Cambridge, MA: Harvard University Press, 1949.

———. *On Moral Ends*. New York: Cambridge University Press, 2001.

———. *On Obligations*. New York: Oxford University Press, 2000.

Clough, David. *Ethics in Crisis*. Burlington, VT: Ashgate, 2005.

Cloutier, David. *The Vice of Luxury*. Washington, DC: Georgetown University Press, 2015.

Coco, Linda. "The Cultural Logics of the Bankruptcy Abuse Prevention and Consumer Protection Act of 2005: Fiscal Identities and Financial Failure." *Critical Sociology* 40, no. 5 (2014): 711–27.

Colish, Marcia L. *The Stoic Tradition from Antiquity to the Early Middle Ages*. New York: E. J. Brill, 1990.

Collins, Harry, and Robert Evans. "The Third Wave of Science Studies." *Social Studies of Science* 32, no. 2 (2002): 235–96.

Congregation for the Doctrine of the Faith. *Instructions Dignitas Personae on Certain Bioethical Questions*. Nairobi: Pauline Publications Africa, 2009.

Crawford, Matthew B. *The World Beyond Your Head*. Farrar, Straus & Giroux, 2016.

———. *Why We Drive*. New York: HarperCollins, 2020.

Crouter, Richard. "H. Richard Niebuhr and Stoicism." *Journal of Religious Ethics* 2, no. 2 (1974): 129–46.

Csikszentmihalyi, Mihaly. *Flow*. New York: HarperCollins, 1994.

Curran, Charles. "Conscience in the Light of the Catholic Moral Tradition." In *Conscience*, edited by Charles Curran, 3–24. Readings in Moral Theology 14. Mahwah, NJ: Paulist Press, 2004.

Cyprian. "On Jealousy and Envy." In *Hippolytus, Cyprian, Caius, Novation*. Vol. 5, *Ante-Nicene Fathers*. Peabody, MA: Hendrickson, 1996.

Danaher, John, Sven Nyholm, and Brian Earp. "The Quantified Relationship." *American Journal of Bioethics* 18, no. 2 (2018): 3–19.

Dastin, Jeffrey. "Amazon Scraps Secret AI Recruiting Tool That Showed Bias against Women." Reuters, October 9, 2018. www.reuters.com/article/us-amazon-com-jobs-automation -insight/amazon-scraps-secret-ai-recruiting-tool-that-showed-bias-against-women-idUSK CN1MK08G.

Daston, Lorraine. *Classical Probability in the Enlightenment*. Princeton, NJ: Princeton University Press, 1995.

David, Marie. "AI and the Illusion of Human-Algorithm Complementarity." *Social Research* 86, no. 4 (2019): 887–908.

Davis, Joseph E. *Chemically Imbalanced*. Chicago: University of Chicago Press, 2020.

———. "Social Physics Comes to the Workplace." *Hedgehog Review* 22, no. 2 (2020): 58–72.

Dean, Mitchell. *Governmentality*. Thousand Oaks, CA: Sage, 1999.

Deane-Drummond, Celia. *Christ and Evolution*. Minneapolis: Fortress Press, 2009.

Defert, Daniel. "Popular Life and Insurance Technology." In *The Foucault Effect*, edited by Graham Burchell, Colin Gordon, and Peter Miller. London: Harvester Wheatsheaf, 1991.

Delumeau, Jean. *Rassurer et Proteger*. Paris: Fayard, 1989.

Dempsey, Bernard. *Interest and Usury*. Washington, DC: American Council on Public Affairs, 1943.

Dennett, Daniel C. *From Bacteria to Bach and Back: The Evolution of Minds*. New York: Norton, 2017.

Desrosieres, Alain. *The Politics of Large Numbers*, translated by Camille Naish. Cambridge, MA: Harvard University Press, 1998.

Doneson, Daniel. "The Conquest of Fortune: On the Machiavellian Character of Algorithmic Judgement." *Social Research* 86, no. 4 (2019).

Douglas, Mary, and Aaron Wildavsky. *Risk and Culture*. Berkeley: University of California Press, 1982.

Dreyfus, Hubert L. *What Computers Can't Do*. Revised ed. New York: HarperCollins, 1978.

Droge, Mitchell. "What Is Quantified Self?" *Quantified Self Institute* (blog), October 18, 2016. http://qsinstitute.com/about/what-is-quantified-self/.

Dudley, John. *Aristotle's Concept of Chance*. Albany: State University of New York Press, 2012.

Dumit, Joseph. *Drugs for Life*. Durham, NC: Duke University Press, 2012.

Dupuy, Jean-Pierre. *The Mechanization of the Mind*. Princeton, NJ: Princeton University Press, 2000.

———. *Pour un catastrophisme eclaire*. Paris: Seuil, 2002.

———. *A Short Treatise on the Metaphysics of Tsunamis*, translated by Malcolm DeBovoise. East Lansing: Michigan State University Press, 2015.

Edwards, Paul. *The Closed World*. Cambridge, MA: MIT Press, 1997.

Ehrenreich, Barbara. *Natural Causes*. New York: Twelve, 2018.

Elbow, Matthew. *French Corporative Theory, 1789–1948*. New York: Columbia University Press, 1953.

Eliade, Mircea. *The Myth of Eternal Return*, translated by Willard Trask. New York: Pantheon, 1954.

Elliot, David. "The Christian as Homo Viator: A Resource in Aquinas for Overcoming 'Worldly Sin and Sorrow.'" *Journal of the Society of Christian Ethics* 34, no. 2 (2014): 101–21.

Ellul, Jacques. *The Technological Society*, translated by John Wilkinson. New York: Vintage Books, 1964.

Elster, Jon. *Ulysses and the Sirens*. Cambridge: Cambridge University Press, 1984.

Emanuel, Ezekiel, Govind Persad, Ross Upshur, et al. "Fair Allocation of Scarce Medical Resources in the Time of COVID-19." *New England Journal of Medicine* 382 (2020): 2049–55.

Epictetus. *Discourses, Books 1–2*, translated by W. A. Oldfather. Loeb Classical Library 131. Cambridge, MA: Harvard University Press, 1998.

Epstude, Kai. "Counterfactual Thinking." In *The Psychology of Thinking about the Future*, edited by Gabriele Oettingen, A. Timur Sevincer, and Peter Gollwitzer, 110–26. New York: Guilford Press, 2018.

Eubanks, Virginia. *Automating Inequality*. New York: St. Martin's Press, 2018.

Ewald, Francois. *L'etat providence*. Paris: Grasset, 1986.

Fager, Jeffrey. "Land Tenure in the Biblical Jubilee: A Moral World View." *Hebrew Annual Review* 11 (1987): 59–68.

Farmer, Paul. *Pathologies of Power*. Berkeley: University of California Press, 2004.

Fergusson, David. *The Providence of God*. New York: Cambridge University Press, 2018.

Finnis, John. *Natural Law and Natural Rights*. 2nd ed. Oxford: Oxford University Press, 2011.

Fisher, Irving, and Eugene Fisk. *How to Live*. 16th ed. New York: Funk & Wagnalls, 1922.

Fleming, Julia. *Defending Probabilism: The Moral Theology of Juan Caramuel*. Washington, DC: Georgetown University Press, 2007.

Foucault, Michel. *The Birth of Biopolitics: Lectures at the Collège de France, 1978–79*, edited by Michel Senellart. New York: Palgrave Macmillan, 2008.

———. *The Care of the Self*. New York: Pantheon Books, 1986.

———. *Discipline and Punish*. New York: Pantheon Books, 1977.

———. *The History of Sexuality*. Vol. 1. New York: Pantheon Books, 1978.

———. "On the Genealogy of Ethics: An Overview of Work in Progress." In *Ethics, Subjectivity, and Truth*, edited by Paul Rabinow, 253–80. New York: New Press, 1998.

———. *The Order of Things*. New York: Vintage Books, 1994.

———. *Security, Territory, Population: Lectures at the Collège de France, 1977–78*, edited by Michel Senellart and translated by Graham Burchell. New York: Palgrave Macmillan, 2007.

———. *Society Must Be Defended: Lectures at the Collège de France, 1975–76*, edited by Mauro Bertani and Alessandro Fontana and translated by David Macey. New York: Picador, 2003.

Foucault, Michel, Graham Burchell, Colin Gordon, and Peter Miller. *The Foucault Effect: Studies in Governmentality*. Chicago: University of Chicago Press, 1991.

France, R. T. *The Gospel of Matthew*. New International Commentary on the New Testament. Grand Rapids: Wm. B. Eerdmans, 2007.

Francis. *Evangelii gaudium*, 2013. www.vatican.va/content/francesco/en/apost_exhortations/documents/papa-francesco_esortazione-ap_20131124_evangelii-gaudium.html.

———. *Fratelli tutti*, 2020. www.vatican.va/content/francesco/en/encyclicals/documents /papa-francesco_20201003_enciclica-fratelli-tutti.html.

———. *Gaudete et exsultate*, 2018. http://w2.vatican.va/content/francesco/en/apost _exhortations/documents/papa-francesco_esortazione-ap_20180319_gaudete-et -exsultate.html.

———. *Laudato si'*, 2015. http://w2.vatican.va/content/francesco/en/encyclicals/documents /papa-francesco_20150524_enciclica-laudato-si.html.

———. *Patris corde*, 2020. www.vatican.va/content/francesco/en/apost_letters/documents /papa-francesco-lettera-ap_20201208_patris-corde.html.

Franklin, James. *The Art of Conjecture*. Baltimore: Johns Hopkins University Press, 2001.

Franks, Christopher. *He Became Poor: The Poverty of Christ in Aquinas's Economic Teaching*. Grand Rapids: Wm. B. Eerdmans, 2009.

Freddoso, Alfred. "Introduction." In *On Divine Foreknowledge: Part IV of the Concordia*, by Luis de Molina, 1–83. Ithaca, NY: Cornell University Press, 2004.

Gadamer, Hans-Georg. *The Enigma of Health*. Stanford, CA: Stanford University Press, 1996.

Garber, Daniel, and Sandy Zabell. "On the Emergence of Probability." *Archive for History of Exact Sciences* 21, no. 1 (1979): 33–53.

Garrigou-Lagrange, Reginald. *Providence*, translated by Bede Rose. Saint Louis: Herder, 1937.

Giddens, Anthony. *The Consequences of Modernity*. Stanford, CA: Stanford University Press, 1991.

Gigerenzer, Gerd. "On the Supposed Evidence for Libertarian Paternalism." *Review of Philosophy and Psychology* 6 (2015): 361–83.

———. *Rationality for Mortals*. New York: Oxford University Press, 2008.

Gigerenzer, Gerd, Zeno Swijtink, Theodore Porter, Lorraine Daston, John Beatty, and Lorenz Kruger. *The Empire of Chance*. Cambridge: Cambridge University Press, 1990.

Gill, Christopher. "Did Chrysippus Understand Medea?" *Phronesis* 28, no. 2 (1983): 136–49.

Goldin, Ian, and Mike Mariathasan. *The Butterfly Defect*. Princeton, NJ: Princeton University Press, 2015.

Goldschmidt, Victor. *Le système stoïcien et l'idée de temps*. 2nd ed. Bibliotheque d'histoire de la philosophie. Paris: Vrin, 1969.

Gould, Stephen Jay. *The Mismeasure of Man*. 2nd ed. New York: W. W. Norton, 1996.

———. *Time's Arrow, Time's Cycle*. Cambridge, MA: Harvard University Press, 1987.

Grant, George. "Knowing and Making." In *The George Grant Reader*, edited by William Christian and Sheila Grant, 407–17. Toronto: University of Toronto Press, 1998.

Graver, Margaret. *Stoicism & Emotion*. Chicago: University of Chicago Press, 2007.

Greene, Jeremy A. *Prescribing by Numbers*. Baltimore: Johns Hopkins University Press, 2008.

Greene, Joshua, R. Brian Sommerville, Leigh Nystrom, John Darley, and Jonathan Cohen. "An FMRI Investigation of Emotional Engagement in Moral Judgment." *Science* 293, no. 5537 (2001): 2105–8.

Gregersen, Niels Henrik. "Risk and Religion: Toward a Theology of Risk Taking." *Zygon* 38, no. 2 (2003): 355–76.

Guardini, Romano. *Conscience*, translated by Ada Lane. New York: Benziger Bros., 1932.

———. *Das Ende Der Neuzeit*. Basel: Hess Verlag, 1950.

———. *The End of the Modern World*. Wilmington, DE: ISI Books, 2001.

———. *Freedom, Grace, and Destiny*, translated by John Murray. New York: Pantheon, 1961.

———. "The Jewish Problem: Reflexions on Responsibility." *Dublin Review* 227, no. 459 (1953): 1–14.

Guillaume, Philippe. *Land, Credit, and Crisis: Agrarian Finance in the Hebrew Bible.* Sheffield, UK: Equinox, 2012.

Gusterson, Hugh. "Introduction: Robohumans." In *Life by Algorithms,* edited by Catherine Besteman and Hugh Gusterson, 1–27. Chicago: University of Chicago Press, 2019.

Guynn, Jessica. "Google Photos Labeled Black People 'Gorillas.'" *USA Today,* July 1, 2015. www.usatoday.com/story/tech/2015/07/01/google-apologizes-after-photos-identify -black-people-as-gorillas/29567465/.

Habermas, Jürgen. *The Future of Human Nature.* Malden, MA: Polity, 2003.

Hacker, Jacob. *The Great Risk Shift.* New York: Oxford University Press, 2019.

Hacking, Ian. *The Emergence of Probability.* 2nd ed. Cambridge: Cambridge University Press, 2006.

———. *An Introduction to Probability and Inductive Logic.* New York: Cambridge University Press, 2001.

———. *Logic of Statistical Inference.* Cambridge: Cambridge University Press, 1965.

———. *The Taming of Chance.* Cambridge: Cambridge University Press, 1990.

Hadot, Pierre. *Philosophy as a Way of Life,* translated by Arnold Davidson. Cambridge, MA: Blackwell, 1995.

———. *The Present Alone Is Our Happiness.* Stanford, CA: Stanford University Press, 2009.

HAPI.com. "HAPIfork." No date. www.hapilabs.com/product/hapifork.

Haring, Bernard. *The Law of Christ.* Vol. 1, *General Moral Theology,* translated by Edwin Kaiser. Westminster, MD: Newman Press, 1966.

Harrison, Peter. *The Fall of Man and the Foundations of Science.* New York: Cambridge University Press, 2007.

Harvey, David. *A Brief History of Neoliberalism.* Oxford: Oxford University Press, 2007.

———. *The Condition of Postmodernity.* Cambridge, MA: Blackwell, 1990.

Haskell, Thomas. *Objectivity Is Not Neutrality.* Baltimore: Johns Hopkins University Press, 2000.

Hasselberger, William. "Ethics beyond Computation: Why We Can't (and Shouldn't) Replace Human Moral Judgment with Algorithms." *Social Research* 86, no. 4 (2019): 977–1000.

Hauerwas, Stanley. *A Community of Character.* Notre Dame, IN: University of Notre Dame Press, 1991.

Haueter, Niels Viggo, and Geoffrey Jones. *Managing Risk in Reinsurance.* Oxford: Oxford University Press, 2017.

Hayek, Friedrich A. von. *Individualism and Economic Order.* Chicago: University of Chicago Press, 1948.

———. *Law, Legislation, and Liberty.* Vol. 1, *Rules and Order.* Chicago: University of Chicago Press, 1973.

———. *New Studies in Philosophy: Politics, Economics, and the History of Ideas.* Chicago: University of Chicago Press, 1978.

Hayles, N. Katherine. *How We Became Posthuman.* Chicago: University of Chicago Press, 1999.

Hefner, Philip J. *Technology and Human Becoming.* Minneapolis: Fortress Press, 2003.

Heidegger, Martin. *Being and Time,* translated by John Macquarrie and Edward Robinson. New York: HarperCollins, 2008.

———. "The Question concerning Technology." In *The Question concerning Technology, and Other Essays,* 3–35. New York: Harper Torchbooks, 1977.

Herman, Barbara. *The Practice of Moral Judgment.* Cambridge, MA: Harvard University Press, 1993.

Hesiod. "Theogony." In *Hesiod I*, translated by Glenn Most, 2–85. Loeb Classical Library 57. Cambridge, MA: Harvard University Press, 2006.

———. "Works and Days." In *Hesiod I*, translated by Glenn Most, 86–153. Loeb Classical Library 57. Cambridge, MA: Harvard University Press, 2006.

Hirschfeld, Mary. *Aquinas and the Market*. Cambridge, MA: Harvard University Press, 2018.

HM Treasury. "The Orange Book: Management of Risk—Principles and Concepts." London: HM Treasury, 2004.

Hobbes, Thomas. *Leviathan*. Indianapolis: Hackett, 1994.

Hollenbach, David. *The Common Good and Christian Ethics*. Cambridge: Cambridge University Press, 2002.

Husserl, Edmund. *The Crisis of European Sciences and Transcendental Phenomenology*. Evanston, IL: Northwestern University Press, 1970.

Illich, Ivan. *Deschooling Society*. New York: Harper & Row, 1971.

International Theological Commission. "In Search of a Universal Ethic: A New Look at the Natural Law," 2009. www.vatican.va/roman_curia/congregations/cfaith/cti_documents /rc_con_cfaith_doc_20090520_legge-naturale_en.html.

Janssens, Louis. "Ontic Evil and Moral Evil." In *Moral Norms and the Catholic Tradition*, edited by Charles Curran and Richard McCormick, 40–93. Readings in Moral Theology 1. New York: Paulist Press, 1979.

Jarzabkowski, Paula, Rebecca Bednarek, and Paul Spee. *Making a Market for Acts of God*. Oxford: Oxford University Press, 2015.

Jasanoff, Sheila. "Breaking the Waves in Science Studies." *Social Studies of Science* 33, no. 3 (2003): 389–400.

Jensen, Steven. *Good and Evil Actions*. Washington, DC: Catholic University of America Press, 2010.

John of Damascus. "Exposition of the Orthodox Faith." In *Hilary of Poitiers, John of Damascus*, edited by Philip Schaff and Henry Wace, 9:1–101. Nicene and Post-Nicene Fathers. 2nd ed. Peabody, MA: Hendrickson, 2012.

John Paul II. *Salvifici doloris*, 1984. https://w2.vatican.va/content/john-paul-ii/en/apost _letters/1984/documents/hf_jp-ii_apl_11021984_salvifici-doloris.html.

———. *Veritatis splendor*, 1993. http://w2.vatican.va/content/john-paul-ii/en/encyclicals /documents/hf_jp-ii_enc_06081993_veritatis-splendor.html.

Joint Statement. "Moral Guidance on Prioritizing Care during a Pandemic." *Public Discourse*. No date. www.thepublicdiscourse.com/2020/04/62001/.

Jonas, Hans. *The Imperative of Responsibility*. Chicago: University of Chicago Press, 1985.

Jonsen, Albert. *Responsibility in Modern Religious Ethics*. Washington, DC: Corpus Books, 1968.

Jonsen, Albert, and Stephen Toulmin. *The Abuse of Casuistry*. Berkeley: University of California Press, 1988.

Junkersfeld, Julienne. "The Aristotelian-Thomistic Concept of Chance." PhD diss., University of Notre Dame, 1945.

Kahneman, Daniel. *Thinking, Fast and Slow*. New York: Farrar, Straus & Giroux, 2013.

Kant, Immanuel. *Groundwork of the Metaphysics of Morals*, translated by Jens Timmermann. New York: Cambridge University Press, 2012.

Kaveny, M. Cathleen. "Tax Lawyers, Prophets, and Pilgrims." In *Cooperation, Complicity, and Conscience*, edited by Helen Watt, 65–88. Oxford: Linacre Center, 2005.

Kaye, Howard. *The Social Meaning of Modern Biology*. New Haven, CT: Yale University Press, 1986.

Keenan, James F. *A History of Catholic Moral Theology in the Twentieth Century.* London: Bloomsbury Academic, 2010.

Ketteler, Wilhelm Emmanuel von. *The Social Teachings of Wilhelm Emmanuel von Ketteler,* translated by Rupert Ederer. Washington, DC: University Press of America, 1981.

Kevles, Daniel. *In the Name of Eugenics.* Cambridge, MA: Harvard University Press, 1995.

Keynes, John Maynard. *A Treatise on Probability.* London: Macmillan, 1921.

Kierkegaard, Søren. "The Cares of the Pagans." In *Christian Discourses: The Crisis and a Crisis in the Life of an Actress,* translated by Howard V. Hong and Edna H. Hong. Kierkegaard's Writings XVII. Princeton, NJ: Princeton University Press, 1997.

———. *The Concept of Anxiety,* translated by Albert B. Anderson. Princeton, NJ: Princeton University Press, 1981.

———. *Consider the Lilies,* translated by A. S. Aldworth and W. S. Ferrie. London: Daniel Company, 1940.

———. *The Sickness unto Death,* translated by Howard V. Hong and Edna H. Hong. Princeton, NJ: Princeton University Press, 1983.

Kirzner, Israel. *Competition and Entrepreneurship.* Chicago: University of Chicago Press, 1973.

Kishkovsky, Sophia, and Oleg Matsnev. "Stanislav Petrov, Soviet Officer Who Helped Avert Nuclear War, Is Dead at 77." *New York Times,* September 18, 2017.

Kleinman, Daniel Lee, and Sainath Suryanarayanan. "Dying Bees and the Social Production of Ignorance." *Science, Technology & Human Values* 38, no. 4 (2013): 492–517.

Knauer, Peter. "The Hermeneutic Function of the Principle of Double Effect." In *Moral Norms and the Catholic Tradition,* edited by Charles Curran and Richard McCormick, 1–39. Readings in Moral Theology 1. New York: Paulist Press, 1979.

Knight, Frank H. *Risk, Uncertainty, and Profit.* Ithaca, NY: Cornell University Library, 2009; orig. pub. 1921.

Koch, Antony. *A Handbook of Moral Theology,* vol. 1., edited by Arthur Preuss. Saint Louis: Herder, 1918.

Koninck, Charles De. "The Problem of Indeterminism." In *The Writings of Charles De Koninck,* edited by Ralph McInerny, 1:355–400. Notre Dame, IN: University of Notre Dame Press, 2008.

———. "Reflections on the Problem of Indeterminism." In *The Writings of Charles De Koninck,* edited by Ralph McInerny, 1:401–42. Notre Dame, IN: University of Notre Dame Press, 2008.

Koolhaas, Rem. "Rem Koolhaas Asks: Are Smart Cities Condemned to Be Stupid?" *ArchDaily* (blog), December 10, 2014. www.archdaily.com/576480/rem-koolhaas-asks-are-smart-cities-condemned-to-be-stupid/.

Koselleck, Reinhart. *Futures Past,* translated by Keith Tribe. New York: Columbia University Press, 2004.

Krugman, Paul. "An Insurance Company with an Army." *New York Times Opinion* (blog), April 27, 2011. https://krugman.blogs.nytimes.com/2011/04/27/an-insurance-company-with-an-army/.

La Mettrie, Julien Offray de. *L'homme machine,* edited by Aram Vartanian. Princeton, NJ: Princeton University Press, 1960.

LaCugna, Catherine. *God for Us.* San Francisco: Harper, 1993.

Langholm, Odd. *Economics in the Medieval Schools.* New York: Brill, 1992.

Larson, Erik J. *The Myth of Artificial Intelligence.* Cambridge, MA: Belknap Press, 2021.

Lears, Jackson. "Animal Spirits." *Hedgehog Review* 19, no. 2 (2017).

———. *Something for Nothing: Luck in America.* New York: Viking, 2003.

Leftow, Brian. *Time and Eternity.* Ithaca, NY: Cornell University Press, 1991.

Legaspi, Michael. *Wisdom in Classical and Biblical Tradition.* New York: Oxford University Press, 2018.

Leo XIII. *Rerum novarum,* 1891. www.vatican.va/content/leo-xiii/en/encyclicals/documents /hf_l-xiii_enc_15051891_rerum-novarum.html.

Levinas, Emmanuel. *Otherwise than Being or beyond Essence,* translated by Alphonso Lingis. Dordrecht: Kluwer, 1978.

———. *Totality and Infinity,* translated by Alphonso Lingis. Pittsburgh: Duquesne University Press, 1969.

Lewis, Charlton. "Probabilis." In *An Elementary Latin Dictionary.* New York: American Book Company, 1890. www.perseus.tufts.edu/hopper/text?doc=Perseus%3Atext%3A1999.04 .0060%3Aentry%3Dprobabilis.

———. "Probabilitas." In *An Elementary Latin Dictionary.* New York: American Book Company, 1890. www.perseus.tufts.edu/hopper/text?doc=Perseus%3Atext%3A1999.04.006 0%3Aentry%3Dprobabilitas.

Lewis, C. S. *The Abolition of Man.* New York: Simon & Schuster, 1978.

———. *The Screwtape Letters.* New York: HarperCollins, 1996.

Lewis, David. *On the Plurality of Worlds.* Oxford: Blackwell, 1986.

Lewis, Dyani. "Where COVID Contact-Tracing Went Wrong." *Nature* 588 (2020): 384–87.

Lewontin, Richard. *Biology as Ideology.* New York: Harper Perennial, 1991.

Lonergan, Bernard. *Insight.* San Francisco: Harper & Row, 1957.

Long, A. A., and D. N. Sedley. *The Hellenistic Philosophers.* New York: Cambridge University Press, 1987.

Long, D. Stephen. *Divine Economy.* New York: Routledge, 2000.

Loomes, Graham, and Robert Sugden. "Regret Theory: An Alternative Theory of Rational Choice under Uncertainty." *Economic Journal* 92 (1982): 805–24.

Luhmann, Niklas. *Risk,* translated by Rhodes Barrett. New Brunswick, NJ: Aldine Transaction, 2005.

Lupton, Deborah. *The Quantified Self.* New York: Polity, 2016.

Luz, Ulrich. *Matthew 1–7: A Commentary,* translated by James Crouch. Hermeneia–A Critical and Historical Commentary on the Bible. Minneapolis: Fortress Press, 2007.

Machiavelli, Niccolò. *Discourses on Livy,* translated by Harvey Mansfield and Nathan Tarcov. Chicago: University of Chicago Press, 1996.

———. *The Prince.* 2nd ed., translated by Harvey Mansfield. Chicago: University of Chicago Press, 1998.

MacIntyre, Alasdair. *After Virtue.* 2nd ed. Notre Dame, IN: University of Notre Dame Press, 1984.

———. *Dependent Rational Animals.* Chicago: Open Court, 1999.

———. *Ethics in the Conflicts of Modernity.* New York: Cambridge University Press, 2016.

———. *Three Rival Versions of Moral Enquiry.* Notre Dame, IN: University of Notre Dame Press, 1990.

———. *Whose Justice? Which Rationality?* Notre Dame, IN: University of Notre Dame Press, 1988.

Macrobius, Ambrosius Aurelius Theodosius. *Commentary on the Dream of Scipio.* New York: Columbia University Press, 1990.

Mahoney, John. *The Making of Moral Theology.* New York: Oxford University Press, 1989.

Maritain, Jacques. *Bergsonian Philosophy and Thomism*, translated by Mabelle Andison and J. Gordon Andison. Notre Dame, IN: University of Notre Dame Press, 2007.

———. *The Degrees of Knowledge*. Notre Dame, IN: University of Notre Dame Press, 1995.

———. *The Person and the Common Good*, translated by John J. Fitzgerald. Notre Dame, IN: University of Notre Dame Press, 1973.

Marmot, Michael. "Social Determinants of Health Inequalities." *Lancet* 365 (2005): 1099–1104.

Martin, Emily. *Flexible Bodies*. Boston: Beacon Press, 1995.

Mattison, William. *The Sermon on the Mount and Moral Theology*. New York: Cambridge University Press, 2017.

McCall, Brian. *The Church and the Usurers*. Ave Maria, FL: Sapientia Press, 2013.

McCormick, Richard. *Ambiguity in Moral Choice*. Père Marquette Theology Lecture 1973. Milwaukee: Marquette University Press, 1973.

———. "A Commentary on the Commentaries." In *Doing Evil to Achieve Good*, edited by Richard McCormick and Paul Ramsey, 193–267. Chicago: Loyola University Press, 1978.

McKenny, Gerald. *The Analogy of Grace: Karl Barth's Moral Theology*. Oxford: Oxford University Press, 2010.

———. "Responsibility." In *The Oxford Handbook of Theological Ethics*, edited by Gilbert Meilaender and William Werpehowski. Oxford: Oxford University Press, 2007.

———. "Transcendence, Technological Enhancement, and Christian Theology." In *Transhumanism and Transcendence*, edited by Ronald Cole-Turner, 177–92. Washington, DC: Georgetown University Press, 2011.

McKeown, Thomas. *The Modern Rise of Population*. London: Edward Arnold, 1976.

McKinnon, Susan. *Neo-Liberal Genetics*. Chicago: Prickly Paradigm Press, 2005.

Menconi, Michael. "COVID-19 Ventilator Allocation Protocols Are Poised to Disadvantage African Americans." *Voices in Bioethics* 6 (2020). https://doi.org/10.7916/vib.v6i.6210.

Merchant, Carolyn. *The Death of Nature*. New York: HarperCollins, 1980.

Merriell, Donald. *To the Image of the Trinity*. Toronto: Pontifical Institute of Mediaeval Studies, 1990.

Milbank, John. *Theology and Social Theory*. Oxford: Blackwell, 1993.

Milbank, John, and Adrian Pabst. *The Politics of Virtue*. Lanham, MD: Rowman & Littlefield, 2016.

Mirowski, Philip. *Never Let a Serious Crisis Go to Waste*. New York: Verso, 2013.

———. *Science-Mart: Privatizing American Science*. Cambridge, MA: Harvard University Press, 2011.

Mirowski, Philip, and Dieter Plehwe, eds. *The Road from Mont Pelerin: The Making of the Neoliberal Thought Collective*. Cambridge, MA: Harvard University Press, 2009.

Mises, Richard von. *Probability, Statistics, and Truth*, translated by J. Neyman, D. Sholl, and E. Rabinowitsch. New York: Macmillan, 1939.

Moltmann, Jürgen. *Theology of Hope*. New York: Harper & Row, 1975.

Monod, Jacques. *Chance and Necessity*. New York: Vintage Books, 1972.

Moore, G. E. *Principia ethica*. Cambridge: Cambridge University Press, 1922.

Moses, Julia. *The First Modern Risk*. New York: Cambridge University Press, 2019.

Mounk, Yascha. *The Age of Responsibility*. Cambridge, MA: Harvard University Press, 2017.

Murphy, Roland. *The Tree of Life: An Exploration of Biblical Wisdom Literature*. 3rd ed. Grand Rapids: Wm. B. Eerdmans, 2002.

Nell-Breuning, Oswald von. *Reorganization of Social Economy*, translated by Bernard Dempsey. New York: Bruce, 1936.

Newman, John Henry. *A Letter Addressed to His Grace the Duke of Norfolk on Occasion of Mr. Gladstone's Recent Expostulation.* New York: Catholic Publication Society, 1875.

Niebuhr, H. Richard. *The Responsible Self.* New York: Harper & Row, 1963.

Nolt, Steve. "Problems of Collectivity and Modernity: Midcentury Mennonite Conflicts Involving Life Insurance and Biblical Hermeneutics." *Mennonite Quarterly Review* 72, no. 2 (1998): 207–24.

Noonan, John. *The Scholastic Analysis of Usury.* Cambridge, MA: Harvard University Press, 1957.

Northcott, Michael S. *The Environment and Christian Ethics.* New York: Cambridge University Press, 1996.

Nowak, Martin A., and Sarah Coakley, eds. *Evolution, Games, and God: The Principle of Cooperation.* Cambridge, MA: Harvard University Press, 2013.

Nussbaum, Martha C. *The Fragility of Goodness.* New York: Cambridge University Press, 2001.

Obermeyer, Ziad, Brian Powers, Christine Vogeli, and Sendhil Mullainathan. "Dissecting Racial Bias in an Algorithm Used to Manage the Health of Populations." *Science* 366, no. 6464 (2019): 447–53.

O'Byrne, Anne. *Natality and Finitude.* Bloomington: Indiana University Press, 2010.

O'Donovan, Oliver. *Finding and Seeking: Ethics as Theology.* Vol. 2. Grand Rapids: Wm. B. Eerdmans, 2014.

Odozor, Paulinus Ikechukwu. *Moral Theology in an Age of Renewal.* Notre Dame, IN: University of Notre Dame Press, 2003.

O'Malley, Pat. "Governmentality and Risk." In *Social Theories of Risk and Uncertainty*, edited by Jens Zinn, 52–75. Malden, MA: Blackwell, 2008.

Oreskes, Naomi, and Erik Conway. *Merchants of Doubt.* New York: Bloomsbury Press, 2010.

Panofsky, Dora, and Erwin. *Pandora's Box: The Changing Aspects of a Mythical Symbol.* Bollingen 52. New York: Pantheon, 1956.

Pascal, Blaise. *Pensées and the Provincial Letters.* New York: Modern Library, 1941.

Paul VI. *Gaudium et spes*, 1965. www.vatican.va/archive/hist_councils/ii_vatican_council /documents/vat-ii_const_19651207_gaudium-et-spes_en.html.

Payne, Christopher. *The Consumer, Credit and Neoliberalism.* New York: Routledge, 2012.

Peng, Xinyan. "'We've Always Worked': Professionalizing Life among White-Collar Women in Contemporary Urban China." PhD diss., University of Virginia, 2019.

Pentland, Alex. "The Death of Individuality: What Really Governs Your Actions." *New Scientist* 222, no. 2963 (2014): 30–31.

———. *Social Physics.* New York: Penguin, 2014.

Perrow, Charles. *Normal Accidents.* Princeton, NJ: Princeton University Press, 1999.

Peter, Carl. *Participated Eternity in the Vision of God.* Vol. 142. Analecta Gregoriana. Rome: Gregorian University Press, 1964.

Petri, Thomas. *Aquinas and the Theology of the Body.* Washington, DC: Catholic University of America Press, 2018.

Pfau, Thomas. *Minding the Modern.* Notre Dame, IN: University of Notre Dame Press, 2013.

Pieper, Josef. *Prudence.* New York: Pantheon Books, 1959.

Pinckaers, Servais. "Conscience and Christian Tradition." In *The Pinckaers Reader*, edited by John Berkman and Craig Steven Titus, 346–66. Washington, DC: Catholic University of America Press, 2005.

———. "Conscience and Virtue of Prudence." In *The Pinckaers Reader*, edited by John Berkman and Craig Steven Titus, 367–81. Washington, DC: Catholic University of America Press, 2005.

————. *The Sources of Christian Ethics*. 3rd ed., translated by Mary Thomas Noble. Washington, DC: Catholic University of America Press, 1995.

Pinker, Steven. *The Blank Slate*. New York: Viking, 2002.

Pius XI. *Quadragesimo anno*. 1931. www.vatican.va/content/pius-xi/en/encyclicals/documents /hf_p-xi_enc_19310515_quadragesimo-anno.html.

Plato. *Laws*. In *Complete Works*, edited by John Cooper and translated by D. S. Hutchinson, 1318–1616. Indianapolis: Hackett, 1997.

Plomin, Robert. *Blueprint*. Cambridge, MA: MIT Press, 2018.

Polanyi, Karl. *The Great Transformation*. 2nd ed. Boston: Beacon Press, 2001.

Pope, Stephen J. *The Evolution of Altruism and the Ordering of Love*. Washington, DC: Georgetown University Press, 1994.

————. *Human Evolution and Christian Ethics*. New Studies in Christian Ethics 28. Cambridge: Cambridge University Press, 2007.

Popper, Karl. *The Logic of Scientific Discovery*. New York: Routledge, 2002.

————. "The Propensity Interpretation of Probability." *British Journal for the Philosophy of Science* 10 (1959): 25–42.

Porter, Jean. *Natural and Divine Law*. Grand Rapids: Wm. B. Eerdmans, 1999.

————. *Nature as Reason*. Grand Rapids: Wm. B. Eerdmans, 2004.

Porter, Theodore. *The Rise of Statistical Thinking 1820–1900*. Princeton, NJ: Princeton University Press, 1986.

————. *Trust in Numbers*. Princeton, NJ: Princeton University Press, 1996.

"Probability." In *OED Online*. Oxford University Press, June 2020. www-oed-com.proxy01.its .virginia.edu/view/Entry/151690?redirectedFrom=probability.

Puffer, Matthew. "Taking Exception to the Grenzfall's Reception: Revisiting Karl Barth's Ethics of War." *Modern Theology* 28, no. 3 (2012): 478–502.

Rabinow, Paul, and Nikolas Rose. "Biopower Today." *Biosocieties* 1, no. 2 (2006): 195–217.

Ratzinger, Joseph. *Fundamental Speeches from Five Decades*. San Francisco: Ignatius Press, 2012.

————. "Technological Security as a Problem of Social Ethics." *Communio* 9 (1982): 238–46.

Rawls, John. *A Theory of Justice*. Cambridge: Belknap Press, 1971.

Reydams-Schils, Gretchen. *The Roman Stoics*. Chicago: University of Chicago Press, 2005.

Richardson, Rashida, Jason Schultz, and Kate Crawford. "Dirty Data, Bad Predictions: How Civil Rights Violations Impact Police Data, Predictive Policing Systems, and Justice." *New York University Law Review* 94, no. 15 (2019): 15–55.

Rist, John M. *Augustine Deformed*. New York: Cambridge University Press, 2014.

Roediger, Henry. "What Happened to Behaviorism?" *Observer*, 2004. www.psychological science.org/observer/what-happened-to-behaviorism.

Rosa, Hartmut. *Social Acceleration*. New York: Columbia University Press, 2013.

Rosenbaum, Eric. "IBM Artificial Intelligence Can Predict with 95% Accuracy Which Workers Are about to Quit Their Jobs." CNBC, April 3, 2019. www.cnbc.com/2019/04/03/ibm-ai -can-predict-with-95-percent-accuracy-which-employees-will-quit.html.

Rosser, Gervase. *The Art of Solidarity in the Middle Ages: Guilds in England, 1250–1550*. New York: Oxford University Press, 2015.

Rousseau, Jean-Jacques. *Emile*, translated by Allan Bloom. New York: Basic Books, 1979.

Rowe, C. Kavin. *One True Life: The Stoics and Early Christians as Rival Traditions*. New Haven, CT: Yale University Press, 2016.

Sahlins, Marshall. *The Use and Abuse of Biology*. Ann Arbor: University of Michigan Press, 1976.

Savage, Leonard. *The Foundations of Statistics*. 2nd ed. New York: Dover, 1972.

Savulescu, Julian. "In Defence of Procreative Beneficence." *Journal of Medical Ethics* 33, no. 5 (2007): 284–88.

———. "Procreative Beneficence: Why We Should Select the Best Children." *Bioethics* 15, no. 5/6 (2001): 413–26.

Scherz, China. *Having People, Having Heart*. Chicago: University of Chicago Press, 2014.

Scherz, Paul. "Grief, Death, and Longing in Stoic and Christian Ethics." *Journal of Religious Ethics* 45, no. 1 (2017): 7–28.

———. "Living Indefinitely and Living Fully: *Laudato si'* and the Value of the Present in Christian, Stoic, and Transhumanist Temporalities." *Theological Studies* 79, no. 2 (June 1, 2018): 356–75.

———. "Prudence, Precaution, and Uncertainty: Assessing the Health Benefits and Ecological Risks of Gene Drive Technology Using the Quasi-Integral Parts of Prudence." *The Thomist* 81, no. 4 (2017): 507–37.

———. "Risk, Health and Physical Enhancement: The Dangers of Health Care as Risk Reduction for Christian Bioethics." *Christian Bioethics* 26, no. 2 (2020): 145–62.

———. "Risk, Prudence, and Moral Formation in the Laboratory." *Journal of Moral Education* 47, no. 3 (2018): 304–15.

———. *Science and Christian Ethics*. Cambridge: Cambridge University Press, 2019.

Schmidt, Harald, Dorothy Roberts, and Nwamaka Enanya. "Rationing, Racism and Justice: Advancing the Debate around 'Colourblind' COVID-19 Ventilator Allocation." *Journal of Medical Ethics* 48, no. 2 (2022): 126–30.

Schull, Natasha Dow. "Abiding Chance: Online Poker and the Software of Self-Discipline." *Public Culture* 28, no. 3 (2016): 563–92.

———. *Addiction by Design*. Princeton, NJ: Princeton University Press, 2012.

———. "The Data-Based Self: Self-Quantification and the Data-Driven (Good) Life." *Social Research* 86, no. 4 (2019): 909–30.

———. "Data for Life: Wearable Technology and the Design of Self-Care." *Biosocieties* 11, no. 3 (2016): 317–33.

———. "Sensor Technology and the Time Series Self." *Continent* 5 (2016): 24–28.

Schumpeter, Joseph. *The Theory of Economic Development*, translated by Redvers Opie. Cambridge, MA: Harvard University Press, 1968.

Schwartz, Barry. *The Battle for Human Nature*. New York: W. W. Norton, 1986.

———. *The Paradox of Choice*. New York: HarperCollins, 2004.

Schweiker, William. *Responsibility and Christian Ethics*. Cambridge: Cambridge University Press, 1999.

Searle, John. "Minds, Brains, and Programs." *Behavioral and Brain Sciences* 3, no. 3 (1980): 417–57.

Seneca. "De Providentia." In *Moral Essays, Volume I*, translated by John W. Basore, 2–47. Loeb Classical Library 214. Cambridge, MA: Harvard University Press, 1928.

———. *Epistles 1-65*, translated by Richard M. Gummere. Loeb Classical Library 75. Cambridge, MA: Loeb Classical Library, 1917.

Servick, Kelly. "Cornell Nutrition Scientist Resigns after Retractions and Research Misconduct Finding." *Science*, September 21, 2018. www.sciencemag.org/news/2018/09/cornell-nutrition-scientist-resigns-after-retractions-and-research-misconduct-finding.

Shadle, Matthew. *Interrupting Capitalism*. Oxford: Oxford University Press, 2018.

Shakespeare, William. "Macbeth." In *The Complete Works of William Shakespeare*, 1045–70. New York: Avenal Books, 1975.

Shrader-Frechette, Kristin. *Science Policy, Ethics, and Economic Methodology: Some Problems of Technology Assessment and Environmental-Impact Analysis*. Boston: Springer, 2013.

Sidgwick, Henry. *The Methods of Ethics*. Chicago: University of Chicago Press, 1962.

Simon, Herbert. "Rational Choice and the Structure of the Environment." *Psychological Review* 63, no. 2 (1956): 129–38.

Skinner, B. F. *About Behaviorism*. New York: Alfred A. Knopf, 1974.

———. *Beyond Freedom and Dignity*. New York: Alfred A. Knopf, 1971.

———. *Walden Two*. New York: Macmillan, 1976.

Sorabji, Richard. *Emotion and Peace of Mind*. New York: Oxford University Press, 2000.

———. *Moral Conscience through the Ages*. New York: Oxford University Press, 2014.

———. *Time, Creation, and the Continuum*. Chicago: University of Chicago Press, 2006.

Sorel, Georges. *The Illusions of Progress*, translated by John Stanley and Charlotte Stanley. Berkeley: University of California Press, 1969.

Spaemann, Robert. "Bourgeois Ethics and Non-Teleological Ontology." In *A Robert Spaemann Reader*, edited by D. C. Schindler and Jeanne Heffernan Schindler, 45–59. Oxford: Oxford University Press, 2015.

———. "In Defense of Anthropomorphism." In *A Robert Spaemann Reader*, edited by D. C. Schindler and Jeanne Heffernan Schindler, 77–96. Oxford: Oxford University Press, 2015.

———. "Individual Actions." In *A Robert Spaemann Reader*, translated by D. C. Schindler and Jeanne Heffernan Schindler, 139–53. New York: Oxford University Press, 2015.

———. *Persons: The Difference between "Someone" and "Something,"* translated by Oliver O'Donovan. Oxford: Oxford University Press, 2017.

Spanneut, Michel. *Le stoïcisme des pères de l'église, de Clément de Rome à Clément d'Alexandrie*. Patristica Sorbonensia 1. Paris: Éditions du Seuil, 1957.

Standen, William. *The Ideal Protection*. New York: US Life Insurance Company, 1897.

Starr, Paul. *The Social Transformation of American Medicine*. New York: Basic Books, 1984.

Stavrianakis, Anthony, and Laurence Anne Tessier. "Go Suppress Yourself." *Somatosphere* (blog), May 20, 2020. http://somatosphere.net/2020/go-suppress-yourself.html/.

Stein, Edith. *Essays on Woman*, edited by L. Gelber and Romaeus Leuven. Washington, DC: ICS, 1987.

———. *Finite and Eternal Being*. Washington, DC: ICS, 2002.

———. "Martin Heidegger's Existential Philosophy," translated by Mette Lebech. *Maynooth Philosophical Papers* 4 (2007): 55–98.

———. *Potency and Act*. Washington, DC: ICS, 2009.

Stoddart, Eric. *Theological Perspectives on a Surveillance Society*. London: Routledge, 2016.

Sullivan, Meghan. *Time Biases*. Oxford: Oxford University Press, 2018.

Sulmasy, Daniel, and Nathaniel Hibner. "Catholic Ethics and the Challenge of COVID-19 Part 2." No date. www.rev.com/transcript-editor/Edit?token=U-2FWP0qHem8s10v0O Juls7bUxRs6oEn0LHUbvYn9SUOQ_O5LIXSjCuEjip8yl1eNNFcwlcbGmM1opBr5m 2zk8LguRA&loadFrom=DocumentHeaderDeepLink.

Sunstein, Cass. *Laws of Fear: Beyond the Precautionary Principle*. Cambridge: Cambridge University Press, 2005.

———. *Worst-Case Scenarios*. Cambridge, MA: Harvard University Press, 2007.

Taleb, Nassim Nicholas. *Antifragile*. New York: Random House, 2014.

———. *The Black Swan*. New York: Random House, 2007.

Tanner, Kathryn. *Christianity and the New Spirit of Capitalism*. New Haven, CT: Yale University Press, 2019.

———. *God and Creation in Christian Theology*. Minneapolis: Fortress Press, 1988.

———. "Grace without Nature." In *Without Nature?* edited by David Albertson and Cabell King, 363–76. New York: Fordham University Press, 2010.

Tartak, Jossie Carreras, and Hazar Khidir. "US Must Avoid Building Racial Bias into COVID-19 Emergency Guidance." NPR, April 21, 2020. www.npr.org/sections/health -shots/2020/04/21/838763690/opinion-u-s-must-avoid-building-racial-bias-into-covid -19-emergency-guidance.

Taylor, Charles. *A Secular Age*. Cambridge, MA: Belknap Press, 2007.

———. *Sources of the Self*. Cambridge: Cambridge University Press, 1992.

Tertullian. "Against Hermogenes." In *Ante-Nicene Fathers*. Vol. 3, *Latin Christianity—Its Founder, Tertullian*, 477–502. Peabody, MA: Hendrickson, 2012.

Thaler, Richard H., and Cass Sunstein. *Nudge: Improving Decisions about Health, Wealth, and Happiness*. New York: Penguin, 2009.

Theresa of Avila. *Interior Castle*, translated by E. Allison Peers. New York: Image Books, 1961.

Thomas Aquinas. *On Kingship*, translated by Gerald Phelan. Amsterdam: Academische Pers, 1967.

———. *Summa theologica*, translated by Dominicans of the English Province. New York: Benziger Bros., 1947.

Thorsteinsson, Runar. *Roman Christianity and Roman Stoicism*. Oxford: Oxford University Press, 2010.

Tomczyk, Pawel. "The Presence of Virtue Ethics in the Thought of Karol Wojtyła / John Paul II." Catholic University of America, 2017.

Toner, Jules. *Discerning God's Will: Ignatius of Loyola's Teaching on Christian Decision Making*. Saint Louis: Institute of Jesuit Sources, 1991.

Tracy, Myles. "Insurance and Theology: The Background and the Issues." *Journal of Risk and Insurance* 33, no. 1 (1966): 85–93.

Turner, Fred. *From Counterculture to Cyberculture*. Chicago: University of Chicago Press, 2006.

Tutino, Stefania. *Uncertainty in Post-Reformation Catholicism: A History of Probabilism*. Oxford: Oxford University Press, 2018.

Twenge, Jean. *IGen*. New York: Atria, 2017.

United Nations. "Rio Declaration on Environment and Development." 1992. www.un.org /en/development/desa/population/migration/generalassembly/docs/globalcompact/A _CONF.151_26_Vol.I_Declaration.pdf.

Vallor, Shannon. *Technology and the Virtues*. New York: Oxford University Press, 2016.

Varda, Agnes. *The Gleaners and I* (*Les glaneurs et la glaneuse*; "The gleaners and the female gleaner," in French). Documentary film, 2000.

Vera, Luis. "Augmented Reality and the Limited Promise of 'Ecstatic' Technology Criticism." *Journal of Moral Theology* 9, no. 2 (2020): 147–74.

Vogler, Candace. *Reasonably Vicious*. Cambridge, MA: Harvard University Press, 2002.

Wade, Nicholas. *A Troublesome Inheritance*. New York: Penguin, 2014.

Waldenfels, Bernhard. *Phenomenology of the Alien*, translated by Tanja Stahler and Alexander Kozin. Evanston, IL: Northwestern University Press, 2011.

Watson, John B. *Behavior*. New York: Henry Holt, 1929.

Waugh, Evelyn. *Unconditional Surrender*. In *The Sword of Honour Trilogy*, 479–710. London. Random House, 1994.

Wawrykow, Joseph P. *God's Grace and Human Action: "Merit" in the Theology of Thomas Aquinas*. Notre Dame, IN: University of Notre Dame Press, 2016.

Weber, Max. "Politics as a Vocation." In *From Max Weber*, edited by H. H. Gerth and C. Wright Mills, 77–128. New York: Oxford University Press, 1958.

Weil, Simone. "The Love of God and Affliction." In *Essential Writings*, 41–70. Maryknoll, NY: Orbis, 2003.

Welch, H. Gilbert, Lisa Schwartz, and Steven Woloshin. *Overdiagnosed*. Boston: Beacon Press, 2011.

Welch, Sharon. *A Feminist Ethic of Risk*. Minneapolis: Fortress Press, 1990.

Werpehowski, William. "Karl Barth and Just War: A Conversation with Roman Catholicism." In *Commanding Grace*, edited by Daniel Migliore, 60–82. Grand Rapids: Wm. B. Eerdmans, 2010.

Westberg, Daniel. *Right Practical Reason: Aristotle, Action, and Prudence in Aquinas*. New York: Clarendon Press, 1994.

White, Heath. *Fate and Free Will*. Notre Dame, IN: University of Notre Dame Press, 2019.

White, Lynn. "The Historical Roots of Our Ecologic Crisis." In *Philosophy and Technology*, edited by Carl Mitcham and Robert Mackey, 259–65. New York: Free Press, 1983.

Williams, Bernard. *Moral Luck*. Cambridge: Cambridge University Press, 1982.

Wilson, Edward O. *On Human Nature*. 2nd ed. Cambridge, MA: Harvard University Press, 2004.

Witt, John. *The Accidental Republic*. Cambridge, MA: Harvard University Press, 2006.

Wolterstorff, Nicholas. *Justice: Rights and Wrongs*. Princeton, NJ: Princeton University Press, 2008.

Wynne, Brian. "Seasick on the Third Wave? Subverting the Hegemony of Propositionalism." *Social Studies of Science* 33, no. 3 (2003): 401–17.

Yates, Frances. *The Art of Memory*. Chicago: University of Chicago Press, 1966.

Yoder, John Howard. *Karl Barth and the Problem of War*. Nashville: Abingdon Press, 1970.

———. *The Politics of Jesus*. 2nd ed. Grand Rapids: Wm. B. Eerdmans, 1994.

Yuengert, Andrew. *Approximating Prudence*. New York: Palgrave Macmillan, 2012.

Zaloom, Caitlin. *Out of the Pits*. Chicago: University of Chicago Press, 2010.

Zeelenberg, Marcel. "Anticipated Regret: A Prospective Emotion about the Future Past." In *The Psychology of Thinking about the Future*, edited by Gabriele Oettingen, A. Timur Sevincer, and Peter Gollwitzer, 276–95. New York: Guilford Press, 2018.

Zelizer, Viviana. *Morals and Markets: The Development of Life Insurance in the United States*. New York: Columbia University Press, 1979.

Zigon, Jarrett. "Can Machines Be Ethical? On the Necessity of Relational Ethics and Empathic Attunement for Data-Centric Technologies." *Social Research* 86, no. 4 (2019): 1001–22.

———. *"HIV Is God's Blessing": Rehabilitating Morality in Neoliberal Russia*. Berkeley: University of California Press, 2010.

Zuboff, Shoshana. *The Age of Surveillance Capitalism*. New York: PublicAffairs, 2019.

Index

About the Author

PAUL SCHERZ is an associate professor of moral theology and ethics at the Catholic University of America. He is the author of *Science and Christian Ethics* and coeditor of *The Evening of Life: The Challenges of Aging and Dying Well.*